Almost Everything You Need to Know About

Cockapoos

Diane Klumb

Table of Contents

CHAPTER ONE:

Cockapoo Basics

Long before the media coined the term "Designer Dog", and long before Doodles of every conceivable stripe started appearing across America, there were Cockapoos.

Although many people are unaware of it, the totally adorable Cockapoo is not a "new invention" by any stretch of the imagination— in fact, he's been around far longer than most of today's most popular hybrids and is actually older than at least a couple of AKC-recognized breeds!

The venerable Oxford Dictionary first added an entry for the Cockapoo *over 50 years ago,* and the name itself first appeared in print earlier than that, when his "parent" breeds, the Cocker Spaniel and the Poodle, were vying for top position as America's most popular AKC purebred. The idea of deliberately crossing the two most popular breeds into a single shaggy package of uncommon charm and intelligence simply made a lot of sense back then.

It still does.

In fact, for a multitude of reasons, the qualities inherent in the Cockapoo make it an even *more* attractive choice for today's modern family, which probably accounts for the breed's sudden surge in popularity after decades of relative obscurity.

For example, although housewives in the 1960s no doubt appreciated his low-shedding coat, no one gave much thought to its hypoallergenic qualities, because few Americans suffered from allergies back then. Today, when nearly *one in five* Americans suffers from allergies, this becomes a much more important consideration, and is largely responsible for the recent rise in popularity of the Cockapoo.

Likewise, back in 1960, the concept of a Therapy Dog was unknown, and Service Dogs were pretty much limited to guiding the blind. Today, Therapy and Service dogs can be found performing a multitude of tasks, and the versatile Cockapoo excels at virtually all of them.

His hypoallergenic coat, outgoing temperament and compact size combined with his intelligence and easy trainability, makes him well-suited for Therapy work in a variety of settings and make him a Service Dog second to none, whether running errands for those with limited mobility or as a Medical Alert Dog. (The natural capability for scent discrimination inherited from his Cocker ancestors make him especially well-suited to diabetes, seizure alert and response and allergen-alert work... in fact, in laboratory studies, Cockers have been shown to be stunningly accurate in cancer detection work.)

Another very specific area in which the Cockapoo excels that simply didn't exist in the 1960s involves autism, which, like allergies, was pretty rare back in 1960.

The Cockapoo's compact size and physical sturdiness
combined with his innate love of and patience with children
make him especially well-suited for working with kids on the autism spectrum,
both as a Therapy Dog in a clinical setting
and in a one-on-one in-home setting as an Autism Service Dog.

As autism rates in the US have reached 1 in 50 and continue to skyrocket, many Cockapoos are filling this critical need, and more will no doubt continue to do so in the future. In fact, when it comes to his affinity for special needs kids, the Cockapoo surpasses most breeds its size and is easily on par with the much larger Goldendoodle.

Which brings us neatly to the other wonderful advantage of the Cockapoo– his size. As impressive as both the Labradoodle and the Goldendoodle are in many ways, both breeds have tendency to run to ...well...*huge*....easily reaching 80 to 100 pounds.
This is simply "more dog" than a lot of modern families need or even have room for. Breeders have

tried to address the problem by crossing in smaller Poodles to produce "mini doodles", but size is one of the hardest qualities to control in dog breeding, and very few honest breeders will guarantee adult size. (Given the number of "mini" doodles that have ended up standing close to 24 inches at the shoulder and weighing 50 pounds or more as adults, this is probably a Good Thing!)

The Cockapoo, on the other hand, *counts no large dogs among his ancestors at all.* As a result, he's pretty much incapable of producing those "big dog throwbacks" that continue to plague his larger hybrid cousins even after multiple generations of backcrosses. When size is a deal-breaker in the final choice of a breed, the Cockapoo is simply a better bet than a breed originally descended from significantly larger sporting breeds. A "better breed"? Wait a minute....

Is the Cockapoo Actually a *Breed?*

If you're reading this book, odds are you fall into one of two categories—you already own a Cockapoo or you are considering adding one to your family. In either case, you've probably done some internet research along the way before you got here.

Which means you've probably run into a lot of "internet experts" quick to explain that the Cockapoo, like the Goldendoodle, the Labradoodle and the Puggle, is not a "breed" at all, but rather a "hybrid" or "mixed breed".

And to further confuse things, according to *another* whole group of "experts", since the parents are from the same species these dogs do not even qualify as hybrids, but are simply "overpriced mutts" with cutesy names produced by greedy commercial breeders and puppy mills for quick profit.

Unfortunately, like much of what is written by self-appointed internet experts, ALL of this so-called "information" is incorrect. Actually, it's incorrect on so many levels one hardly knows where to *begin.* But as somebody wiser than yours truly once pointed out , 90% of all arguments can be settled with a dictionary, and this is certainly one of those cases, so let's start there.

To begin with, the term *breed* is not even used in the field of *taxonomy*, that branch of science responsible for the defining of groups of biological organisms on the basis of shared characteristics. (This is not to be confused with *taxidermy*, which is the preserving of those biological organisms for display in Natural History museums and the walls of hunters and fisherman, usually by stuffing them.)

In taxonomy, all domestic dogs, purebred and mongrel alike, are classified as members of the **species** *Canis Lupus Familiaris,* which is a member of the **genus** *Canis*, which is a member of the much larger **family** *Canidae,* which is a member of the **order** *Carnivore.* (Taxonomy is very organized.)

Subspecies are commonly divided into landraces, races, strains or breeds by breeders and livestock geneticists, *but not by taxonomists.*

The reason for this is simple— without human intervention, most landraces, strains, races, strains and breeds will happily revert back to their larger subspecies. (In the case of domestic dogs, they tend to revert back to the phenotype common among "street dogs" all over the world—medium-sized, short-haired, long-legged, with a long muzzle and erect or semi-erect ears— simply because these are all dominant traits.)

In other words, since a "breed" is an entirely man-made phenomenon, and so there is no scientific classification for it in taxonomy. However, it can be found in any dictionary or glossary of dog terms, and both Merriam Webster and the venerable American Kennel Club define it similarly:

breed: a race of animals, selected and maintained by humans, with a characterized appearance and a common gene pool.

OK, so let's put the Cockapoo to the test….

Is the Cockapoo selected and maintained by humans?
Yes. There is no evidence that the Cockapoo exists in the wild.

Does the Cockapoo have a characterized appearance?
Yes. As a quick Google search of "Cockapoo images" will reveal, they all look remarkably similar.

Do Cockapoos share a common gene pool?
Yes. ALL Cockapoos are descended entirely from Cockers and Poodles, just as all Golden Retrievers are descended entirely from Yellow Retrievers and Tweed Water Spaniels.

Gee, that seems pretty straightforward, doesn't it? *So why are people still arguing about this?*

Well, aside from the fact that a lot of purebred fanciers simply don't *like* the idea of anyone deliberately crossing existing breeds to produce new ones, even for the sole purpose of eliminating a serious genetic disorder (and there's frankly no sense arguing with this group), there is still some legitimate confusion about this whole breed/hybrid/purebred thing among the less narrow-minded.

Although the Cockapoo is clearly a *breed,*
the Cockapoo is NOT is a *purebred,* which is the source of most of the confusion.

Although many people use the terms interchangeably, they mean very different things. To sort it out, we need to go back to the American Kennel Club, inarguably the "subject matter experts" on purebred dogs in the US. Here's how they define the term:

purebred dog: a dog whose sire and dam belong to the same breed and are themselves of unmixed descent since recognition of the breed.

This whole idea of "unmixed descent", or genetic purity, represents the heart and soul of the American Kennel Club for the last 130 years. (It has also led to an alarming lack of genetic diversity in the genes responsible for immune function in nearly every breed studied to date.) "Recognition" implies recognition by a registry or studbook, and by definition requires that studbook to be *closed* (like AKC's), which means that once established, no new foundation stock from the original parent breeds can be added. This "closed studbook" breeding system, which was developed by the Victorian breeders, was believed to be necessary in order for the breed to "breed true." (Actually, this was incorrect— we now know that the presence of *a single gene mutation* floating around in a breed's gene pool can prevent it from "breeding true" even if the stud book has been closed for a hundred years.)

The real *problem* with this closed studbook system is that every subsequent dog of that breed can only inherit the genes carried by the relatively few dogs used in the original crosses— in some breeds that is less than 10 foundation dogs! And as genes are accidentally lost in a remarkably short time through what is called "genetic drift", this small gene pool gets even *smaller* with every succeeding generation.

Geneticists now understand that eventually, this lack of genetic diversity (especially in the area of the genome known as the DLA complex, which regulates immune function) will result in compromised immune function, as well as "locking in" rare genetic disorders, the responsible mutations for which may have been unknowingly carried by the original foundation dogs.

While the Cockapoo breed actually has several registries worldwide (the American Cockapoo Club in the US and the Cockapoo Club of Great Britain in the UK are probably the largest and most active, with up-to-date and informative websites) none of them are "closed registries"— they all wisely register first-generation crosses as well as multi-generational dogs and backcrosses.

In other words, a Cockapoo is a Cockapoo as long as it is descended entirely from Cockers and Poodles— it doesn't matter if those Cockers and Poodles are its parents, grandparents, great-grandparents or some combination thereof.

An *open registry* like this, which allows for the addition of new genetic material (in the form of new foundation stock from either of the designated parent breeds) as needed, will maintain the genetic diversity needed to keep a breed robust and healthy, and will avoid the genetic problems and autoimmune diseases now plaguing so many of the "Victorian-era" breeds.

Hopefully, those organizations working to preserve the Cockapoo breed for the future will continue on this wise path rather than fall prey to the inbreeding problems inherent in the closed studbooks currently required for recognition by the large all-breed registries like AKC.
(Of course, one can also hope that some of these large and monolithic all-breed registries will in the near future take a hard look at the outdated policies that have not served purebreds well and decide to revise their own positions!)

So, if the Cockapoo does not qualify as a "purebred", what exactly IS it?

Well, what it is NOT, in spite of what you may have read by the aforementioned "internet experts" with no apparent access to a dictionary, is a "mongrel" or a "mutt", both of which are defined as *a dog of unknown parentage.* Through the miracle of modern molecular genetics, the parentage of any Cockapoo can now easily be confirmed via a simple DNA test, so these people just need to get *over* themselves.

The Cockapoo is a *hybrid.* Here's how geneticists define the term:

hybrid: the descendents of the deliberate crossing of two or more separate inbred strains, or homogeneous populations.

Notice what is missing from this definition here— a hybrid is NOT limited to the of crossing two separate *species,* which is possible but actually pretty rare. Even if species are closely related, reproductive barriers caused by poor chromosome pairing often produces infertile offspring, which can make "inter

-species hybrids" pretty much of a dead end from a breeding standpoint. (Mules are a classic example of this— the offspring of a cross between a horse and a donkey are famously infertile. Oddly, the offspring of a zebra and a horse —called a "zorse" — are not. Go figure.)

Nor, you may notice, is the definition of a hybrid limited to the *first-generation* result of a deliberate cross, which a lot of people erroneously believe.

A first-generation cross is referred to as an F1 hybrid cross, while successive crosses are variously referred to a F1bs, F2s, F2bs, or F3s (or even F24s or beyond) depending on the breeding formula used. All are considered hybrids. So when does a "hybrid" officially become a "purebred"?

There IS no magic number— it's actually pretty arbitrary, and depends entirely on the rules of the registering body in question and the breeding formula used. For registration purposes, 7 generations with no backcrosses and the addition of *no new foundation dogs* is generally the accepted number. From a purely genetic standpoint, a hybrid may represent the 20th generation of descendents from the original cross or crosses.

Unfortunately, with only two breeds in the original mix, after 7 or more generations of closed breeding, the "new" breed will likely suffer from the same overall lack of genetic diversity that plagues its parent breeds, *so nothing is gained from a health standpoint.* And with a breed like the Cockapoo, sacrificing overall health and a robust immune system for the sort of "pedigree depth" required for recognition from an all-breed registry is not really necessary in order to produce consistency of phenotype.

In fact, unlike many hybrid crosses, the Cockapoo displays remarkable consistency in the FIRST generation.

What this means is that most F1 Cockapoos look remarkably similar, and have remarkably similar temperaments and high intelligence levels. Although a lot of "general information" written on hybrids explains that F1 hybrids can resemble either parent, this is by and large untrue, and especially so for the Cockapoo. And the *reason* it rarely happens is amazingly simple— it's the result of what's called the "mode of inheritance" of particular genes.

Most genetic mutations, whether simple single point mutations or something more complex like retro-gene insertions, are inherited in one of two fashions— they are either *dominant*, which means a single copy of the mutation will produce an observable variation in phenotype in the offspring, or *recessive*, in which case two copies (one from each parent) are needed to effect a variation.

11

By happy accident, most of the traits that make a Cockapoo immediately recognizable happen to be controlled by *dominant* genes, which means only *one copy* of the gene needs to be inherited (from either parent) in order for the trait to be expressed.

Examples of these dominant traits would be the Cocker's silky, wavy coat, which is dominant over the coarser, curly coat displayed by the Poodle, as well as the single retrogene insertion over on canine chromosome 13 that's responsible for all canine facial furnishings, in this case inherited from the Poodle. Structurally, the Poodle's straighter upper arm is a dominant trait that's largely responsible for the Cockapoo's squarish outline.

Other traits, like muzzle length, are controlled by what are called *nucleotide repeats;* in these cases, the first-generation cross tends to display an "intermediate phenotype", which explains why most F1 Cockapoos usually have a longer muzzle than the typical American Cocker but shorter than the Poodle. (F1 Cockapoos with a typically longer-muzzled English Cocker parent, not surprisingly more common in Great Britain, tend to have longer muzzles than those with an American Cocker parent.)

Less immediately obvious traits, including behavior, maturation (this translates to housetraining!) and what breeders have long referred to as general "make and shape" are also controlled in the same way, and in virtually all cases, the Cockapoo simply got lucky.

It's worth noting that this is unfortunately NOT true of all hybrids.

Because other traits, such as short coats, short legs, and erect ears are also controlled by dominant or (even worse) *incompletely dominant* genes, many other hybrids do *not* produce consistently in the first generation, and it can take many generations of selective breeding in order to produce a litter of puppies that even vaguely resemble each other. F1 puppies resulting from these crosses often tend to be "all over the map" —although they all display hybrid vigor and no doubt a wealth of other virtues, lacking the required "characterized phenotype", one would be hard-pressed to consider the F1 crosses produced as a breed per se. (In a breed like the Cockapoo, where most of the *desirable* characteristics are controlled by dominant genes, the least consistency is usually found in the F2 pups, when recessive genes may cause a percentage of pups to resemble the parent breeds.)

The truth is, **not all efforts at hybridization are successful.** Plant breeders, who've been creating new plants through hybridizing since well before the days of Brother Mendel and his peas, generally have to try many different crosses before they get a "winner" that displays all the traits they're looking for. Dogs are really no different. And through nothing more than sheer luck, the Cockapoo turned out to be a winner.

Making Sense of All Those Fs

Now, before we get any farther, it might be a good idea to explain what all these "F"s that breeders use for different generations of hybrids actually mean, where this terminology originally came from, and how important it really is to the pet owner.

The capital letter actually F stands for *filial* (from the Latin word for son, *fili*) and in genetics refers to **"the sequence of generations following the parental generation, with each generation designated by an *F* followed by a subscript number indicating its place in the sequence."**

The designations most commonly found in Cockapoos are:

- **F1 — the offspring of a Poodle and a Cocker**
- **F1b— The offspring of an F1 Cockapoo bred back to a Poodle**
- **F2b— the offspring of an F2 Cockapoo bred back to a Poodle**
- **F2 — the offspring of an F1 Cockapoo bred to any other Cockapoo**
- **F3 — the offspring of an F2 bred to another F2 (or higher) Cockapoo**
- **F4 — the offspring of an F3 bred to another F3 (or higher) Cockapoo**

One can go farther, of course, remembering that each generation moves up one number from the lower-numbered parent.

So which generation is best for the pet owner? *By itself, it really doesn't matter much.*

Although it was once believed that all hybrid vigor was lost after the first generation cross (and many breeders still believe this), new research shows that this just isn't true. It has been shown that *as long as inbreeding* is not employed, the greatest loss of hybrid vigor (maybe 25%) occurs after the first generation and then levels off in the next two or three. Repeated backcrossings to one of the original breeds, on the other hand, will reduce hybrid vigor faster — the key to maintaining diversity is to keep a near-equal balance between the two original strains.

Inbreeding, though (long the mainstay of purebred fanciers because it quickly "sets breed type"), will reduce hybrid vigor with blinding speed— within 4 generations of selective inbreeding, a nearly homozygous population can be developed. (Unfortunately, it now appears that these inbred dogs simply don't have immune systems capable of dealing with the modern world in which we live, where over-vaccination and overuse of antibiotics, as well as pesticides and other pollutants in the water and air, on our lawns, and in our food challenge the immune system at every turn.)

For the pet owner, what is more important than which generation a pup may represent is whether or not the parents have been health-screened for genetic problems like Prcd/PRA, and selected for good temperaments and sound structure, because these traits are also genetic.

Although it can increase disease resistance, longevity and reproductive fitness, hybrid vigor cannot overcome genetic deficiencies in the parent stock.

In other words, crossing two individuals with poor structure or temperament of two unrelated breeds will simply produce robust puppies with poor temperament and structure. Hybridization is not a panacea for all ills that can befall a dog — whether breeding hybrids or purebreds, selection of the best puppies for breeding stock will always produce the best results.

This actually gives the breeder of multigenerational dogs an edge, because they can select the best puppies from their own litters for the next generation.

Breeders who limit themselves to F1s, on the other hand, have to keep purchasing new breeding stock, and as most responsible breeders of purebreds are frankly disinclined to sell their best-quality pups to people who want to cross them with another breed, getting one's hands on quality dogs can be a real challenge. (This is one of the primary reasons many breeders are now moving toward breeding mutigenerational dogs.)

OK, by now it should now be pretty clear that a Cockapoo (whether the product of a first-generation cross or a multigenerational breeding) is a Cockapoo is a Cockapoo— unless of course it's from Australia or New Zealand, where a Cockapoo is a Spoodle. *A Spoodle ???*

That's right. If you're looking for a Cockapoo in that part of the world (where their popularity has literally exploded in the last few years) you'll probably get a lot farther if you do an internet search for "Spoodle puppies".

Exactly *why* the breeders there collectively decided to break with a 50 year tradition here and call their dogs Spoodles is a bit of a mystery, but from a purely technical standpoint, they actually got it quite a bit "righter" than those early breeders in the US did back in 1950.

Contrary to poplar belief, the rules for a "portmanteau" (which is simply one word made from two, like Lewis Carroll's famous "slithy") actually go back a hundred years at least —they weren't just made up by the breeders of Designer Dogs. These rules require that the *first half* of one word be combined with the *second half* of the other ("Labradoodle" is actually a classic portmanteau) rather than using the first half of *both words* as "Cockapoo" does.

Of course, the early breeders really didn't have much of a choice. Let's face it, even if it's technically correct, "Cockoodle" is a non-starter of a name. Even keeping the "er" and then adding an extra D like the Goldendoodles did (in order to avoid becoming Goldenoodles) won't help, because then you end up with a "Cockerdoodle". Yikes.

So faced with these choices, the early breeders just went with "Cockapoo", for which one can hardly blame them. It isn't exactly correct but it sort of works, especially with an extra A thrown in so it flows off the tongue a little better than "Cockpoo", which is truly dreadful on so many levels. (And of course, they're in good company— strictly by the rules, Microsoft should really be Microware, but no doubt even a geek like Bill Gates realized that sounded too much like a bowl you might use in your microwave.)

Now, what obviously occurred to our friends Down Under is that "Cocker" is actually short for "Cocker Spaniel", and the "spaniel" part gives you a little more to work with. Hence…. the Spoodle. Brilliant.

All silliness aside, one very real advantage of "Spoodle" over "Cockapoo" as a name is that should the need arise in the future for more genetic diversity, the Cocker has several closely-related spaniel "cousin" breeds that could be easily pressed into service here without requiring a name change, or engendering the sort of bizarre arguments currently plaguing the Labradoodle world with regard for the possibility of introducing a third breed into one whose name clearly indicates it's made of only two.

OK, now that we've totally beaten this subject to death, let's recap:

- A Cockapoo is a breed descended from English or American Cockers and Poodles (usually of the Miniature and Toy varieties)
- Although clearly qualifying as a breed, the Cockapoo does not qualify as a "purebred", which may actually be an advantage.
- As long as he's descended from only Cockers and Poodles, a Cockapoo is a Cockapoo and may be registered as such whether he is an F1 hybrid *or* the result of a multigenerational breeding of one sort or another.
- If he moves to Australia, a Cockapoo automatically becomes a Spoodle.

And now it's time to answer a far more important question...which is…..

Is the Cockapoo the Right Breed for Me?

Adding a dog to the family is a long-term commitment...in the case of the Cockapoo, it can actually be *a 15 to 20 year commitment*, and possibly even longer. (One of the major advantages of the Cockapoo over many of the "newer" hybrids is that they've actually been around long enough to make some accurate predictions about things like longevity, and there really are Cockapoos who've made it to 22 years old. With hybrids that haven't been around very long, breeders are frankly just guessing.) Because of this, it's really important to figure out at the outset if he's likely to be a good fit.

There really is no single perfect breed of dog. The characteristics of one breed might be perfect for one individual or family, while those very same characteristics may make it a really *bad* match for family next door. And that's where both *breed type* and *breed character* come into play, so let's look at them in terms of the Cockapoo, which will help determine if he's a good match for your family.

The term *breed type* generally refers the physical characteristics that define a breed— a combination of what old breeders called "shape and make" and "fancy points" and what we more commonly refer to as structural characteristics and cosmetics characteristics.

Breed character generally refers to a commonality of behavioral traits found among most well-bred and well-socialized member of an individual breed— in this category falls things like a breed's typical energy level, trainability, and its typical attitude toward kids, strangers and other dogs.

In both area, what's right for one individual or family may be totally wrong for another. This has always been the strongest argument for buying a particular breed in the first place, rather than adopting a puppy of unknown parentage from a shelter. In the latter case, it's virtually impossible to predict adult size, weight, coat type, or personality.

Breed Type and Breed Character....a matter of Genetics

As with most breeds, in both breed type and breed character the Cockapoo is a genetic "blend" of the older breeds from which it was developed, and all well-bred and well-socialized puppies tend to display a lot of the same characteristics. But because some traits are controlled by dominant genes and others by recessive ones, traits from the parent breeds are rarely *evenly* inherited.

In other words, in some areas *the entire Cockpoo breed* displays its Cocker ancestry, while in other areas it displays its Poodle ancestry.

For example, in the area of *breed type*, the Cockapoo's large, soulful eyes with their melting expression are without question a gift from the Cocker alone, while his frame, typically lighter and squarer than the Cocker's by some bit, is much more similar to that of the Poodle, as is his rather light-footed and springy "way of going".

In terms of *breed character*, the Cockapoo's lifelong playfulness and his wonderful patience with children are definitely Cocker traits, but not generally counted among the Poodle's many virtues. On the other hand, the ease with which the typical Cockapoo puppy is housetrained is definitely NOT a gift from the Cocker. Not exactly what one might call the Cocker's strong suit (and I'm being kind here), ease of housetraining is pretty much a given in the Poodle, and thankfully the Cockapoo generally takes after his Poodle ancestors in that regard.

These sorts of "either/or" traits are what geneticists call *complex qualitative* (or binary) traits — they have a dichotomous expression with a *polygenic* genetic background, meaning they are controlled by multiple genes, and represent what's called a "threshold" characteristic. In other words, if a puppy inherits enough of the necessary genes to cross the threshold, he displays the trait.

Although there are no genetic tests for these traits as there are for *simple qualitative* ones (like whether a black dog is capable of producing chocolate puppies) breeders have long been able to control them by using a common-sense technique called "breeding for improvement."
In other words, if a breed is notoriously hard to housetrain, common sense tells you your best bet is to cross it with a breed where the problem is rare to non-existent, which should take the puppies "over the threshold". (This of course explains why the Cocker/Bichon cross has never really gained any traction—what would possibly be gained by deliberately crossing two of the *hardest-to-housetrain* breeds on the planet?)

Much harder to control are what are called *quantitative* traits, which also tend to be polygenic. Rather than falling into discrete, qualitative categories (i.e. present or absent) they instead have a continuous, seemingly smooth spectrum of possible values.

Two examples of hard-to-predict quantitative traits that are relevant to the Cockapoo are size and the amount of wave in the coat. And to further complicate things, quantitative traits are also the ones most likely to be affected by environmental factors.

Although the Cockapoo has a LOT less variance than the Goldendoodle and is never a large dog, very few breeders are willing to predict adult height within less than a couple of inches, and pounds is even iffier, because feeding makes a huge difference there.

And although there is a gene test that will determine if a dog is carrying the Poodle's curly gene or the Cocker's wavy one, there is a real "spectrum of possible values" when it comes to waviness within the Cocker breed. (And as many women can attest, things like hormones and humidity can also affect the amount of wave in hair!)

So with those caveats in mind, let's look at breed type and breed character in the Cockapoo separately, because ideally both areas need to be a good fit.

Cockapoo Breed Type

Breed type is defined as "a particular set of physical characteristics which set one breed apart from all others" and these "typical" characteristics are traditionally laid out in a breed's Standard, which is used when judging that breed in the show ring. However, when researching different breeds, these Breed Standards also provide the best initial clues as to whether or not a given breed might be a good physical match for one's lifestyle and family situation.

For example, if you happen to live in a studio apartment in Manhattan, phrases like "very active" or "shall not be less than 30 inches at the shoulder" in a breed's Standard might be sufficient to give one pause. There's a *world* of difference between a dog described in its Standard as "outgoing" and one described as "reserved with strangers". And odds are that "profuse undercoat" is going to end up on your furniture and clothes, and probably floating in your coffee. Dogs described as "sturdy" rather than "fine-boned" are generally better bets for families with children.

Unfortunately, most of the hybrid dog breeds (unlike hybrid cattle breeds) do not have a Parent Club, a Registry or written Standard, which can make things considerably more difficult. In some of those breeds, the physical descriptions of the breed can vary quite a bit from breeder to breeder, are often limited to colors and weights, and many breeders' websites don't include one at all. (Of course, many of these hybrids are pretty new, and a written Breed Standard would be at best an "educated guess" at what the adult dogs *may* look like!)

Because the Cockapoo has been around so long, breeders know a lot more about what can generally be expected in an adult in terms of size, overall body shape, coat and temperament, as well as in the important areas of health and longevity.

And the American Cockapoo Club actually has a well-written Breed Standard, reprinted here in its entirety, with permission:

18

ACC Breed Standard for the Cockapoo

General Appearance. Cockapoos have a sturdy, squarely-built appearance. The length from the body measured from the breastbone to the rump is approximately the same-to-slightly longer than the height from the highest point of the shoulder to the ground. He stands up well at the shoulder on straight forelegs with a top line that is level-to-slightly sloping toward moderately-bent hindquarters. He is a dog capable of great speed and endurance, combined with agility. The body must be of sufficient length to permit a straight and free stride. Cockapoos should never appear low and long, or tall and gangly, but should always be in proportion.

Size and Weight. Size of Cockapoos can be influenced by either parent's recent background. Adult dogs 10" at the shoulder or less are toy size. Dogs 11"-14" at the shoulder are considered mini size, and those 15" at the shoulder and over are standard size. Cockapoo size is judged by their height, not their weight. Two dogs who are the same size can vary considerably in weight depending both on their overall build and whether one is fat or thin. Weights of individuals will depend on the factors explained above. To give a general idea of weight, a toy would ideally weigh under 12 pounds, a Mini 13-20 pounds and a Standard 21 pounds and up.

Head, Expression. Large, round, well-set, well-spaced eyes with a keen, soulful, endearing and intelligent expression. The color of the eyes should be dark brown on dogs with black noses. Brown dogs have brown noses. Dogs with light-colored noses may have lighter (i.e.: greenish, hazel) eyes. The eyes should not have a droopy appearance. Hair should be scissored back so as not to obstruct the eyes or vision. The ears should hang fairly close to the head, starting above the eyes and hanging to well below eye level. They should be well-feathered, but never erect or carried up over the head. Ideally the bottom of the ears should be level with the beard. The skull is moderately rounded but not exaggerated, with no tendency towards flatness.

Bite. Aligned bite, with neither over- nor under-bite. Level bites (incisors striking edge to edge) are acceptable, but scissors bite (lower incisors striking just behind the uppers) is preferred.

Neck, Top Line, Body.   The neck rises strongly from the shoulders and arches slightly as it tapers to join the head. Carried high and with dignity, the neck is never pendulous (no throatiness - skin tight). The top line is level- to-slightly sloping toward the hindquarters. The chest is deep and moderately wide, with well-sprung ribs, its lowest point no higher than the elbow.

Tail.   The tail is set on line with the back and carried on line with the top line or higher; when the dog is in motion the tail action is merry. The tail can be left long or docked like the parent breeds; both are acceptable. The tail should be well feathered and full coated when left long. If not docked, the tail is to be curled up over the back and left long, never shaven. If docked, tail should be no more and no less than 4 inches.

Forequarters.   The shoulders are well laid back, forming an angle with the upper arm of approximately 90 degrees, permitting easy movement and forward reach. When viewed from the side with the forelegs vertical, the elbow is directly below the highest point of the shoulder blade. Forelegs are parallel, straight, with strong pasterns. Legs should be set close to the body. Front dew claws can be left or removed, back dew claws should be removed. Feet should be in balanced proportion with the dog; however, the feet should be compact, with arched toes and turn neither in nor out.

Hindquarters.   When viewed from behind, the legs are parallel when in motion and at rest. Moderately angled at the stifle, and clearly defined thighs. When standing, the rear toes should be behind the point of the rump.

Coat Types.   As with many other breeds, Cockapoos have three different coat types. There is the tight curly coat, the medium curl, and the flat coat. While we strive for the medium curl, all three coat types are acceptable. It is very common to see all three types within the same litter of pups. This can happen with 1st, 2nd, 3rd (etc.) generation litters.

Coat length. The Cockapoo's coat should be clipped all over in a "teddy bear" type cut of about 2-3". The top of the head should be the same length as the body. If the tail is docked, the hair on the docked tail should be the same length as the body. A Cockapoo should never be shaven. They should have facial hair and a beard, all flowing into each other and trimmed no longer than 4 inches. The ears should be trimmed straight across and even with the bottom of the beard. The face should never be shaven. If the dog is not being shown, then a shorter or longer coat is allowed. Just remember to keep the eyes clear of fur and keep them well brushed.

Color and Markings. Any solid color; parti color (two or more solid colors, one of which must be white); phantom (brown, black or silver body with contrasting color on legs, under tail, eyebrows, side of face, inside ears); sable (may be black, brown, brindle, changing to silver, silver/gold mix, red, brown, other, all with darker points); tri-color (parti color with white base and tan markings over each eye, on the sides of the muzzle/cheeks, on the underside of the ears, on all feet and/or legs and optionally on the chest). Merle and/or roan are also acceptable colors. The nose and rims of eyes should be one solid color. Brown colored dogs may have brown noses, eye rims, lips, dark toenails and dark amber eyes. Black, blue, gray, cream and white dogs have black noses, eye rims and lips, black or self colored toenails and very dark eyes. In light-colored dogs, the liver-colored nose is quite common.

Temperament. Cockapoos are very people-oriented, outgoing, and happy dogs. The playful personality appeals to young and old alike. The Cockapoo has a keen intelligence any adult can appreciate, coupled with a forgiving nature that makes it unparalleled as a children's dog. They are as much at home in an apartment as they are on the biggest farm. They are extremely easy to train in just about any situation, but are people dogs and should not be left alone for extended periods of time.

****

Now there's quite a lot of useful information in here...what we have is a pretty clear "word picture" of the typical Cockapoo, which is what any good standard provides.

Let's look at *size*, which is, as in any good Breed Standard, measured here in the *height at the shoulder* rather than in pounds, because weight really tells us nothing– a Pembroke Welsh Corgi weighs around

28 pounds, and only stands 10 inches at the shoulder, while a Papillion standing 10 inches at the shoulder might be lucky to weigh 8 pounds!

Varying amounts of body fat aside, height-to-weight ratio in dogs is determined by both *proportion* (a dwarf breed like the Corgi is going to weigh a lot more for his height, because if it didn't have the FGF4 mutation that prevented its legs from growing normally, it would be a much bigger dog!) as well as *substance,* which is a "dog term" referring to the amount of bone a dog carries.

As he is not descended from dwarf breeds, the Cockapoo is a "squarely-built" dog and should "never appear long and low".

He is also described as "sturdy", which tells us he is neither fined-boned nor excessively heavy-boned. This general sturdiness makes him a more durable playmate for small children than one more delicately-built. This translates into a dog who might stand about 12 inches at the shoulder and weigh maybe 15 pounds as an adult, depending on gender and condition.

What does 12 inches at the shoulder look like? Take a yardstick and hold it up against your leg. A dog who stands 12 inches at the shoulder will generally measure about 18 inches at the top of the head, because well-proportioned dogs of any breed are roughly one-third leg, one-third body, and one-third neck and head.
This gives you an idea of how far you'll have to bend over to give him a pat on the head, which can be a problem for those with limited mobility.

You will also immediately see that the difference between 10 inches and 15 inches at the shoulder, which is the average height range for the breed, just isn't all that much when it comes right down to it.

The other information provided by a Standard concerns coat, which albeit a "fancy point", is of significant importance. It should be immediately apparent from this one that this is not a "wash-and-wear" breed. In fact, it's pretty *high-maintenance,* coat-wise (which is the price you pay for *any* low-shedding hypoallergenic breed) and that maintenance will cost you either time or money any way you slice it, no matter what length you decide to keep your Cockapoo.

The rest of the clues provided by a good Standard concern *breed character,* so let's look at that next.

Cockapoo Breed Character

As explained earlier, *breed character* generally refers to a commonality of behavioral traits found among most well-bred and well-socialized member of an individual breed— into this category fall things like a breed's typical energy level, and its typical attitude toward kids, strangers and other dogs.

In many ways, *breed character* is a better indicator of whether or not a particular breed will be a good match than *breed type*— a dog who ends up way too big for one's real estate holdings and who may drool and shed a lot more than one might have hoped, but who's also easy to train and great with kids may well be less of a problem in the long run than a small low-shedding dog who's wound like an old-fashioned alarm clock and inclined to snap at strange kids and the poor UPS guy!

In order for ANY DOG to be healthy and happy and to fully meet his genetic potential, there are three very different sets of essential needs that need to be met. These needs, common to all pack animals, are hard-wired into his DNA and have been carried down for millennia from his wolf ancestors. Listed in no particular order as all are equally critical, these are:

- **PHYSICAL NEEDS**
- **SOCIAL NEEDS**
- **INTELLECTUAL NEEDS**

Every breed's Standard, if well-written, provides good clues to what those needs are *in that individual breed*, which is important because they vary greatly from breed to breed. And here's why this is so important:

Without exception, virtually all behavioral problems in dogs are a result of one or more of these essential needs not being met.

It's that simple, really. And because most breeds were developed for very different and often very specific tasks over the years, the requirements for meeting these needs vary from breed to breed (and to a lesser extent from individual to individual) based upon breed *character*.

With most hybrids, especially the newer ones, the only real way to guess at these needs is to look at the parent breeds. But the Cockapoo has a good solid 50 year history behind him, and a Standard that does a good job of describing breed character. So let's look at those needs one by one, and what clues are in the Standard that might tell us how they'll best be met.

Meeting the Cockapoo's Physical Needs

The most obvious physical need of any dog, after food and water, is *exercise,* and most of America's dogs simply don't get enough. The Cockapoo standard states that the breed is **"capable of great speed and endurance, combined with agility",** which should give you a clue that this is not a "couch-potato" breed.

(There *are* a few real couch potato breeds out there, but *none* of them are Poodle crosses, just for the record— the Poodle tends to pass his high-energy tendencies to *all* his descendents, no matter what their size or who their "other parent breed" is. The Poodle could probably bump up the energy levels of *a three-toed sloth* if he was crossed with one.)

Although there's a modern tendency to look for much more complicated psychological reasons, (which keeps a lot of Canine Behavioralists in business) any experienced dog trainer can tell you that simple lack of exercise is the main reason for most of the annoying and destructive behavior in dogs. Here is one of the oldest and truest axioms in the world of dog training:

"A TIRED DOG IS A WELL-BEHAVED DOG."

It is positively amazing how maybe ten or fifteen minutes of hard, all-out *directed* exercise right before you leave will reduce a dog's "separation anxiety" when he needs to be left alone for a while. And popping him outside in a fenced yard by himself is *not* going to do it — in truth, many "city dogs", all of whose exercise is by definition directed, get more exercise than the average suburban Cockapoo with a big fenced yard. Here's why:

Unlike hounds, which as a group are bred to work independently from the handler at sometimes astonishing distances, the Cockapoo is descended from pretty "handler-dependent" hunting dogs on both sides. In the case of the Cocker, a flushing dog, his fieldwork actually requires him to stay within shotgun range at all times, and the breed has been selected for the better part of a hundred years to have a pretty short "psychological check cord" and to take directions from his handler while hunting. Working with a flushing dog is actually more like working with a herding dog than with a hound. Although he's really a pointing dog rather than a flushing dog (and many Cockapoos still display that pointing instinct!) the Poodle afield is not much different, although he is marginally less handler-dependent..

It's pretty obvious that a dog carrying this sort of DNA is not likely to self-exercise, especially when turned into a large square space by himself. (For the record, this is why "kennel runs" are traditionally long and narrow— a single dog is more likely to use a long narrow space than a square yard to self-exercise.)

This *doesn't* mean that you have to take your Cockapoo for a 10 minute walk prior to leaving the house every day, though. Although taking a daily walk around the neighborhood is great for *any* dog, it actually does more to meet his intellectual needs than his need for exercise, unless he's geriatric, really fat, or has little-bitty short legs. Dogs are built for endurance trotting (that word "endurance" is even in the Cockapoo Standard, remember?) and if they are balanced fore and aft, which the Cockapoo is, can do it all day without tiring. So odds are, by the time you're back in the house and ready to plop down on the couch, your dog is barely warmed up. To burn off excess energy and get tired out, a dog really needs to *run*.

However, this does not need to be accomplished by actually running *with* them for miles— in fact, for puppies that's a bad idea, especially on hard sidewalks. A dog's exercise should be the way Nature intended— in short bursts of all-out speed, and preferably on soft surfaces like grass.

Luckily, through a stroke of sheer luck, the Cockapoo, like many dogs descended from Sporting breeds, was endowed by Mother Nature with the perfect method of delivering this needed exercise— it's his natural inborn love of *retrieving*.

Hands-down, the best thing you can do for both your Cockapoo and yourself is to develop and encourage his retrieving skills early on.

This can be started as soon as he comes into your house at 8 or 10 weeks of age— it's amazing how fast puppies catch on to the game, and how quickly they become addicted to it. Once you've got a dog who loves to retrieve, you have the perfect method for exercising him. Ten minutes of a lively game of fetch will go a long way toward burning off excess energy, while requiring a lot less in the way of energy expenditure on the part of the guy doing the throwing. The dog won't mind, though— in fact, he probably won't even notice. Once a dog has developed his retrieving skills (say by 12 weeks of age) it becomes a self-rewarding exercise.— as long as you keep throwing, the dog really doesn't care if you're sitting on your butt reading a book or checking your email, and he certainly doesn't need a treat every time he returns with a tennis ball or a Frisbee.

Because of his compact size, this retrieving can be moved to a long hallway indoors in inclement weather. In good weather, a dog park and even a small fenced backyard will suffice.

Meeting the Cockapoo's Social Needs

There are literally *tons* of clues about what is needed to meet the Cockapoo's social needs in the ACC Standard. Here are a few key phrases:

- "very people-oriented"
- "outgoing"
- " playful "
- "people dogs"
- "should not be left alone for extended periods of time"

In other words, it is generally agreed that the Cockapoo is about as people-oriented as a dog can get. A well-bred and well-socialized Cockapoo views every stranger he happens upon as a friend he simply hasn't met yet. His love of children, even babies, is legendary and (with the exception of maybe the Pug) is frankly rare in a dog his size. But, then, kids love to play, and so do Cockapoos.

The take-home message here is that no matter what a breeder anxious to make a sale may tell you, the Cockapoo is just NOT a good choice for the household where no one is home most of the time. Their social needs are just too great.

However, if that is your situation, and you still are sure that the Cockapoo is the only dog for you, there *are* a couple of things you can do to make it work. They work because like most really social dogs, they don't suffer from an overdose of loyalty….their social needs can easily be met by those outside their immediate family.

Because they typically get along remarkably well with other dogs, Doggy Day Care is a great solution for owners who work full-time. This can be a formal Doggy Day Care facility, or it can involve dropping him off for those hours at the home of a trusted retired dog-loving relative or family friend who might well enjoy the company as well as the extra income. (This can be a more economical option, especially in cities where day care facility costs might be prohibitively high.) What *won't* work is simply having someone come in at noon to take him out and play with him for a few minutes— the lonely hours in between will be agony for this super-social little breed.

In addition, most breeders and owners agree that the Cockapoo gets along remarkably well with other animals— dogs, cats, even some smaller pets like rabbits if they're raised together— which is why so many Cockapoo owners have a pair of Cockapoos rather than just one...sort of doubles the fun, and they can provide company for each other when there are —horrors!—no people around.

Two Cockapoos will also tend to zoom around together in a fenced backyard even if there are no humans in evidence, which will help to meet those exercise needs without the need for you to be out there throwing a tennis ball at least some of the time. (But it also goes without saying that you never, *ever* want to leave them outdoors when you're not home for safety reasons, even if they're having a grand old time. Remember, it's better for a dog to be temporarily bored than permanently stolen.)

Which brings us to the *next* question regarding the meeting of a Cockapoo's substantial social needs, and that would be: is it better to get ….

One Puppy or Two?

Although most "two-dog families" started with one and added the second one later, a sizable minority decide to raise two puppies (often littermates) together, figuring it will take care of that "lonely puppy when no one is home" problem. And it will, no doubt about it.

On the other hand, if anyone on the planet has figured out how to HOUSETRAIN two puppies left alone all day, they've yet to share it with the rest of the world.

Although two puppies will indeed meet each other's social needs if left alone for extended periods, what you'll likely end up with is a pair of happy hooligans. For this reason, many responsible breeders will flat-out *never* sell two littermates to the same family. Others will, but only if someone is home all day to keep a lid on the hooliganism. (One might want to be careful dealing with a breeder who doesn't ask a *lot* of questions before selling a pair of puppies from the same litter, because they may be more motivated by profit than by a desire to see their puppies actually succeed in their new homes.)

For the record, a pair of littermates *can* be successfully trained simultaneously, but it does take more than twice the effort, and it really does require that someone be around 24/7 at least until they're reliably housetrained., as well as a better-than-average sense of humor.

Although "conventional wisdom" claims that puppies raised together will bond with each other rather than with people, this generally only happens when they are left alone together for extended periods, and varies a lot with breed character. Two puppies of a people-oriented breed like the Cockapoo raised together tend to *compete* for human attention rather than ignore it. The hardest part is really early housetraining, because you have to watch *two* puppies for signs they need to pee rather than just one, and odds are they won't need to go at the same time. Considered yourself warned.

27

Meeting the Cockapoo's Intellectual Needs

In the intelligence department, the ACC standard includes the following descriptive phrases:

- Keen intelligence
- Forgiving nature
- Extremely easy to train

Again, this is one of those places where not being a "new" breed provides a decided advantage. Breeders don't have to guess at the expected IQ level and trainability the cross will produce, because they actually have generations of Cockapoos (and Cockapoo owners!) to turn to for information, and the consensus is that like their Poodle ancestors, the breed is uniformly intelligent and easy to train.

A lot of people who want a smaller hybrid will look at the mini Goldendoodle before the Cockapoo mainly because the Cocker, bless his heart, has a reputation as one of the dimmer bulbs in the canine chandelier...sort of the "blondes" of the purebred dog world. This is unfortunate on a couple of levels. To begin with, Cockers really are not so much *dumb* (most are in fact quite intelligent) as they are *chronically immature*— the American Cocker in particular is what is referred to as a *neotenous* breed. In fact, many trainers consider it to be the single most neotenous breed. Cockers are Perpetual Puppies.

Neoteny is a phenomenon that refers to the retention of juvenile characteristics into adulthood.

This fascinating phenomenon, which has been well-studied and not unique to dogs by a long shot, is what makes them so gosh-darned *cute*, even as adults, and why they remain playful even as adults, and make great playmates for kids. On the other hand, it also makes them less than reliable even when they seem like they should be "old enough to know better", and often frustratingly slow to housetrain (Women invariably notice that these are the same character traits displayed in their first husbands, many of whom also suffer from neoteny– you know, those charmers you married back in college who just won't grow up and get a real job?)

The Poodle, on the other hand, is probably one of the *least* neotenous of breeds— as a group, they're the Doogie Housers of the dog world. The difference is obvious just by *looking* at them, since neoteny affects the body as well as the brain in all species. Like those guys who are still "boyishly cute" at 30,

Cockers keep their soft mushy puppy muzzles throughout life, as well as their big puppy paws, whereas Poodle puppies look more like miniature adults right from the get-go. (Whatever their many other virtues, Poodles are not really "cute", even as puppies.) And they are rarely playful as adults like Cockers. But that lightning-fast maturation does translate into easy training, especially in the housetraining department. Their well-recognized intelligence is simply not complicated by chronic immaturity, as it often is in Cockers.

And where does that leave the Cockapoo? Once again, through the serendipity of genetics, he got lucky. The typical Cockapoo is highly intelligent, because intelligence is really coming in from both sides, but the neoteny is reduced significantly in the first cross to the Poodle. He still retains enough to make him a playful, social, and all-around fun dog even as an adult. (It also accounts for the "forgiving nature" which is a boon to training as well as making him great with kids.) But there's not so much neoteny in evidence to make him difficult to housetrain, and like his Poodle ancestors, he is pretty reliable early on. (An amazing number of owners report that their Cockapoo puppy was ringing a bell to go outside at 12 weeks of age!)

On the other hand, this intelligence, combined with his strong social nature, means that the Cockapoo is really a poor choice for hose who aren't interested in training beyond the basics.

This is a breed that takes to training from early puppyhood like a duck to water, and really loves to learn. Without training, he will simply train himself, and that's not really fair to the dog, since the results are rarely what the owner had in mind.

Because he's very social, training classes are a great idea for Cockapoos, and they are often Valedictorians of their puppy classes. But there's no need to wait until he's old enough for classes— even the novice owner can start training right away without screwing it up (that's an upside of that "forgiving nature" thing) and really should. Once the basics have been mastered, there is no end to the games this breed can learn to play, or the various jobs they can master. On the other hand, without the pretty constant intellectual stimulation required of a "high IQ" breed like this, boredom will set in...and boredom invariably leads to behavioral problems.

One of the easiest "non-training" ways to do this is to simply take him for a daily walk around the neighborhood. This is especially important for suburban dogs—although it doesn't occur to most owners, "city dogs" really have an advantage here. Being turned out into a privacy-fenced yard is just not as intellectually stimulating than checking out what's new and interesting in the 'hood.

CHAPTER TWO

The Cockapoo Coat

There is no doubt that the characteristic soft, wavy and somewhat tousled Cockapoo coat contributes in no small part to the overall charm of the breed, as well as contributing in no small part to his killer-cute "Cockapoo face"— whether kept long or scissored into its traditional Teddy Bear cut, and no matter what its color, this soft and eminently pettable coat is just an integral part of the Cockapoo, and somehow fits his personality perfectly.

For a few hours after a bath and a trim and brush-out, the typical Cockapoo looks pretty elegant, but soon reverts to the typical casual shagginess that says this is not a *decorative* dog so much as a *useful* one. This is a dog well-suited for hiking, swimming, and rolling in leaves, one who doesn't mind snow and ice or wet grass as long as he's having fun.

In fact, along with his compact size, kid-friendly temperament and reputation for robust health and longevity, the Cockapoo's "hypoallergenic, non-shedding" coat is one of the chief characteristics that attracts people to the breed. Are these qualities for real, or are they just "breeder hype", as is sometimes claimed?

Let's look at the "hypoallergenic" part first.

Over the past couple of years the term "allergy-friendly" has largely replaced the term "hypoallergenic" on a lot of breeders' websites, as it is now generally accepted that there is "really no such thing as a hypoallergenic dog".

This is an unfortunate mistake. The *only* reason it is now generally accepted that "there is really no such thing as a hypoallergenic dog" is because that particular bit of misinformation been *widely disseminated on the internet*, apparently by persons one can only charitably assume have no access to a dictionary.

From the American Heritage Dictionary:

Hypoallergenic adj. :
Having a decreased tendency to provoke an allergic reaction.

In other words, a "hypoallergenic dog" simply has a *decreased* (i.e. lower) tendency to produce an allergic reaction in people with allergies when compared to a dog that is not hypoallergenic. That's pretty cut-and-dried. (This makes sense if you think about it— "hypoglycemic" refers to *low* blood sugar, not *no* blood sugar, and "hypothyroid" refers to *low* thyroid levels, not *non-existent* ones.)

So why the confusion?

What's actually happened here is that way too many self-styled "internet dog experts" have unfortunately confused *hypoallergenic* with *nonallergenic,* which is an entirely different word with an entirely different meaning.

Nonallergenic adj.:
Not producing an allergic reaction.

There are in fact *many* hypoallergenic breeds, and the Cockapoo is definitely one of them. According to many people who live with them, these breeds simply have a *decreased tendency* to provoke an allergic reaction compared to other breeds. On the other hand, there are no *nonallergenic* breeds at all, even those which are entirely devoid of hair, because all dogs are covered from nose to tail in *skin*, which is where the allergens are produced. To understand why, we need to know a little about...

The Science of Dog Hair

Most dog allergies in humans are produced by reactions to the rather awkwardly named *Can f 1* and *Can f 2* proteins. These proteins are produced in canine epithelial tissue, and end up in the dog's dander (which consists of shed skin cells) some of which sticks to the hair before becoming airborne. (These proteins are also found in canine saliva, which is why dogs that drool heavily are a poor choice for people with allergies.)

Some breeds have been shown to carry measurably greater amounts of these proteins on their hair, and the differences are actually connected to *seborrhoeac levels* rather than hair length. (*Seborrhoeac* in this context simply refers to dogs that naturally produce a lot of *sebum*, as opposed to dogs with a pathological skin condition.)

Sebum is the oily substance produced by the sebaceous gland, a small gland connected to the hair follicle and which lubricates the hair shaft. Not surprisingly, the oilier "waterproof" breeds like Labs were found to have the highest levels of Can f proteins on their hair, because instead of the normal 21-day cycle, the epidermal turnover time of seborrhoeac dogs is only 3-4 days. In other words, oily-coated dogs simply produce more dander. Less oily breeds like the Poodle produce considerably less. The Cocker Spaniel probably falls somewhere in the middle.

Although hair length itself does not affect the amount of Can f proteins produced, the more hair that's shed, the more allergens are dispersed throughout the house. This is where the "non-shedding/low-shedding" part comes in, and hair length (largely determined by variations on the canine RSPO2 and FGF5 genes) is a definite factor in shedding, another area where misinformation abounds. So let's look at that next.

Shedding and Genetic Coat Variations:

To begin with, except for a very few totally hairless breeds, *all dogs shed*.
There is simply no such thing as a non-shedding coated dog, or a non-shedding coated mammal of *any kind,* for that matter. Even *elephants* shed, for Heaven's sake. Some dogs simply contribute less hair to the environment than others, for a couple of different reasons.

Each mammalian hair goes through a basic three-phase cycle – *anagen, catagen* and *telogen* – although not all hairs are on the same cycle. (If that were the case, shorthaired dogs would be totally bald for a couple of weeks several times a year, which they clearly are not.)

Although it can be affected by temperature, daylight, endocrine function and the animal's individual health, most shedding is genetically determined.

Anagen is the "growth" phase, and the length of this cycle varies greatly based on the dog's genes. Longhaired dogs logically spend a lot more time in the anagen phase than short-haired ones do.
Catagen is the "transitional" phase, which lasts 1-2 weeks.
Telogen is the "resting" phase, which lasts 5-6 weeks, during which time the hair doesn't grow. At the end of this cycle, the hair detaches from the follicle and is pushed out, or shed, as a new hair develops beneath it.

So what's happening is basically this: a shorthaired dog is genetically programmed to whip through the anagen or "growth" phase a lot faster than a longhaired one – the anagen phase in a dog like the Lab, whose hair grows to about an inch or two at best, may only last a couple of months, whereas the anagen phase in a Poodle, whose hair can reach 10 inches before shedding out, may last a couple of years. (Although the Poodle coat spends more time in anagen than probably any other breed, contrary to popular belief, a Poodle's hair will *not* continue to grow indefinitely!)

In other words, a shorthaired dog sheds out each *individual* hair a lot more often.
This results in more dog hair lying around, which carries more dander and, depending on the seborrhoeac levels, more Can f proteins.

There are four additional factors affecting shedding that are a lot less straightforward.

The first involves the amount of curl in the dog's hair, which is largely controlled by variations on the KRT71 gene. Although we can't see them, each hair shaft is covered with scales, sort of like a fish. In straighter-coated breeds, these scales lie flat against the hair shaft, whereas on curly or wavy hair, which consists of a series of s-curves, the scales are forced open at each outside curve, sort of like what you'd see if you bent a fish.

When curly or wavy haired breeds shed, the hair that's just been shed
tends to catch in open scales of the surrounding hairs and get stuck there,
rather than falling clean off the dog and landing on the couch.

These breeds are said to "shed into their coats", and if not brushed regularly to remove the shed hairs they will rapidly turn into a matted mess. The tradeoff for this higher grooming requirement, of course, is less dog hair floating around the house.

The second factor in shedding is the *pattern* of coat growth, which is largely controlled by two different genes. A typically longhaired breed like the Cocker carries two copies of a variation on the *FGF5* gene, which causes the hair on the bottom half of the dog to be long while the hair on the face, front of the legs and feet is short, with the hair on the back of intermediate length.

Longhaired breeds shed less than shorthaired breeds because a large percentage of their hair spends more time in the anagen phase.

These breeds are considered to be "moderate" shedders. Many people are surprised to learn that longhaired breeds shed less than shorthaired ones, but it is a fact nonetheless. As anyone who's owned one can attest, in the shedding department the otherwise adorable Pug is the hands-down winner. The Pug's coat is both short *and* dense, which translates to a *lot* of shed hair pretty much everywhere.

To further complicate things, dogs with facial furnishings and furry feet all carry at least one copy of a dominant variant on the *RSPO2* gene which causes the hair all over the dog to stay in a longer anagen cycle.
Breeds that carry two copies of the recessive "longhaired" (FGF5) variant and at least one copy of the dominant "furnishings" (RSPO2) variant have long hair from nose to tail and will logically shed less than a longhaired breed without the RSPO2 mutation. Breeds carrying this genetic combination are referred to as "drop-coated", and include Bearded Collies, Tibetan Terriers, Lhasas and Maltese.

When the gene variants that produce a drop coat are combined with the variants that produce a curly coat you end up with the breeds likely to be lowest-shedding and most hypoallergenic.

The Poodle, the Portuguese Water Dog, and the Bichon Frise all fall into this category. (For reasons not yet fully understood, these breeds also tend not to produce a lot of sebum, which is why they rarely have a "doggy" odor.)

This brings us to the third factor affecting shedding – coat *density*, which is defined as the number of hairs per square inch. The denser the coat, the more hairs are logically shed on a daily basis.

Depending upon the texture, this extra hair will either end up on the furniture or being shed into the coat, where it will rapidly form mats.

Coat density is inherited independently of all the other coat genes. Poodles carry a uniformly dense coat, while coat density in Cockers varies quite a bit. As well as typically carrying more wave, the American Cocker carries a softer, denser coat than the English Cocker does, and both carry more coat than the "field-bred" Cockers both American and English. (Groomers generally agree that the dense coats on show-bred American Cockers are far and away the most difficult to maintain.)

The final factor is the difference between guard hair and undercoat. These are produced by two different types of hair follicles, which cycle differently—as everyone with a dog has probably already noticed, undercoat cycles faster than guard hair.

As juveniles, all mammals produce only undercoat, which is generally softer and finer and is insulating, while guard hair is generally coarser and waterproof. Around six months, some of the undercoat follicles are replaced by those which will produce guard hair. This is the period called "blowing puppy coat", and it generally lasts for several months, during which time tangles form almost overnight —if the puppy is not brushed almost daily he will rapidly become a matted mess.

Even as an adult, the ratio of guard hair to undercoat varies from breed to breed and in the case of the Cockapoo from dog to dog. Because undercoat cycles faster, in general, the greater the proportion of undercoat, the greater the coat maintenance requirements. (It's worth noting that the American Cocker generally carries more undercoat than the English Cocker does.)

It's also worth knowing that research has shown that genetics aside, *the single most effective tool* in reducing the amount of Can f proteins on the dog and by extension in the house is *frequent bathing*.

The amount of Can f allergens dispersed throughout the house can be reduced by up to 84% by simply bathing the dog twice a week.

Which, let's face it, no one is really going to do. But it is a strong argument for considering a dog on the smaller end of the Cockapoo size scale when allergies are a factor.

It's simply a lot less work to bathe a little dog than a big one, and for that reason alone a smaller dog is likely to get bathed more often.

Cockapoo Coat Genetics

One of the reasons relatively few Cockapoo breeders over the years have bred Cockapoo to Cockapoo is because no matter which combinations they try, or how many Poodle backcrosses they do, puppies with "spaniel coats" invariably pop up in litters. Because these "throwbacks" appear to be impossible to eliminate, and are frankly harder to find homes for, many breeders just stick with F1 breedings.

Then in 2009 a team led by researchers from the National Human Genome Research Institute (NHGRI), part of the National Institutes of Health, found that variants in just **three genes** acting in different combinations account for the wide range of coat textures seen in dogs. (These are the same 3 genes that affect shedding.) They looked at these three loci on the genes of 662 dogs from 108 breeds (including Poodles and Cockers) and found that the presence of the mutations or not, in various combinations, *accounted for the variation in coat in 95 percent of the breeds.* Their research was published in the September 2009 issue of the journal *Science,* and within a year or two, inexpensive commercial tests for these genes became widely available. This is *great news* for breeders who want to breed multigenerational dogs…..here's why:

The Cocker (American or English) is genetically *ll, CC, ff.* This means he typically carries two copies of the recessive longhaired variant at FGF5, two copies of the wavy variant at KRT71, and two copies of the recessive "clean-faced" variant at RSPO2 rather than the variant responsible for facial furnishings.

The Poodle is *ll, cc, FF.* This means. Like the Cocker, he also carries two copies of the *l* variant. He also typically carries two copies of the curly variant and two copies of the dominant "facial furnishings" RSPO2 variant.

The chart (or *Punnett square*) to the right shows the predicted results of crossing these two genotypes—ALL pups have the same *ll,Cc,Ff* genotype.

F1 breeding	Parent A (purebred poodle)	ll cc FF long, curly, with furnishings
Parent B (purebred cocker) **ll CC ff** long, wavy, no furnishings	**ll Cc Ff** long, wavy, with furnishings	**ll Cc Ff** long, wavy, with furnishings
	ll Cc Ff long, wavy, with furnishings	**ll Cc Ff** long, wavy, with furnishings

F2 breeding	**Sire** ll Cc Ff long, wavy, with furnishings	
Dam ll Cc Ff long, wavy, with furnishings	ll CC FF long, wavy, with furnishings	ll cc FF long, curly, with furnishings
	ll CC ff long, wavy, no furnishings	ll Cc Ff long, wavy, with furnishings

Now, what happens when you breed two of these F1 Cockapoos together to produce F2s is shown in the Punnett square to the left.

Statistically, half the puppies will have typical wavy Cockapoo coats with facial furnishings, while another 25% will have curly Poodle coats.
Another 25% will look a lot like a purebred Cocker, which are often called "spaniel coats".

These coats are not evident at birth (and obviously they do not come out sporting the show clips used in these diagrams!) but by about 6 weeks, experienced breeders can usually identify them.

Less experienced breeders *may not realize* a particular pup is developing a spaniel coat by the time the pups are ready to go at 8 weeks or so, resulting in a very surprised (and disappointed) owner later on, as the expected Cockapoo head furnishings never develop.

F1b breeding	(Poodle) Parent A ll cc FF long, curly, with furnishings	
(F1 Cockapoo) Parent B ll Cc Ff long, wavy, with furnishings	ll Cc FF long, wavy, with furnishings	ll cc Ff long, curly, with furnishings
	ll cc FF long, curly, with furnishings	ll Cc Ff long, wavy, with furnishings

In an effort to avoid this, many Cockapoo breeders wishing to keep Cockapoo bitches for breeding will breed them back to Poodles, as shown in the diagram at the lower left.

Because the Poodle is FF, these breedings cannot produce any spaniel-coated pups, but usually half the litter will have the tightly curled coat typical of a Poodle.

And, although their pedigrees are actually 3/4 Poodle, half the pups will still carry the RSPO2 mutation for the clean-faced "spaniel coat" and will still pass it on to half their offspring if bred.

Without gene testing, recessive genes, whether for

fairly benign "cosmetic" genes like this one, or more serious problems like PRA, cannot *ever* be completely eliminated from a gene pool even after generations of "selecting away" from the trait.

In the example to the immediate right, we can see that even in an F2b breeding, where the pedigree of the resulting pups is now 7/8 Poodle and only 1/8 Cocker, if the F1b parent happens to be carrying the spaniel coat gene, a percentage of the litter (statistically 50%) will also carry the gene, because the parent carrying that gene will pass it to 50% of his offspring. Because it takes two copies in order for the trait to be displayed and the Poodle parent doesn't have a copy to pass on, none of the pups from this breeding will display the trait.

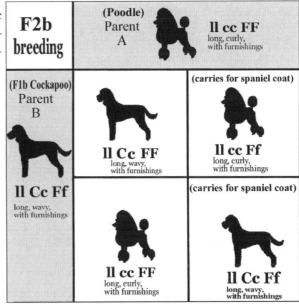

However, if a Cockapoo from that litter who *is* carrying the gene for a spaniel coat is subsequently bred to another multigenerational Cockapoo (like for instance the F2 pup in the lower right-hand corner of the first chart) who happens to be carrying it, It is entirely possible that there will be spaniel-coated pups in the resulting litter.

Although the number of spaniel-coated pups is statistically 25%, that is based on a hundred puppies, which is an impossibly large number for a single litter. In reality, in a normal litter of 4-6 puppies, there may be anywhere from none to 100%. (The latter case will usually send the breeder into a dead faint.) Or it may not show up in the first litter, but will in the second or third.

This is why recessive genes were long thought to "skip a generation", a phrase some breeders still use. In reality, *no generation* is skipped genetically— it just may take several generations to produce a pup who inherits two copies and displays the trait.

tested F2 X untested F1	**Parent A** gene-tested F2, not carrying f allele for spaniel coat, or c allele for curly coat — ll CC FF	
Parent B F1, obligate carrier of both f and c alleles — ll, Cc, Ff	ll, Cc, FF	ll, Cc, Ff
	ll, CC, FF	ll, CC, Ff

On the other hand, with simple non-invasive gene tests (DNA is collected using a cheek swab from pups as young as 3 weeks) currently costing around $60, breeders can now test for both the furnishings gene and the curly gene. (Labs currently offering these tests are listed in the Resources section.)

Puppies from any F2 breeding can now be tested (there's no point to testing F1 puppies as all will be obligate carriers because the Cocker carries 2 copies of the *f*, or "spaniel coat" allele) and those who don't carry the allele can be bred to F1 bitches with no risk of producing spaniel coated puppies.

Testing can also be done for the curly gene at the same time, but as the genes are inherited independently, the *FF* puppies may be carriers of the curly gene, so breeders may have to work on eliminating one trait at a time. Those lucky pups who inherit the *ll, CC, FF* genotype will produce typical Cockapoo coats no matter who they're bred to, even when bred back to either of the parent breeds.

tested F2 X tested F2 breeding	**Parent A** gene-tested F2, not carrying f allele for spaniel coat, or c allele for curly coat — ll CC FF	
Parent B gene-tested F2, not carrying f allele for spaniel coat, or c allele for curly coat — ll, CC, FF	ll, CC, FF	ll, CC, FF
	ll, CC, FF	ll, CC, FF

These gene tests are a great bargain, because they allow breeders to maintain a healthy level of genetic diversity (and play with color!) while still producing Cockapoo puppies with ideal coats. The puppies produced from the breeding shown above can then be gene-tested and those not carrying the *F* and *c* alleles can again be selected for breeding.

Breeders who choose to "go deep" can also breed two tested F2 dogs together. *None of the resulting pups will be carriers* because neither parent has the genes to pass on. These pups are considered "clear by parentage" and do not require testing. This technique is generally used to eliminate recessive genes for serious problems like *PRA/prcd*, but can also be used to eliminate cosmetic traits like spaniel coats...

Cockapoo Coats and Allergies

OK, after all this discussion about breeding for the "ideal" wavy coat, from the pet buyer's standpoint, there is a situation in which a Cockapoo puppy with a different coat would be by far the better choice.

For families where allergies are a problem, or for the owner who simply wants the least possible amount of shedding, these puppies (whose coats will spend more time in anagen and who, when they do shed, will shed into their coats rather than end up on the floor) are far and way the best choice.

These coats generally look better (and mat less!) when kept in a short clip, but the family where allergies are an issue is going to want to do that anyway, because it's much easier to keep a short coat bathed once (or even twice) a week, which research has shown will significantly reduce the amount of *Can f* proteins in the environment.

These coats are most likely to be found in F1b and F2 litters (as well as untested multigenerational breedings) rather than in F1 litters, so if allergies are a problem, those are the best litters to look at. Even with the gene tests available, they are not going to disappear, because they will inevitably turn up in F2 breedings– in that case, gene testing will simply allow breeders to identify which puppies are carrying which genes, and can make breeding decisions based on that.

Even with these curlier coats, however, it's important to remember that *hypoallergenic* does NOT mean the same as *nonallergenic,* so it's a really good idea for the allergy sufferer to spend some time playing with Cockapoos (petting is really important here, just looking won't do it!) in an indoor environment before making a final decision.

And because allergic reactions generally do not occur until the *second* exposure (after the IgE antibodies have been "primed" by the first exposure), it's really important to do it more than once. If the second exposure, which sets off the allergic reaction, does not happen until you bring a new puppy home, it's not going to turn out well for anybody, including the poor puppy.

For those owners where allergies and shedding are not deal-breakers, but who would like the lowest-maintenance coat while still enjoying the Cockapoo temperament, trainability, and robust health, the spaniel-coated puppy might be the perfect choice. These are really the only "wash-and-wear" Cockapoos.

Some Cockapoo colors and patterns, like this tan-pointed sable
(shown here as a newborn, a puppy, and as an adult)
change a lot from birth to adulthood.

CHAPTER FOUR

Cockapoo Colors

Surely one of the coolest things about Cockapoos is their absolute *plethora* of colors they come in. If you can think of a color or pattern known to dogs, odds are pretty good there's a Cockapoo somewhere on the planet wearing it, and it seems like breeders are coming up with new ones all the time.

From the pet owners point of view, the genetics of color really doesn't matter— in the final analysis, color is really nothing more than personal preference, and when it comes to choosing a puppy, individual differences in temperament, energy level and sometimes size are usually way more important.

For the Cockapoo *breeder,* understanding the genetics of color can be a lot more important. It allows the breeder to actually produce litters in the colors they *want* instead of simply being surprised, and in a few cases can actually prevent some fairly serious health problems, especially when breeding multi-generational dogs. For this reason, even breeders who find the whole subject of genetics coma-inducing really need to study this section. Some pet owners may find it interesting as well.

So what we're going to do here is take a look at the color genes commonly found in Cockapoos, what colors and patterns they can produce, and how they are inherited.

Since the 1940s, most of what was known about canine color genetics came from one source— a book called **the Inheritance of Coat Color in Dogs** by Clarence C. Little, a Harvard-educated geneticist and founder of the world-famous Jackson Laboratory, which is where he did his color research. (The Jackson lab now breeds genetically-engineered Jaxmice for cancer research.)

(Unfortunately, Dr. Little was also possibly *the world's most boring writer,* which goes a long way toward explaining why so few breeders really understand color genetics to this day. Although many have tried, it's virtually impossible for the average breeder to make it all the way through this seminal work on canine color genetics without actually slipping into a coma...)

Anyhow, what Little hypothesized (primarily through test breedings as there were no other genetic techniques available at that time) was that **virtually all colors and patterns seen in domestic dogs** were the result of a combination of variations (called *alleles*) in at least ten different genes located on 10 different *loci* (or "addresses" within the genome) which had arisen over time and were inherited in unique combinations in each puppy within a litter. He also determined that some of these alleles were recessive to the original "wild type" genes seen in the wolf, while a few were dominant over them.

Half a century later, when a new breed of geneticists had the technology to actually examine these genes at the molecular level, it turned out that Little was basically right. In fact, the letters that Little used to denote each locus are still used today, mostly because it's easier than referring to the genes by their actual names (like *CBD103* or *TRYP1)* which let's face it, don't exactly slide off the tongue.

The loci responsible for color and pattern in canines are **A, B, C, D, E, G, I, K, M, S, and T. (**All these loci were hypothesized by Little way back in the 40s except K, and the actual genes for most of them have now been located on various chromosomes on the canine genome.) Cockapoos appear to be variable at most of them, which explains all the color variations in the breed.

So what we're going to look at are the bare basics of what *causes* the various colors and patterns seen in Cockapoos, the genes responsible, and which variants are dominant and which are recessive, in some sort of logical order. Let's start with pigment itself, which is produced in the body by *melanin.*

There are two types of melanin in mammals: the brown or black *eumelanin* and the reddish-yellow *pheomelanin*, both produced by cells called *melanocytes* in the skin and hair. The color and pattern we see on a dog is determined primarily by which of these pigment types predominates, by the distribution of the *pigment granules*, and how the eye "reads" these combinations.

What we see as "coat color" is determined by various genes
which instruct the body on *how much* of these pigments to produce, *where* to produce them,
and sometimes *when to start and stop* producing them.
It's that simple.

"True white", on the other hand, is what the eye sees when there are no pigment granules at all in the hair. It is caused by *the absence of any pigment development* in the developing embryo and can occur with any color or pattern. Lack of pigment granules in the skin of the dog's nose causes it to appear pink, and in the iris of the eye to appear blue.

OK, so all the colors and patterns seen in Cockapoos are determined by variations in the amount and distribution of eumelanin and pheomelanin in the hair, skin, and eyes, which is determined by the actions of various *gene alleles* acting in combination. Simple enough.

Some of these "color genes" have only two allelic variations, while others have several. However, no matter how many variations there are on a given gene, a dog can only inherit TWO of them, one from each parent. He may inherit two of the same alleles (in which case we say the dog is *homozygous* for that allele), or two different ones (in which case we say he is *heterozygous*). Generally, one of the alleles is dominant over the other. A heterozygous dog will "display" the dominant allele and "carry for" the recessive one, which he will pass to half his offspring randomly. So let's look at each locus and what it can produce:

The K locus

The K locus is home to a *canine beta-defensin gene* called CBD103. This is probably the *most important* locus to understand, because it affects every other color and pattern gene the dog inherits. (Ironically, this is the one Dr Little missed, although he recognized that dominant inheritance of a black coat was different in dogs than in other animals.) To date, three different alleles have been identified on this gene, all of which can affect Cockapoo coat color:

- K^B —often called "dominant black", this one really causes all the hair that's not "true white" to be *a single color*. All Labradors—black, chocolate, or yellow— have two copies of this allele (they're all K^B/K^B) which is why "dominant black" is a really dumb name for it. "Self-colored" is probably more accurate.
- Because it is the most dominant gene in the series, one copy of K^B is enough to make a dog self-

colored— no matter what other pattern genes the dog inherited (with the exception of white spotting), this gene will pretty well mask them.

- **k^{br}** —this mutation causes brindling, a series of darker and lighter colored hairs on the coat in a striped pattern. Not found in Cockers, brindling *does* occur in Poodles (just Google *'brindle poodle images'* to see what it looks like) and, since it only takes *one copy* of this allele to produce a brindle dog, it can show up even in F1 Cockapoos, although it's pretty rare. Since k^{br} is recessive to K^B, **the brindle gene cannot show in a dog who inherits a single copy of K^B. (**Brindle dogs are generally either k^{br}/k^{br} or k^{br}/k^y.) Since dogs that are "e/e" at this locus have a dysfunctional *melanocortin 1 receptor* and are unable to make black hairs anywhere on their body, a dog with an "e/e" genotype could carry brindle and it would not be expressed. This dog could produce brindle pups with the right mate.

- **k or k^y** —sometimes called the "sable gene" (which it's not) the Stanford group who identified this gene named this allele k^y since it allows yellow (*pheomelanin*) pigment to show. *Where* it shows depends on which alleles at the A locus a dog also happened to inherit— in Cockapoos, that could be clear or shaded sable, fawn, or tan patterned. But because this allele is recessive to both the solid **(K)** and brindle (k^{br}) alleles, a dog must inherit a copy from each parent (in other words he must be k^y/k^y) in order to display those patterns, although he may carry the genes for them.

The A locus

Located on canine chromosome 24 and home to the *agouti signal peptide* gene (called *ASIP* for short), the A locus is responsible for several different *patterns,* including the various forms of sable. These patterns can occur on an array of "base" colors So far three alleles have been identified on this gene, and three of them affect Cockapoos. (A fourth allele, the original "wolf pattern" agouti gene that produces banded hairs, is mostly found in German Shepherds and Nordic breeds.)

- **A^y**—this allele causes sable in many breeds, which can vary quite a bit. *Shaded sable* puppies are born dark, and the coat lightens as it grows out, often ending up with dark tips. *Clear sable* dogs are a clear shade of red or fawn and are often confused with the red shades produced by the **e/e** phenotype. (The main difference is the **e/e** dog will have *no black hairs in his coat* anywhere even at birth, where the sable usually will, although they may disappear.)

-
a^t——This allele is responsible for the classic *tan pattern* or *tan points* in all breeds; it shows up on many

coat colors and patterns, including merle. (A black, chocolate, red or merle dog with white markings along with a^t/a^t tan points will be "tri-colored".) Because it's recessive to A^y, a dog must be a^t/a^t to display tan points. Many e/e and K^B/K^B dogs are a^t/a^t; although they can't display it themselves, they can produce tan-patterned puppies.

- **a** —- this allele, recessive to all the others, causes a solid black coat; because it is found in Poodles, it probably is responsible for some solid black Cockapoos who are k^y/k^y.

Note: In Cockapoos (and Poodles) tan pattern is often called "phantom", but they're really two different things. In Cockers, "phantom" is specifically used for a dog who displays *incomplete expression* of the tan pattern. These dogs are usually K^B / k^y as well as a^t/a^t . Without the second k^y allele, the tan pattern is often subtle and hard to see (hence the term "phantom") and sometimes doesn't make its appearance at all until the dog is several years old! The easiest place to see "phantom tan" on a black puppy is under the tail.

The B locus

Although at least four alleles have been identified at this locus, there are really only two possible phenotypes— *black* noses and *brown* noses. The gene at the B locus is *Tyrosinase Related Protein 1 (TYRP1)* on canine chromosome 11. Three variations in this gene all affect *eumelanin synthesis*, causing hair and pigment on the nose, lips, pads and eye rims that would otherwise appear black to appear brown. In Cockapoos, this is called *chocolate,* as it is in both parent breeds. (In others, this same color may be called *liver*, and sometimes *red*.)

- **B** — is the dominant allele in the series; a dog with even one copy can produce black pigment.

- b^S, b^d, b^c— all recessive to **B**, *any two of these alleles* will produce brown pigment, whether the dog inherits the same two alleles (such as b^d/b^d) or two different ones (b^d/b^c); to make things simpler, all are simply referred to as **b.**

(Cockapoos carry all three recessive **b** alleles, as do both parent breeds.) Because brown is recessive, a black dog may be **B/B** or **B/b**—the latter dog, who's "carrying for chocolate", can produce chocolate when bred to a chocolate **(b/b)** or another heterozygous black dog (**B/b**). **Helpful Hint: Because so many other genes can affect coat color in Cockapoos, it's really much easier to think of the B locus in terms of *nose* color rather than *coat* color.**

- A black Cockapoo who inherits **b/b** will have a chocolate coat and a brown nose.
- A buff, gold or red Cockapoo with **b/b** will be born buff, gold or red with a brown nose.
- A sable Cockapoo with **b/b** will be a "chocolate sable"— with brown tipping and a brown nose.
- A merle Cockapoo with **b/b** will be a chocolate merle, with a brown nose..
- A black and tan Cockapoo with **b/b** will be chocolate and tan, with a brown nose.
- A black cocker with **b/b** and the "silvering" gene (**G/g** or **G/G**) will start out deep chocolate and lighten to "café au lait", with a brown nose.

Because white is inherited independently, any of these dogs may also display varying amounts of white. And because it only affects eumelanin, any dog who can genetically display tan points will still do so.

The E Locus

This locus is home to the *Melanocortin Receptor 1 gene* (MC1R) on canine chromosome 5. Although several mutations have been identified on this gene, there are really only three that appear to affect Cockapoo coat color, so this one is pretty easy, too :

- **E**— the dominant E allele allows for the normal production of brown/black pigment (*eumelanin*) in the hair. Dogs with black (or b/b brown) anywhere in the coat are **E/E, E/e, or E/eh.**

- **eh**— recessive to **E** and dominant over **e,** this allele also produces sable in Cockers– Cockapoos may carry both **A^y** and **eh** sable mutations. The **eh/eh** sable may also have tan points.

- **e**— the recessive e allele restricts the normal production of *eumelanin* in the hair, but allows it to be produced normally in the skin. An **e/e** dog will always appear as a shade of cream, buff, gold or red, with no visible black (or brown if he's also **b/b**) hair anywhere, even at birth.

Now, the **e/e** dog may be anything from cream to deep red, but this difference appears to be caused by the action of a separate gene. Because the **e** allele *only* affects the pigment granules in the hair, the pigmentation on the nose, eye rims, lips and pads will still be black —or, in the presence of **b/b,** brown. (A red, buff, or gold Cockapoo with brown pigmentation in those areas is a genetic chocolate— his genotype would be **b/b, e/e.**)

The most important thing to remember about **e/e** is because it restricts the production of *eumelanin* pigment in each and every hair, *it will totally mask the effects of virtually every other allelic variation on the coat, including those responsible for tan points, chocolate, sable and merle.* As shown at right with **at** (tan points), the necessary genes for the pattern may be there (and the dog will be able to pass them on) but you won't be able to *see* them.

Although it was long believed that two copies of the **e** allele causes *no eumelanin at all* to be produced in the hair, this may not be true— recent analysis of human hair revealed that black hair can contain 99% eumelanin and 1% pheomelanin; some shades of blonde actually contain 95% eumelanin and 5% pheomelanin; and red hair actually contains 67% eumelanin and 33% pheomelanin. It's really how the eye "reads" these combinations that matters.

B/B, E/e, at/at
black and tan
(carries for red/gold/buff)

B/B, E/E, at/at
black and tan

B/B, E/e, at/at
black and tan
(carries for red/gold/buff)

B/B, E/e, at/at
black and tan
(carries for red/gold/buff)

B/B, E/e, at/at
black and tan
(carries for red/gold/buff)

B/B, e/e, at/at
red/gold/buff

The G Locus

Little described "graying" as a progressive change resulting in a lightening of the hair coat as the dog ages, and so assigned it the **G** locus. The gene itself has not yet been identified, but in all breeds in which it occurs, it is dominant over its "wild type" counterpart— in other words, it only takes one copy for a dog to display this progressive lightening.

(This is different than the recessive "dilution" gene on the D locus —causing **d/d** pups to be born with apparently diluted color in both hair and pigmentation of the nose, eye rims, lips and pads— which is extremely rare if it exists at all in the Cockapoo.)

Dogs that are **G/g** or **G/G** are *born* black (or chocolate or red or gold or even sable or tan-patterned) and progressively lighten as they mature. Usually the process is complete by the time the dog is two years old, and sometimes much earlier.

The lightening process pretty much affects all colors—a red puppy who inherits a **G** allele from a silver Poodle parent will generally end up apricot or cream. Even a G/g or G/G merle will lighten.

Although not seen in Cockers, the **G** allele is common in Poodles— virtually all silver poodles are born black, and many apricots start out red. Because it is dominant, it only takes one copy to cause the lightening effect, so it can and does show up in F1 Cockapoos. (In fact, if the Poodle parent is a silver, half the litter will lighten no matter what color the Cocker parent is.) Unlike the **d/d** phenotype, this gene affects *only the hair*— the nose, lips and pads more or less stay whatever color they started out.

The I Locus

The gene variants controlling the *intensity* of **e/e** red in dogs have long been assumed to be on the C locus, home of a gene called *TYR*, which codes for *Tyrosinase* and where the gene mutation for albinism is located in several species. (A different mutation in *TYR* causes the classic Siamese pattern in cats.) However, no mutations have been found in the *TYR* gene in dogs that correspond with varying shades of red/cream. **As a result, a new locus has been hypothesized for pheomelanin intensity in dogs— the Intensity locus.** Currently, it is not known which gene is involved, how this locus actually works, or even how many alleles are present on it. However, the general idea is that mutations here affecting pheomelanin will lighten or darken the appearance of recessive **e/e** red dogs from birth, as well as the red areas on some tan-patterned dogs.

The M Locus

The flashy merle pattern is becoming more and more popular in Cockapoos. Although not currently acceptable in either breed's standards anywhere on the planet (and its existence has caused a LOT of controversy in both breeds) the gene variant for merle pattern exists in both Poodles and Cockers, and so may be introduced to the Cockapoo from either side of the pedigree.

In all breeds studied to date, the same mutation (**M**) in the *SILV* gene located on chromosome 10 causes some of the eumelanin pigment to be diluted in distinctive random patches all over the body.

Two variations at this locus have been identified in dogs so far:
- **M**— the dominant allele that causes merling.

- **m**— the "wild-type" allele (called "non-merle" rather than "solid" because the dog may actually be any pattern, including parti, as long as no part of the coat is merled) which is the original gene.

Because the mutation that causes merling is dominant over the "normal" gene, it only takes one copy of the merle gene (**M**) to produce the distinctive merle pattern— technically, dogs can't "carry for merle". *However,* in Cockapoos, a dog may *be* a genetic merle (**M/m**) who cannot *display* the merle pattern because he is also an **e/e** buff, gold or red. These dogs are essentially "masked" or "hidden" merles. (In some breeds so-called "red merles" are actually **b/b, E/E** chocolates, where merle is totally visible. It is the **e/e** phenotype, with or without **b/b,** that masks the merle pattern.

This can be a serious problem for breeders. Although a single copy of the merle mutation (**M/m**) does not appear to cause any problems, two copies of merle (**M/M**) can cause some really *serious* problems. In most merle breeds (especially those who also carry the piebald gene, which many Cockapoos do), so-called "double merles" are born with excessive white in their coats and are usually born deaf in one or both ears, often vision-impaired and sometimes totally blind. In the worst-case scenario, the **M/M** pup may be *anaphthalmic* —born without any eyes at all.

Obviously, no sane breeder wants to bring these poor puppies into the world intentionally, and for this reason most breeders know better than to breed two merles together, as 25% of the resulting litter will statistically be double merles.

But any e/e buff, gold or red dog with a merle parent has a 50/50 chance of being M/m himself, and if bred to another merle, these "hidden merles" can produce double merles as shown at right.

To *further* complicate things, some apparently non-merle solid black or chocolate dogs may actually be **M/m**, but may display so little merling (like a dime-sized patch in some obscure place,) that it will go unnoticed, or they may display no merling at all.
Long called "cryptic merles", these dogs can produce merle puppies bred to a non-merle, and can also produce double merles if bred to another merle.

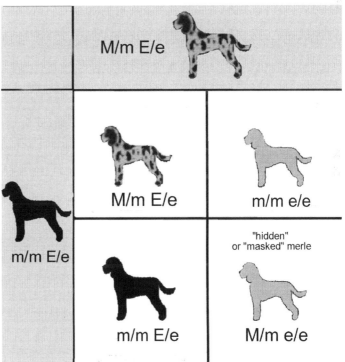

The mystery behind the "Cryptic Merle" was solved by Dr Leigh Anne Clark when her lab actually isolated the merle gene a few years ago.

Turns out the merle "mutation" is really an unstable, short piece of DNA known as a "short interspersed element" (SINE) inserted into the normal *SILV* gene. The SINE is organized into 3 parts: a head, a body and a tail; the latter contains a long string of repeated *adenine nucleotides* (called polyA).

For a dog to produce the merle phenotype, it must have both the SINE insertion *and* a polyA tail that is of sufficient length (90-100 adenine repeats). The "A" tail may shorten or lengthen each time it is copied. The length of the "A" tail controls the degree of merling, because it is this polyA string that interferes with the production of SILV protein needed to form pigmented melanosomes. A dog with the merle SINE mutation but 65 or fewer adenine repeats will present as a cryptic.

These dogs may produce more cryptic merles like themselves, which can carry the problem forward another generation, because now you have a dog with no obvious merle *parents* who can produce merles, even when bred to a non-merle!

Thankfully, an apparently non-merle dog with a merle parent can now be gene-tested for merle prior to breeding. In Cockapoos especially, where e/e dogs are common and the number of cryptic merles is unknown, this may be a wise idea.

The S Locus

The S locus is home to the *Microphthalmia-associated Transcription Factor* (MITF) gene. The "S" stands for "spotting", because at least one mutation here is responsible for a lot of the white spotting seen in dogs. So far, two alleles have been identified at this locus:

- **S—** The dominant allele, this allows for the normal distribution of melanocytes during embryonic development. If there is any displayed at all, the amount of white on an **S/S** or **S/S**P dog will be generally restricted to the feet, chest, muzzle, and the tip of the tail (called *Irish pattern*).

- **S**P— called the "piebald" gene, this allele, which like merle is caused by a SINE insertion, restricts the normal migration of melanocytes during embryogenesis; areas with no melanocytes will appear white, because the melanocytes are the pigment-producing cells.

Amounts of white can vary greatly— in some breeds (like Boxers and Bull terriers) **S**P appears to be *co-dominant* with **S**. Heterozygotes in these breeds typically display the Irish (or tuxedo) pattern, while **Sp** homozyotes are mostly white. Little hypothesized a third allele for "extreme white" **(s**w**)** but so far all "high white" dogs have tested as **S^P/S^P** instead. (This is a different "white" than what is found in white Poodles—they're generally **e/e red** dogs with modifying genes that also restrict pheomelanin production, leaving the coat nearly colorless.)

In many breeds, white spotting is associated with an increased risk for congenital deafness. (Although American Cockers have not been studied, in English Cockers parti-colored dogs have been found to be 7 times more likely to be deaf in one or both ears than solid-colored dogs.) In breeds such as Boxers and Bull Terriers, up to 1/3 of the "extreme white" puppies in a litter produced by two **S/S^P** dogs may be deaf in one or both ears.

This occurs because the **S^P** insertion disrupts normal melanocytes migration in the developing embryo, and in addition to color, ***melanocytes also appear to be involved in normal development of the inner ear.*** Research in affected breeds has shown that parti-colored dogs with two colored ears are less likely to be deaf than parti-colored dogs with one or two white ears. (Contrary to popular belief, though, it's also been shown that unilaterally deaf dogs with one colored ear are equally likely to be deaf in the *colored* ear as in the white ear, which indicates that the path for melanocyte migration in the developing embryo may be different for the inner and outer ear.

Now, in some breeds, another mutation entirely can also produce the Irish (or tuxedo) pattern. Although they may look exactly like the **S/s^P** dogs, gene-testing reveals that dogs of breeds homozygous for the Irish pattern trait do *not* carry the MITF piebald mutation. (Basenjis and Bernese Mountain Dogs are two such breeds.) In these breeds, when two Irish-patterned dogs are bred together, all the resulting pups will be Irish-patterned rather than the "25% solid, 50% Irish, 25% extreme white" results expected when two **S/s^P** dogs are bred together. Oddly, this "true Irish pattern" is NOT associated with deafness.

Whether the mutation for "true Irish pattern" is caused by another mutation on the S locus or on another gene entirely is not known at this point, but some breeds do appear to carry both mutations. The recent availability of a gene test for the SINE mutation at MITF now allows breeders in those breeds to determine whether or not that gene is causing Irish pattern in their dogs.

Cockapoos display both the piebald (parti) pattern caused by the SINE insertion as well as the Irish pattern (usually called tuxedo). To date, no gene-testing has been done to see if these Irish-patterned dogs are carrying a single copy of the piebald allele or whether it is caused by a different mutation.

The T Locus

Many Cockers (especially English Cockers) develop small colored flecks or "ticking" (hence the T) in the white parts of their coats several weeks after birth. In Cockers, this pattern is referred to as *roan*. They may be lightly or heavily marked, with some looking like a dark merle.

Although the causative gene has not been identified at this point in time, the roan pattern in English Cocker Spaniels has been mapped to a specific region on canine chromosome 38. The same scientists subsequently studied the trait defined as "ticking" in English Springer Spaniels and found it mapped to a nearby region.
(The trait in Dalmatians was also mapped to a nearby region, apparently one of 3 genes that contribute to their distinctive spotting pattern. It is believed that a second gene (SLC2A9) may affect the size of the eumelanin spots, making them larger than the ticking displayed in other breeds.)

In Cockapoos, there appear to be two variable alleles at the **T** locus:

- T— the mutation that causes ticking appears to be the dominant one here. However, although the ticking will be the same base color as the hair in that area, it can *only* appear in white areas. A solid-colored dog may be **T/T**, **T/t** or **t/t.**

- t— this allele leaves the white areas free of ticking— they will appear pure white. Because it is recessive to **T**, a dog with no ticking in the white areas is probably **t/t.** (These are more likely to be found in Cockapoos that are descended from American Cockers, as roan is pretty-well dispersed throughout the English Cocker breed.)

Twenty-first Century Color Breeding

Now, a lot of breeders will insist that color doesn't really *matter* in a dog, and they do have a point… hound breeders have long insisted that "a good hound can't come in a bad color", and the same can be said for any dog, because things like health and temperament really do matter more to the pet owner in the long run.

But as long as the breeder does not sacrifice health or temperament or structural soundness in pursuit of it, there's nothing really wrong with breeding for a specific color or pattern. In fact, as many have pointed out over the years, it's probably the most challenging and fun part of dog breeding, especially for those breeders who are fascinated by genetics. And for those breeders, the availability over the last few years of inexpensive, non-invasive gene color gene tests has changed the whole ball game, and new color genes are being identified at a dizzying rate. And with the exception of the merle test (which must be submitted to the lab by a licensed vet for some unknown reason) the rest of the color gene tests now available can be submitted directly to the testing lab by the breeder or owner without even leaving the house!

Here's how it works:
After ordering the test kit online, the breeder simply collects a sample of the cells from the inside of the cheek with a swab or two from a pup as young as 3-5 weeks, sticks them in an envelope, mails them off to the lab and —voila!— the dog's genotype is revealed, usually within a matter of weeks.

Here's why it's so cool:
A dog's "phenotype" is essentially what you see. In the case of color, he will generally display the *dominant* genes at each locus. The recessive genes he inherited will be hidden, so in most cases we only know half his "genotype". (The exception is if one of his parents displayed a trait like chocolate (**b/b**) that requires two copies of the gene in order to be displayed. In that case, since we know the parent did not have the dominant gene (**B**) to pass on, all the offspring would be what are called "obligate carriers" of **b**.)

In every other case, the time-honored way to tell if a dog was carrying for a particular recessive color or pattern was to breed him to a dog displaying it, in which case statistically half the litter should be that color or pattern. (These are called "test breedings".) But because that 50% is based on a thousand puppies, it could sometimes take several litters before the first pup from that 50% actually put in an appearance, especially if the litters were small.

Now puppies can be tested at a few weeks old, and breeders can use the results to help decide which puppies they want to add to their breeding programs based on what colors they can produce. They can also use color tests to avoid producing double piebalds and double merles, both of which are associated with congenital deafness in many breeds. And maintaining all of these colors is actually advantageous in Cockapoos, because in most species, breeds with a lot of color variation also display more genetic diversity, and that translates into more robust immune systems and better disease resistance.

All that said, it's also important to remember that life will be easiest with a healthy puppy whose energy level and temperament best match your family's needs, which is less likely to happen if you lock yourself into a particular color. As with hounds, a good Cockapoo can't come in a bad color!

CHAPTER FOUR:

Finding that Perfect Puppy

Unfortunately, puppy buyers as a whole seem to put a lot more time and energy into choosing the RIGHT BREED than they put into choosing the RIGHT PUPPY. Once they've done their research and decided that a particular breed fits the needs of their family, way too many otherwise intelligent people immediately go out and buy the first available puppy of that breed that they find on the internet as if they were all cranked out at the same factory like iPads, and all you had to worry about was price, color, availability and shipping costs.

This is a *really* big mistake.

As is true in any other breed, all Cockapoo puppies are NOT created equal, nor are all the breeders producing them. Your odds of getting the "right puppy"– ideally a healthy, happy, east-to-train fellow that's going to end up with the looks, coat type and temperament you want – are really pretty dependent upon choosing the *right breeder*, since the breeder is really the "manufacturer" here, and the breeder's kennel name is really their "brand name". The breed itself is more general— deciding on Cockapoo rather than another breed is a lot like choosing a tablet over a full-sized laptop … there's still lots of quality differences within each category!

Now, finding the right breeder can be daunting. But *daunting* is NOT the same as *impossible* .

And it's a lot easier if you know what to steer clear of right out the gate— among other things, it wastes a lot less of your valuable time and precludes the possibility of disappointment when things don't work out, which they invariably won't. So let's look first at what you *definitely want to avoid*:

Pet Shops

Buying a dog from a pet shop is a poor choice on many levels. It does not allow you to see the parents or to get any sort of idea how the puppy was raised in the critical early weeks of his life, both of which are important factors that affect things like inherited temperament, sociability, trainability, and lifelong adaptability to new situations.

It also keeps substandard breeders in business, because no matter what the nice kids in the pet shop tell you, responsible breeders do *not* sell their puppies through pet shops. Only the bottom-feeders of the dog-breeding world sell puppies wholesale. Because of that, you'll *also* want to avoid:

Virtual Pet Shops (aka Online Dog Brokers).

Buyers who want to avoid pet shops usually end up looking on the internet, where the odds are the first puppies they will find will be offered for sale in *virtual pet shops*, otherwise known as *dog brokers*.

The main difference between brick-and-mortar pet shops and their "virtual" counterparts is that in the latter case, most people don't realize that they are buying from one.

And because these guys usually have cleverly-designed websites and pay top-dollar for website optimization, they pop up at the top of the results on an internet search for *almost any breed*. How to avoid them? Here are a couple of clues that should tip you off that you're really visiting an online pet store:

Clue #1

The first clue is that they have a LOT of breeds available. With very few exceptions, responsible breeders rarely have more than a couple breeds at most, and more often only one.
This is because all breeds are different, and have different temperaments and different genetics (just look at the chapter on color!) and very few people can really learn all they need to know about a whole

bunch of breeds to do a good job with them all. But since these guys are not actually breeding these puppies themselves, they can offer *dozens* of breeds. And they often do.

Clue #2

The second clue is that they ONLY display "staged" photos of adorable puppies...there are never any parent dogs in evidence, and you never see pictures of their houses or lawns, even as natural background...usually the puppies are displayed on cutsie baby blankets with seasonal props.

 In fact, if you visit their sites repeatedly, you may notice that the same puppy photos often appear over and over, with different names attached – this month's "Freddy" may well be next month's "Phoebe". And some of these pictures are actually swiped from other breeders' websites, honest to God, which means you're actually getting a *totally different puppy* than the cutie you fell in love with.

Just like the brick-and-mortar pet shops, these guys are buying puppies wholesale from bottom-feeding commercial breeders and selling them retail – *they're just less honest about it*. And unlike a neighborhood pet shop, they don't have any ties to the community – in fact, since the puppies are often drop-shipped from the breeder, it's often pretty hard to figure out just where on the planet they are located. (The largest one in the US is based in Florida but their puppies are dropped-shipped from all over the country.) And because of an unfortunate glitch in the law, there are no USDA inspections or even bare-minimum standards for the care and condition of their dogs, as are required for breeders who sell to pet shops.

These guys are the worst of the worst, and unfortunately they practically OWN the internet when it comes to online puppy sales. Steer clear of them. You want to deal only with a real breeder.

Sorting Out the "Real" Breeders

OK, so what you want to find is a BREEDER, which in simple legal terms means the person selling you the puppy is the same person who owns the dam, bred her, and raised the litter.

But because they come in all stripes, and all advertise in pretty much the same places, even after you actually locate a couple you're still not home free, because along with *responsible breeders* (which is what we are looking for) a lot of breeders who advertise puppies on the internet or in newspapers are what we might euphemistically call SUBSTANDARD BREEDERS.

 These substandard breeders may be actual puppy mills, or they may be smaller home-based breeders, but either way they represent the worst of dog-breeding.

Buying a puppy directly from a substandard breeding operation either in person or over the internet because you feel sorry for him (which some kindhearted people actually admit to doing) may SEEM like a kindness but in the long run it's entirely counterproductive – every puppy purchased for this reason ensures that another one will be produced right behind him.

Buying a puppy from a substandard breeder because ***you didn't realize you were dealing with one*** is really no better (because of course the end result is the same) but unfortunately this happens a lot more often. And thanks to the internet, it's getting more frequent every year.

The scary truth is this: ANY dog breeder can make himself look good on the internet.

No matter how irresponsible or downright awful they may be, absolutely *no one* advertises themselves as an "irresponsible breeder".

Absolutely no *one runs* an internet ad for puppies explaining that they're just cranking out puppies to make a quick buck, even if they really *are* just cranking out puppies to make a quick buck.

And absolutely *no one* runs an internet ad for puppies explaining that their puppies are born and raised in an unused chicken coop out back, even if they *are* born and raised in an unused chicken coop out back.

Nope, what substandard breeders invariably tell the buying public is this:
"We raise dogs as a family hobby."
"Our pups are raised underfoot with lots of love."
"Our pups get lots of socialization playing with our kids/grandkids."
"Our dogs and puppies are health-checked by our vet."
"Our puppies are de-wormed and are current on all vaccinations."
 And my personal favorite:
"Our puppies come pre-spoiled", which is ironically true in ways these guys do not even understand… and about as intelligent as selling pre-spoiled groceries.

The problem with all this, of course, is that a whole lot of perfectly responsible breeders say a lot of the same things. (Of course, the big difference is they're probably telling the truth.) But by itself, this list does not guarantee or even indicate you're dealing with a responsible breeder, and if that's all they've got, it's a big red flag and you'd do better to look elsewhere.

Buying Local

The "buy local" movement is gaining purchase in the US, and whether one is looking at produce or puppies, it has much to commend it, not the least of which it is environmentally sound.

The *best* way to determine if a breeder's advertising is an honest representation or a load of horse manure is to simply visit, meet the parent dogs and see where and how their puppies are raised. This gets a whole lot easier if the breeder lives within an hour or two of you.

Do bear in mind that, though, that breeders do NOT run petting zoos, and potential buyers who visit multiple breeders can track viruses like parvo on their shoes from one to another.
In order to avoid this, some breeders now require that you put down an actual deposit on a pup before visiting, with the option of getting it back if you are not happy with what you find. As a policy, this one's hard to argue with.

And of course when he's ready to go home you can just drive over and pick your puppy up without worrying about the time and costs involved in getting him from one end of the country to another.

And, even best of all, if several or all the puppies in a litter end up in the same area, they can get together for play days… and their owners can take turns pet sitting for each other when needed.

Unfortunately, finding a breeder nearby is a lot harder than it used to be back when people advertised puppies for sale in their local newspaper, and it's *amazing* how many people buy a puppy from another state only to find out later there's a great breeder right in their own city. This is one of the places where the internet has just *not made things easier*, but we're stuck with it, so the internet it is.

Now, before you even BEGIN your internet search for a local breeder, you need to be aware of this unfortunate turn of events:

If you now Google the name of almost any breed along with the name of your state or city, an appalling number of the websites that pop up first will actually be dog brokers masquerading as local breeders.
These bandits have collectively purchased *thousands* of those "local" domain names, in every breed and including every state and major metro area in the domain name itself. (According to an investigation launched by HSUS, one Florida-based broker alone owns over 800 of these "local" domain names and ships a reported 20,000 puppies a year.)

Because they are invariably better at marketing than breeding, these commercial brokers swarmed in like a plague of locusts early on with a lot of internet savvy as well as cold hard cash and now practically *own* the internet when it comes to online puppy searches.

So be sure your "local breeder" is really local—- do your homework, get references, and make sure the puppies are really being raised locally *before* putting down a deposit!!!

Now, one of the advantages of the Cockapoo having been around longer than most hybrids is that, like purebreds, they actually have active Parent Clubs both in the US and in Great Britain, which is a great place to begin looking for a breeder. Both the American Cockapoo Club and the Cockapoo Club of Great Britain maintain lists of member/breeders by geographic region, and are worth checking out.

The British club has specific health-screening requirements for breeders who list litters on their site; the ACC does not—although many of the breeders listed there do health screen, you'll have to check their websites or ask. In fact, whether you find a breeder on a Cockapoo Club website or one on the internet at large, you should still always ask about health-screening, because it's one of the marks of a responsible breeder, and that's what you're looking for.

Besides health-screening, what separates a responsible breeder form the rest of the herd?

Redefining "Responsible Breeder"

There's a lot of information on the internet defining what constitutes responsible dog breeding, but most of the time what you're really getting is someone's personal opinion, and usually that person is a longtime purebred dog show enthusiast. In other words, a "show breeder". This can be a problem.

Although the best of them are also concerned with health and temperament, show breeders are *primarily* breeding for **conformation to the standard of their breed** – in other words, their breeding decisions are largely based on *looks*, which is what dogs are judged on in the ring. The ultimate goal of a show breeder is to produce a dog that perfectly conforms to its written standard.

Those puppies which do not closely match the written standard of their breed, or do not have the "look at me" personality required of a successful show dog are sold as pets.

Unlike show dogs, hybrids are produced exclusively as companions and service animals, and so conformation to a detailed physical standard is usually less important than a good temperament, trainability, soundness, health, and longevity, all of which also are (or at least should be) important to show breeders but are frankly not that upon which they ultimately base their breeding decisions.

Decades out of Date

And a lot of the criteria for responsible breeding laid forth with such certainty by show breeders is frankly out of date even if you are looking for a purebred, because the sport is graying rapidly and so most of them are, well....OLD...and haven't exactly kept up with the technological advances of the modern world.

A spectacular example of this is found on one of the many "How to Identify a Responsible Breeder" websites out there, which states unequivocally *(and I swear I am not making this up)* that "only puppy mills accept PayPal", and so acceptance of PayPal should be considered a red flag. ***Excuse me????*** With the exception of Amazon, pretty much the whole WORLD takes PayPal, and how accepting only handwritten checks via snail mail could somehow make one a more *responsible breeder* simply defies the imagination. (Actually, when it comes to payment, the only *real* red flag is the breeder who accepts "cash only", because without an electronic trail of some sort you've got little recourse if things go south.)

So, with all that in mind and without further ado, here's what you need to look for to find a responsible breeder of Cockapoos on the internet:

Look for reviews...and get recommendations

One of the greatest advances of the twenty-first century surely came from Amazon. In fact, it's completely revolutionized the way America makes its collective purchasing decisions. You guessed it....it's the consumer review. And it's the best thing that's ever happened to puppy buyers.

Many breeders' websites now have testimonial letters from previous puppy buyers, with accompanying photos of said puppies all grown up in their new homes, which is pretty cool. But don't assume that's enough by itself, because unfortunately many brokers also now have "testimonials" from buyers on their websites as well. (Are they real? Hard to tell.) But a responsible breeder will also provide you with names and contact information for people who own their puppies if you ask.

Bottom line is this: No matter what breeders say about themselves or their dogs, it's not going to be nearly as useful as what *people who actually own the puppies they've bred* have to say.

Now it goes without saying that breeders who've been at it the longest, and those who've produced a lot of puppies, are going to have more puppy owners out there than those who breed less frequently, so don't assume tons of references on the internet are automatically better than a few phone numbers – this is one of those "quality-over-quantity" issues.

Responsible Breeders are Knowledgeable

Let's face it, any idiot can put two dogs together in the back yard and end up with puppies. But breeding healthy, physically and mentally sound dogs requires a knowledge base. This is ESPECIALLY true with Cockapoos, because there is at least one potential and very serious genetic problem in this breed that will not be magically erased by "hybrid vigor". If breeders do not even know the potential for a problem exists, how can they assure buyers their puppies won't be affected? **When producing hybrids, a responsible breeder is knowledgeable about *the health issues in its parent breeds*, and is current on research regarding them.**

There are also a wealth of books on canine structure and anatomy, genetics, behavior, health and reproduction available to the aspiring breeder to expand their knowledge base, and responsible breeders will avail themselves of them. Even longtime breeders need to keep up, as what we knew "for a fact" 20 years ago may have recently been discovered to be totally wrong.

One quick way to tell if a breeder is knowledgeable is by the *terminology* that they use. Dog-breeding, like medicine, engineering, law or any other discipline, has its own terminology, especially as regards canine anatomy, and knowledgeable breeders are familiar with it.

Just as you'd be hesitant to hire a contractor who called his hammer a "pounder", a puppy buyer should be hesitant about turning over his cash to a breeder who thinks a brood bitch is called a "dame" rather than a "dam", or that the physiology of a dog is its "confirmation" instead of its "conformation.". Or one who thinks that a dog's nose is attached to its "snout". **Dogs don't HAVE snouts, pigs do. Dogs have "muzzles".**

If a breeder is too lazy to learn basic canine structure and terminology, odds are they don't know much about genetics or health-screening or socialization, either.

Responsible breeders provide information on the parents.

The laws of genetics being what they are, the parents of any particular puppy, even a hybrid, offer the best clues about how it's likely to turn out. Ideally, photos of the parents and information about them should be on the breeder's website, **including all health-screening performed**.

And people….the photos should be more than a blurry head shot, and the description of the individual personality should be more than "Sadie loves belly rubs". (What dog *doesn't?*) Those are too often the mark of a substandard commercial breeder posing as a "hobby breeder"—and even if they're not, in this day of cell-phone cameras, why would you want to buy from someone who's too lazy to take a decent photo of the whole dog?

Responsible breeders keep only as many dogs than they can care for.

Despite what you may read elsewhere, *there's really no magic number here*. It depends entirely on the individual's breeding goals and resources— obviously, you want to be wary of a breeder whose goals clearly outstrip their resources, because these breeders inevitably end up cutting corners.

Many breeders simply keep a couple of bitches in their home full-time as house pets and breed a litter or two a year, while breeders with a larger breeding program often have a separate kennel facility, which is NOT automatically a "bad thing". As long as the dogs are clean, comfortable and well-socialized, kennels allow multiple dogs to get more fresh air and exercise than will a stack of crates in the house. Kennels should be safe, clean, well-shaded with plantings and surfaced with something like pea rock or pavers so they may be easily cleaned. And you should be allowed to see it, even if the breeder doesn't want you mucking around in there petting everybody and spreading germs, which is understandable.

Some breeders use "guardian homes" for some of their breeding dogs, which is generally a win/win situation. The best pups are placed in nearby pet homes as pups and come back to the breeder's home to be bred and whelp a litter or two, after which time they are spayed and spend the rest of their lives as pets in the same home they started out in. This allows the breeder to maintain more genetic diversity in their line than they would under the traditional breeding system (where it's often limited by the number of dogs a breeder can practically keep) and it's a terrific deal for the dogs themselves. In fact, when most people are now restricted by law or practicality in the number of dogs they can own, the "guardian home system" probably represents the future of dog breeding.

Responsible breeders have a sales contract.

Every breeder should provide one, and usually they are posted on their website. If it's not, ask for a copy *prior to putting down a deposit*. Sales contracts assure that both the breeder and the buyer understand and agree on what will be done in any contingency that may arise both prior to and after sale of the puppy. Read through these *carefully* before committing yourself to a puppy, because they're NOT all the same, and the devil is in the details.

Responsible breeders often accept deposits:

Most breeders accept deposits to hold a puppy, and some to hold a place in line on an upcoming litter. Some are refundable if they cannot provide a puppy meeting your requirements within a specified time, and some are flat-out non-refundable for any reason whatsoever. Few if any breeders will refund a deposit if you've simply changed your mind, nor should they be expected to.

Responsible breeders ask YOU questions.

Responsible breeders will either ask you to fill out an application or will conduct a phone interview (or both) prior to accepting a deposit. They will ask lots of questions about your living situation, the hours that you work, and your family. Because they want their puppies to be successful in life, they want to find out in advance if one of their puppies is likely to be a good fit for your family situation, and will tell you flat-out if they don't think it is. An irresponsible breeder will ask no questions and will take anyone's money.

Responsible breeders provide ongoing support.

Responsible breeders are there 24/7 to answer questions, no matter how dumb they may be, for the life of the dog. They provide *written instructions* for things like vaccination, worming, housebreaking, early training, grooming and all the other things you need to know to get off to a good start. And they are available for advice at any hour by phone in an emergency. DO NOT, under any circumstances, buy a puppy from a breeder who will not provide you with his/her personal phone number—odds are, there's a good reason **why.**

Responsible breeders take dogs back.

All responsible breeders are concerned with the welfare of puppies they've bred even after they have been sold, and will take them back and/or assist in rehoming them if the owner cannot keep them for any reason at any time in the dog's life. Some will reimburse the owner for part of the purchase price while others do not. (The breeder's policies in this regard should be clearly stated in writing in the sales contract.)

But beware *anyone* who is unwilling to offer a place in their home to any dog whose existence they've called into being, because *they are the people responsible for dogs ending up in shelters.* In fact, don't buy a puppy from them.

Responsible breeders want you to come and pick up your puppy.

This one is probably the most important of all, and a lot of people get it wrong. Because of the possibility of infectious diseases like distemper and parvo, most breeders cannot allow their home or kennel to be used as a petting zoo by everyone considering the possible purchase of a puppy. In fact, some breeders only allow those puppy buyers who actually have a deposit on a puppy to visit after the puppies have received their first vaccinations for this reason. But that said, you should never buy a dog from a breeder who will not allow you on the premises to pick up your puppy. NEVER.

Before you plunk down a single red cent (and even if the breeder is half a continent away), *always* ask if you can come and pick up the puppy. If the breeder demurs and immediately offers to ship or meet you *anywhere* other than their home, they have not just raised a red flag... *they've hoisted the JOLLY ROGER*, and odds are pretty good you're dealing with a pirate.

Responsible breeders may ask you to remove your shoes, or wash your hands, but they will *not* keep you from entering their homes, or seeing the whole litter, or the mother, or the area where the dogs live, even if it's from a "safe" distance.

Responsible breeders do not hand puppies over to their new owners and collect payment for them in the Wal-Mart parking lot. They just don't.

OK, now that you have enough information to sort out the many Cockapoo breeders out there and narrow it down to the good ones, you're down to finding one with whom you "click", and whose expectations match your own.

Some breeders really encourage their puppy buyers to stay in close contact, and buying a puppy from one of them immediately makes you " family". (These are most likely to be breeders of the "puppy-lover" variety and the ones who most often maintain forums and e-lists for their buyers.) Others are there for you if you have a question or problem, and certainly welcome updates and photographs, but assume you already have enough friends and family.

Neither is intrinsically better than the other; it's really a matter of personal preference.

Choosing the Right Puppy

Choosing a good *breeder* makes choosing the right *puppy* in a litter a whole lot easier, because you will have what amounts to professional help, but there's a lot you can do to help the breeder in this regard.

Dispelling the "pick of the litter" myth.

If one phrase should disappear from the world of dogs, that phrase should be "pick of the litter." Unless one is looking for a show dog, THERE IS NO SUCH THING. (Even then it's pretty dicey – many a Westminster Winner over the years was "third-pick puppy" in his litter!)

Since puppies are in essence fraternal rather than identical twins, every puppy in a given litter is going to be a little different, in both looks and personality. As with human siblings, one puppy is invariably going to be the liveliest, one the smartest, one the most assertive, and one the most easy-going.

A good breeder will spend time interviewing each new owner either in person or by phone and will try to match each puppy with the family into which he best fits.

For example, the most assertive puppy is probably not the best choice for a family with very young children. The "genius puppy" in a litter is probably not the best choice for an owner who is not all that interested in doing a lot of training – remember, in general, the higher the puppy's IQ, the more challenging training him will be. The liveliest puppy is not the best choice for the most sedentary owner.

A good breeder has spent a lot of time with the puppies by the time they are 7 weeks old, which is really when neurological development is pretty much complete in the canine and its innate personality is revealed. What the owner sees in an hour's visit may not be reality at all – for example, the "live-wire" puppy may simply be tired at that point from running around all morning and consequently give a pretty good impression of Mr. Mellow, which will change once he gets home and has a chance to recharge his little batteries.

Choosing a puppy based on photographs is not a great idea either.

The most PHOTOGENIC puppy in a litter—the guy who mugs for the camera and is so cute you could just scoop him up right off your computer screen– is almost guaranteed to be the most challenging, while the one who looks a little like he's facing a firing squad is likely to be the easiest to live with. No one EVER believes me on this, by the way, but 40 years of taking puppy pictures has convinced me that I'm right. So if you want to live with the Mick Jagger of Cockapoos, go for it.

Color and gender are two other areas where people put more emphasis than they should when choosing a puppy.

If you end up with a higher-energy puppy than you intended, or one whose personality is not a good match for your household, gender or color is not going to matter much. If a puppy you reserved based on color appears to be the wrong puppy for you based on temperament or energy level as they develop, a good breeder will advise you of this and may suggest a switch. *Trust them.* In the world of dogs, the majority of people who make a mistake that they later come to regret when choosing a puppy chose that puppy based on his *color* and not his *personality*.

Unfortunately, the internet has made it worse, because light-colored dogs simply photograph better than their dark-colored siblings, who may actually be much cuter in person.

In the end, it's really best to explain your family situation, previous dog-owning (or child-rearing) experience and what sort of dog appeals to you and then let the breeder, who interacts with the puppies 24/7, choose the right puppy for you.

For reasons no one has really ever figured out, most good breeders have an intuitive gift for choosing the right puppies for each family. (Puppy owners will often attest to this, which is why it's good to read the reviews.) Maybe it's just part of being a good breeder. But whatever the reason, when choosing which puppy is right for your family, it's really in the new owner's best interest to trust a good breeder's judgment.

What About Price...?

Currently, the price of a Cockapoo puppy ranges anywhere from around $400 to maybe $1,500, depending on several factors. Many breeders charge more for the flashier colors and patterns and often more for breeding-quality pups, but by and large the differences in price reflect the differences in experience levels, breeding expertise, customer support provided and marketing skills that exist among breeders.

At the highest end are generally the breeders who put the most time, money and energy into their breeding program, and offer the greatest amount of support both prior to and after purchase. (*The exception to this is the broker with a slick website, who often charges $1500 for a puppy he paid $400 for wholesale. But hopefully you know how to spot them by now.*)

When it comes to deciding how much you are willing to spend on the initial price of a puppy, it's always good to remember that the cost of the puppy is a mere drop in the bucket when compared to the cost of feeding, grooming and providing veterinary care for that dog over his lifetime.

And in some cases, NO amount of money spent on veterinary care will help. In the Cockapoo breed, both parents can carry the recessive gene for prcd/PRA, which causes irreversible blindness in the unlucky puppies who inherit two copies, often as early as two years of age.

Paying a few hundred dollars extra upfront to purchase a puppy who is guaranteed free of prcd/PRA because the breeder gene-tests for it prior to breeding is a VERY good bargain in the long run.

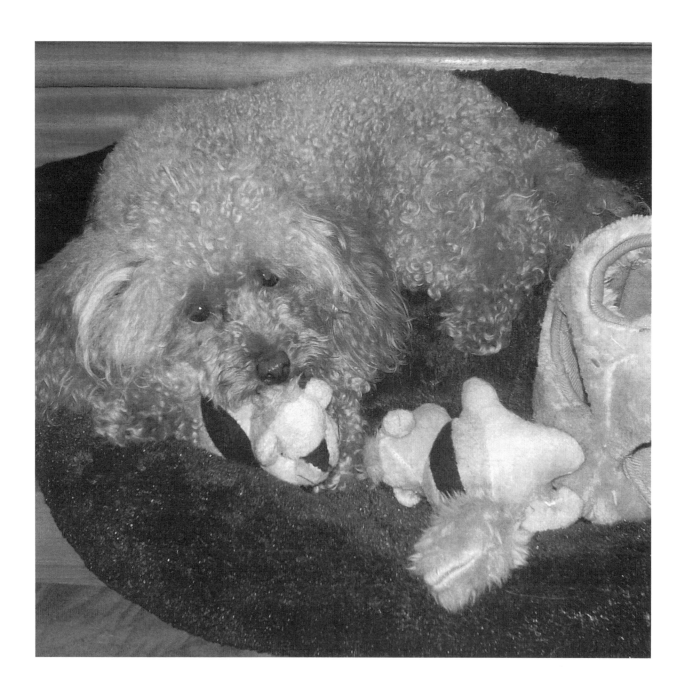

CHAPTER FIVE:

The Right Stuff

(or...how to spend lots of money waiting for your puppy)

Now, unless your timing happens to be perfect, odds are there may be some lag time between when you reserve your puppy and when you can actually bring him home.

This time can best be used for collecting the astonishing amount of equipment, supplies and assorted paraphernalia required for successful puppy management, getting your home ready for the new family addition, and learning what you need to know to make the transition as smooth as possible for everyone concerned.

Raising a Puppy the Way Nature Intended

At 8 weeks, a puppy of any breed is still pretty immature. It is important to understand that removing him from his mother and littermates at that age is *not* the natural course of events for a canine. In the wild, most wolf cubs commonly stay with their parents for up to a year and if resources permit, often for life. The same is true of foxes and coyotes – in most wild canids, packs are really extended families, and domestic dogs are still psychologically hard-wired for that lifestyle.

What we are doing when we "adopt" a puppy is taking an incredibly immature pack animal out of his natal pack and incorporating him into another *very different* pack – one that's comprised of members of another species altogether, and (unless there's another dog in the family) one where no one speaks his language nor shares the same social rules of the pack into which he was born. It's really a credit to the inherent adaptability of the dog that so many of them manage to do so well…just try to imagine for a moment how well the process would work in reverse!

Raising a puppy successfully is a lot easier
if we work *with* his psychological hard-wiring instead of *against* it.

In order to do that, we need to understand what Mother Nature intended, and the best way to do that is to look at how wolf cubs develop and are raised in the wild, and try to adapt that to our own situation, because that's also how *our* puppies are also hard-wired.

Wolf cubs are born in a den, and stay there for the first few weeks of life with their mother. She rarely leaves them during this time, and her food is provided by the litter's sire (usually the alpha male) who delivers it to her door, bless his heart. At 4 weeks or so, the cubs first toddle outside the den into the spring sunshine, where they are greeted enthusiastically by the entire pack. At this point, the litter is beginning to be weaned, and the other pack members provide regurgitated solid food for them.

When the cubs are around 8 weeks old (not coincidentally when neurological development in the canine is completed), the pack moves them from the den to a carefully chosen *rendezvous site* within the pack's territory where they will stay until they are 7-8 months old, at which time they are nearly full-grown and are ready to become full-fledged members of the pack.

During this time, they are usually left in the care of a babysitter (most often a young wolf from the pack of either gender) during the day, and alone when necessary. Their days are spent playing with "toys" and learning the skills they'll need to become useful functioning pack members. Food is still delivered to them, and they sleep with the pack at night. These rendezvous sites are chosen carefully by the pack, with the physical needs (like access to shallow water) and safety of the cubs given highest priority. They are taken on short outings as they grow, but are still largely confined to the rendezvous area until they are mature.

Because this method has worked so well for untold millennia, it simply makes sense to stick to it when raising our own puppies, who share over 99% of their DNA with their wolf ancestors, including those that determine neurological and psychological development.

This method also requires THE RIGHT STUFF in order to work.
Luckily, most of it can be purchased online, and a lot of it is available on Amazon.

This really beats the heck out of driving across town only to find they don't have what you need.

And to save hours searching online, you can just go to **www.dianeklumb.com**, where a lot of it is actually pictured and items can be purchased directly from the suppliers with a single mouse click. If you're not already an Amazon Prime member, signing up before you buy will save you a fortune in shipping. How easy is THAT?)

Setting up the Rendezvous Area

When we bring an 8-10 week old pup home, what we need to do is transition from the "den with mom" to the next naturally-occurring phase, which is moving him to a *rendezvous area*. We are also moving him into a new pack, which is going to be fairly stressful for the first week or two.

The territory of this new pack comprises your entire house and yard, and at his age, your pup should not have the run of it any more than a wolf cub would in the wild, and for exactly the same reason – safety. It is absolutely astonishing how much trouble a puppy can get himself into if he is granted full territorial privileges before he's ready for them.

So what the new owner needs to do before the puppy arrives is decide which area of the house is going to be the *rendezvous site*, and plan on confining him to that area, (usually with baby gates or an ex pen) when he is unattended.

As in the wild, this area should be the place where the older pack members congregate to relax when they are not working. This will vary from family to family and depends upon the layout of the house, but it is usually the kitchen/family room area. In some homes, if it is directly off the kitchen and not isolated but can be blocked off with a gate, a laundry area can work. It should also include a corner for the puppy's crate, which is where he will sleep during the day, and a door that leads directly to the area (whether that is the back yard, a terrace or the sidewalk) where he will eliminate, so he can learn to go directly to the door to signal when he needs to go outside.

Never, ever use a bathroom or laundry room with the door shut- for a young pack animal, that constitutes psychological torture, plain and simple.

Pet Gates...An Absolute Necessity!

Since it is entirely counterproductive to give a young puppy free access to the entire "pack territory", this rendezvous area will need to be cordoned off with baby gates—how many you will need depends entirely upon layout. It should also have flooring other than carpeting for purely practical reasons.

With Cockapoo puppies, an "exercise pen" can serve as an excellent rendezvous area —in fact it's what your puppy was probably raised in at the breeder's. Usually around 4 x4 when set up, some owners use them as a safe area when they're not home for the first year or longer.

Ex pens, beloved by dog show people for decades, come in three basic materials:

- **Folding wire pens**— the "original" dog show ex pen, these still have much to commend them. Chew proof and practically indestructible (unless you accidentally back over it with your car) the best are finished in black epoxy— Midwest makes the best ones. Be sure and get one with a door. Tops can also be purchased for climbers.

- **Folding plastic pens**— these are usually lighter weight and less likely to scratch the floor, but puppies will sometimes gnaw on them which may cause the ingestion of plastic even if they can't gnaw their way out. They are usually available in white and some are pretty attractive.

- **Folding nylon mesh pens**— sort of a doggy version of the Pack N Play, these are really not a good idea for puppies, because they can chew their way out lickety-split.

With any expen, it's a good idea to use a piece of marine-grade vinyl (aka naugahyde) underneath when the puppy is young to protect the floor from accidents and water and food spills as well as scratches. Buy enough to make two mats—this stuff goes right through the washer and dryer beautifully. Color options are endless, so you can choose something that fits your décor.

With a squishy bed, water, a few safe toys and a piddle pad or litter box, a young puppy can spend several hours in an expen unattended, which he really cannot do in a crate.

Pet Gates

Even if you use an ex pen, you'll still need gates for when you are home. You'll need one made with vertical bars or fine mesh, with *no horizontal crossbars* between the top and the bottom. These are the only gates that are climb-proof and *nothing* is more discouraging than installing a new gate only to watch your puppy immediately scamper over it like an oversized squirrel. There's not much purpose in a gate under 30 inches, and for an agile breed like the Cockapoo, 36 inches is even better.

The choice of materials (plastic, wood or metal) and color is really up to you, and you might as well get something that isn't going to look downright ugly. Wood gates should be sprayed with bitter apple before use, though, or they'll soon look like they've been attacked by demented beavers.

Exactly where to put the gates is a matter of traffic flow- it's a good idea to figure this out and live with it for a while *before the puppy arrives,* because you may well decide to move it. Better to figure that out before he gets there than to confuse him by rearranging it after a week or two.

Puppy-proofing

Once you've decided where the gates are going to go, everything inside that becomes the rendezvous area and needs to be *puppy-proofed*. You need to remove everything that can potentially be dangerous or disassembled that's within maybe three feet of the floor – electrical cords (there is an unknown magnetic force that attracts puppies to outlets with electrical cords plugged into them), houseplants, knickknacks, books, magazines, antiques, sporting equipment, electronics and anything else of value that you do not wish to have damaged or turned into confetti by industrious little puppy teeth. The best way to do this is to get down on your knees, lay your forearms flat on the floor, and look around. You now have the puppy's view of his new world, and it's amazing what you'll see that you may have missed standing up.

Anything that cannot be removed (like the woodwork!) should be sprayed with bitter apple *before* the puppy sinks his teeth into it rather than after. So you'll want to put a spray bottle of **Bitter Apple** on your growing list of Things You Absolutely Need.

Food and Water

The rendezvous site should also contain the puppy's water and food dishes because this is where he is going to eat. As with pretty much everything else, there's a wide variety from which to choose, ranging from the most utilitarian to the most decorative. (As you've probably figured out by now, the days when dog ownership required a dog house, a feed pan, a water bowl and a nice butcher's bone are long gone....of course, those were also the days when a kid owned one pair of shoes, used a bicycle to get everywhere he needed to go and got an orange in his Christmas stocking. Right.)

Choosing the Right Bowls and Dishes

A good bowl is chew-proof, easy to clean (i.e. dishwasher-safe) and not easily tipped over or carried. The kind with sloped sides and a non-slip base are a good choice, and stainless steel is the easiest to keep clean, the least toxic, and the most durable. (Heavy ceramic is a close second and usually more attractive, although it can break.) Stay away from plastic— it fails on all counts.

Some owners prefer "double diners" because they tend to keep the dishes tidily in one place- if you go this route, make sure the dishes are easily removable from the platform for cleaning.

Dog Food Storage

If you plan to feed dry dog food, you will need something in which to store it to avoid creating a fast-food drive-thru for the local rodentia, which is what will happen if you leave it in the bag.

The best choice here is probably a tall plastic dog food storage bin with a tight flip-top lid and little castors so you can roll it out to fill it. It is *not* a good idea to keep this in the rendezvous area, however, because even a toy-sized puppy with motivation and a set of industrious little teeth can turn a plastic storage bin into a self-feeder in no time flat by gnawing a hole in the bottom corner – the laundry room or pantry is a better choice. If you absolutely need a chew proof one, you can also get stainless steel model, but it will cost you about a hundred dollars more.

Yes, you DO need a crate!

No matter what PETA says, a crate is not a cage, it's a *den*. And when properly introduced, a crate is an invaluable asset to training. It will help speed the housetraining process considerably, as well as preventing property destruction when a young dog needs to be left unattended.

Some Cockapoos will outgrow the need for a crate when they reach maturity (rarely before a year and often closer to two), while others consider the crate to be their personal "den" and prefer to sleep in it their whole lives; the difference is largely temperamental. Either way, you're going to end up needing a crate large enough to comfortably hold a 15-25 lb dog.

Crates come in a dizzying array of sizes, shapes and materials, and once again, the best place to start looking is Amazon, which pretty much carries every dog crate known to man. For Cockapoos, the wire crate is usually better than the plastic "airline crate", because these are social dogs who like to know what's going on around them.

You can also buy really nice-looking wooden crates that look like furniture, but these are really only appropriate for dogs with no teeth or no imagination, because any other dog (even amazingly small ones) will turn them into a big pile of toothpicks in short order. Been there, done that.

In the "wire crate" world, Midwest crates are an overall good value – many show breeders have been hauling the same Midwest crates around to dog shows decades, subjecting them to a lot more abuse than anything the average pet owner can come up with.

And one of *the absolute best improvements in crates over the last 40 years* has come from Midwest— their new "Ovation" line of crates have a door that opens up (sort of like a garage door) and lies flat on the top of the crate. This is nothing short of brilliant.
It's much easier to open and close in a car. It totally ends trying to position your crate in the house so that the dog doesn't have to negotiate a maze to get in (which makes teaching the "kennel up!" com-

mand much easier!) or out. It takes up a lot less space. AND it comes with a *free* divider, so you can block off half when your puppy is little….how cool is that?

It's also a great improvement for those dogs who like to use their crate as a sleeping area with the door open. With these crates, puppies can have their crate, with a comfy bed inside and the door securely attached to the top, right in their ex pen without worrying that he may get his collar caught on the open door's latch when there's no one around to extricate him, which happens more often than one might imagine. (This is why many breeders do not recommend leaving a crate in an expen.)

And even better, these crates are now available on Amazon. (In the interest of saving time, a quick trip to **www.dianeklumb.com** will take you right to them—because they're brand-new, you'll never find them just scrolling unless you remember " Midwest Ovation", which you probably won't...)

The basic Midwest Ovation wire crate sizes for Cockapoos are:
Medium: 31 X 22 X 24 high......fit most standard-sized Cockapoos
Small: 25.5 X 19 X 21 high....... for the guys on the smaller end

Other brands and lines may vary by an inch or two. In general, it's best to err on the side of too big rather than too small, because a dog who feels cramped is going to put up more of a fuss in his crate.

Even if he has an expen for daytime use, during the first few months most young puppies are going to do better sleeping in a crate in the bedroom with their new "senior pack members", and all of them need to be crated in the car until they're old enough for a seat-belt harness. In fact, if he has an expen, you can just keep his crate in the bedroom for nighttime use.

Crate Pads and Dog Beds

Now that we've got the crate issues sorted out, it's time to look at dogs beds, and there are lots of options here as well. In fact, the world of dog beds has expanded to the point where it's almost impossible to figure out where to start!

The major factors to consider in choosing dog beds are washability, durability and good looks, since it's going to be part of your home décor for years to come unless it gets chewed up. Many gorgeous and very pricey dog beds score well in the "good-looks" area, but fall down badly in the first two, which are really more important.

When he's still a baby, it's pretty simple – the best choice in bedding is a fluffy bath towel. You'll actually need two, so they can be laundered as needed. In spite of everyone's best efforts, puppies and accidents go hand in hand, and there's no sense in getting upset about it.

Some "experts" claim that if a puppy pees in his bed once,

he'll do it all his life, but this is sheer idiocy

and causes a lot of undue worry on the new owner's part.

Hey, *think* about this for minute…little kids wet the bed with appalling regularity, yet most outgrow it and enjoy many years of a dry bed…at least until very old age sets in and we end up back where we started in the bladder-control department. It's much the same scenario with dogs. Where people come up with this stuff is a mystery. (That said, it's important *not to set the puppy up for an accident.*)

When taking him for a ride in the car in his crate, it's a good idea to take the extra towel along for the ride, because puppies also upchuck, although 99.99% of them outgrow that, too.

Helpful Hint: Put the extra towel in a small plastic bag in the car – that way, if he barfs on the first one you can just switch them around and tie the bag closed, which will keep the car smelling much fresher for the duration of the trip than it would if you didn't have the bag…many a perfectly good towel has ended up in a rest-stop trash can for this very reason.

When it comes to choosing a "grownup" bed for his crate, the most popular one among dog owners is probably **Midwest's Quiet Time Bolster Pet Bed,** which is available pretty much everywhere. (It currently ranks #26 in Amazon's Pet Products with 486 reviews at the time of writing.) Get two, so you can launder them frequently…they wash easily and dry fast, and can be laundered probably 100 times without falling apart. These beds are specifically sized for Midwest crates, which makes choosing the right size a whole lot easier.

Floor beds

Most dog owners also have a dog bed or two on the floor…in fact, some have one in every room, honest to God. Essentially "dog furniture", they may help keep him off yours. Or not. Just make sure they're machine washable— the kind with removable covers are great.

Grooming Stuff

Unless you are planning to have your dog groomed professionally on a weekly basis, you will need some basic grooming tools and supplies to keep him clean and mat-free between scheduled appointments. (Matting is invariably caused by the owner using the wrong grooming tools at home, resulting in a dog that looks good on the outside, but is often matted at the skin, which requires the dog be shaved down.) Trying to figure out which tools you need, however, can be a little daunting, because there are literally hundreds of dog brushes and combs on the market, all very different.

So to make it easier, here's a list of what you really need to have on hand when your Cockapoo puppy arrives, so you can get off to a positive start.. (Proper grooming techniques are covered farther along in the Grooming Chapter.)

Grooming table and grooming post

There's simply no way around it – with few exceptions, like all Poodle hybrids, Cockapoos are a high-maintenance breed, and yours will require a fair amount of grooming over his lifetime. This will be a whole lot easier for everyone concerned if the dog is trained to being groomed on a table. **In fact, it's probably close to impossible to keep your Cockapoo truly free of mats without one.**

If you buy your grooming table before your puppy arrives, and you put him on it every single time you run a comb or brush through him from his first day at home, you will have a dog that is a piece of cake to groom. If you don't, you won't, and it will get worse and worse as he grows. It's that simple.

Unless you are a professional, a grooming table that can be folded flat and easily carried to whatever location you prefer is by far the best choice. (In nice weather, you may want to groom outside on a patio or deck, and move into the laundry room or basement in inclement weather.) The grooming post attaches easily to the table with a screw-on clamp and comes off for storage. The best place to check out the available options is once again Amazon, where you have the advantage of being able to read the reviews.

Virtually all Cockapoos will fit on a 36" grooming table. They stand about 33" high, which puts the dog at just the right height for most people to groom without a lot of back strain. (Those who are a lot taller or shorter than average, may want to consider a table with adjustable legs.) If your Cockapoo weighs 20 lbs or under, you can get by with one of the less expensive tables. (These start at under $70 including the post.) On the other hand, if you want a sturdier table, you'll probably want to buy Midwest's 36" model, which is both sturdy and comes with a grooming post. It costs around $130 on Amazon with the post included, and will probably outlast your dog.

Comb, Small Scissors and Brush

A comb (the kind with rotating teeth that literally slide through the coat without pulling are best for puppies), a Chris Christensen mini T-brush and a 5-6 inch straight grooming scissors with rounded tips (for trimming hair around his eyes, pads, and under his tail, as well as cutting out things like gum that may get stuck in his coat and are impossible to brush out) are the other grooming tools you really need to have on hand when the puppy arrives. The rest of the grooming supplies you'll need are listed in Chapter Eight.

Toys and Chew Bones

This may well be the longest treatise ever written on dog toys and dog chews, but **reading through it before you buy a single toy** can save you literally thousands of dollars and several trips to the vet's office, so it's probably well-worth the effort.

In order to satisfy his needs for both intellectual stimulation and chewing, your puppy will require lots of toys. In order to keep him safe, these need to be broken down into two categories – the kind he can play with under supervision, and the kind that can go into his crate with him when he's left alone. (The latter category is frankly pretty limited.)

Besides the more immediate and often life-threatening dangers of choking, every year hundreds of dogs end up having whole plastic, rubber and nylon "chew toys" as well as various parts of said chew toys surgically removed from their digestive tracts via extremely expensive gastric surgery because of intestinal blockage.
(In the last few years, the number of dogs – primarily those of the sporting breeds – who've had to have entire cell phones surgically removed from their guts has been on the increase as well…consider yourself warned.)

Along with hard chew toys, soft stuffed "plush" toys are immensely popular – virtually every Cocka-poo puppy loves to play with them, and will usually retrieve them endlessly. He also loves to snuggle with them and have his picture taken while being so totally adorable.

On the other hand, this same puppy is entirely capable of totally eviscerating his favorite beloved stuffed toy (and ingesting both its stuffing and its squeaker) in ten minutes flat when no one is looking for no apparent reason and with apparently very little forethought. This puzzles owners no end – they simply cannot understand why a dog would systematically destroy (and very probably ingest) what was obviously a favorite toy.

The short answer is…..*they do it because they're dogs.*

Before buying a single dog toy, you need understand the hard-wired instincts driving a puppy's behavior, because once again you will be more successful
working *with* a dog's DNA rather than *against* it.

In the wild, when a litter of wolf cubs is moved to its rendezvous area, the adults deliver whole small animals and birds as well as "leftovers" (like legs and antlers) from large kills as soon as the cubs have graduated beyond the regurgitated-food stage.

These items provide training, entertainment *and* nutrition all in the same package – Mother Nature is nothing if not efficient.

The bony leftovers and antlers satisfy the need to chew during teething while providing needed calcium and trace minerals for the growing cubs.
Small whole animals are dual-purpose as well – they are "hunted", captured and played with, tossed, used for games of tug-o-war, and then ultimately *eviscerated*, because in addition to protein, the internal organs provide vital nutrients like Vitamin A, various amino acids and cholesterol, all critical for optimum physical and brain development in the cubs.
(Ironically, these highly nutritious organs are all classified by law as "byproducts" by the FDA and no one wants them in their dog food.)

Once the insides are eaten, the cubs will then ultimately consume around 85% of the rest, including hide, fur and feathers, all of which provides protein and fiber.

So what happens is when we, as "senior pack members", present our own cub with toys
(often modeled after human baby toys), his ancient canine DNA takes over.

Consequently, he will gnaw industriously on his brightly-colored hard plastic teething toys shaped like car keys or baby pacifiers until he can break them into pieces he can ingest, even though they have zero nutritional value, and he will play with his latest plush "gingerbread man" or soccer ball until he gets bored, at which points his eviscerating instincts take over and he guts it, eats the polyester stuffing and the plastic squeaker, and then shreds the rest of it.

This happens because he is a baby *canid,* not a **baby** *human.*

As with humans, "playing" for immature canids is how they practice the skills they will need as an adult, and their "toys" often reflect that. (If this makes you wonder why anyone would design toys for an animal lacking opposable thumbs in the shape of *keys* you're not alone...chalk it up to a bad case of anthropomorphism.)

Unfortunately for his digestive system, however, a puppy's DNA does not allow him to distinguish between plastic and natural bone, real fur and acrylic, or even entrails and polyester fiberfill – it is the *behaviors themselves* that are hard-wired in.

This is the same reason that a dog will "bury" a bowl of food on a tile floor with imaginary dirt and leaves in an elaborate ritual and then smugly walk away, satisfied that it is well-hidden even though it's clearly still in plain sight.

Once we understand what Mother Nature had in mind and work with it, choosing both the right chew toys and soft toys gets a whole lot easier. Amazon reviews also help a lot, since virtually every bone and dog toy they sell has multiple reviews—one has an astonishing 959 reviews as of today. (That's not a typo, that's actually *959 reviews for a ten-dollar dog toy...* I swear I am not making this up.)

Although the ultimate decisions are of course yours, the following rundown of the most popular will at least give you a place to start, so you don't have to spend the better part of the rest of your natural life reading dog toy reviews on Amazon.

(If you want to save some time, the best of these can also be found on **www.dianeklumb.com.**)

Chew Toys.

All puppies need something acceptable to chew on, especially when they are teething. With only one possible exception, none of them are totally without risk, but then, neither is driving a car – the key is to find a risk level you are personally comfortable with.

Chew toys can be divided into two basic categories- inedible (usually made of plastic and rubber) and edible (usually substances that used to be working parts of animals). Which you prefer is largely a matter of individual temperament and personal philosophy, because puppies will chew up and swallow pretty much anything. Those who don't like the idea of their dog constantly gnawing on and ultimately ingesting artificially-colored rubber and various plastic polymers will probably want to go the more "natural" route, while those who are not comfortable having parts of dead animals lying around their house will probably prefer the "artificial" options, which is what we'll start with.

Fake Stuff for Dogs to Chew On

In the artificial category, **Nylabone** products are probably among the best-known and the safest, if your puppy will chew on them – some will while others just ignore them completely. The larger bone-shaped and wishbone-shaped nylon Nylabones are good choices as long as someone's in the house. (The manufacturer specifically warns against leaving their products with an unattended dog.)

One thing worth knowing about classic Nylabones however is if swallowed in whole or in part *they do not show up on an x-ray,* which can be problematic. Nylabone's puppy keys and teething rings are certainly cute and fun for small puppies, but probably only for the first few months from a safety standpoint. (The good news is that at least the bright colors mean they'll show up on an x-ray if ingested.) *Most Nylabone products average 3-4 star ratings from Amazon customers.*

The ubiquitous **Kong** is another popular chew toy, and being made of rubber it also bounces, which makes it fun. Filled with peanut butter, it will usually keep a puppy entertained for quite a while, but again, should not be left with an unattended dog.
You might as well start right off with a big one so you never have to worry about it being accidentally swallowed. **Kong's Stuff-a-Ball** is one of the more durable and popular "treat toys" (as well as the hands-down quietest) and the **Kong Extreme Ball** rates a solid 5 stars, although it's not really a chew toy. *Kong products average 3.5 to 4.5 stars across the board.*

Real Stuff for Dogs to Chew On

In the "natural" department, let's start with what you DO NOT want to give your puppy, and those are chopped and compressed "bone-shaped things" of any sort. Although most big dogs can crunch them up, swallow the pieces and manage to get them all the way through their digestive tracts, they represent a real hazard for puppies and smaller dogs, who can pretty easily break off a chunk just large enough to choke on or to cause an intestinal obstruction.
For the record, the ubiquitous Greenie falls in this category—although the manufacturer clearly states they are only for *adult dogs* weighing over 15 pounds, it seems like everyone knows someone who's lost a small dog or a puppy to a Greenie.

Stay away from anything that uses the word "compressed" or looks like it's made from chopped-up stuff.

Real Bones

When it comes to bones, **Marrow and knuckle bones** are the time-honored natural chew toys for dogs, who've been happily gnawing on them for untold millennia, but they are not without inherent risk either; leaving a dog alone with even a huge one when no one is around is not recommended by anyone.

- **Cooked bones** can splinter, presenting a risk of both choking and intestinal perforation, even though untold thousands of them are consumed by dogs around the world every single day without incident.

- **Raw bones,** as their proponents are quick to point out, do not splinter as easily, but they do come with the inherent risk of food-borne pathogens like e-coli, campylobacter, and salmonella, to name just a few. Although dogs are indeed less susceptible to them than are people, most dogs *live* with people and can spread these pathogens via their saliva to their human pack members.

- **Smoked bones,** with bits of meat attached are a favorite of nearly all dogs, but they *are* strong-smelling and fairly messy, and many owners limit them to outdoors or crates for that reason. Both raw and cooked bones can cause stomach upset in some dogs, while others have no problem with them at all. Always monitor bone-chewing carefully and replace bones when they start to get small or chunks start to get chewed off. ***Overall, most natural bones get an average rating of 3.5-4.5 stars from Amazon's dog-owning customers.***

Assorted Animal Parts

An alternative to actual bones are various other "natural parts", all of which puppies and indeed dogs of all ages adore, all of which are pretty nutritious and some of which you may find palatable enough to actually have around. The downside of all these "natural" chews, however, is that they're all pretty expensive.

This is really pretty hilarious if you consider that when they used to be routinely included in dog food as a cheap protein source, FDA required them to be labeled as "byproducts".

When dog owner decided they didn't want to feed their dogs food that contained "byproducts", those parts ended up dried, smoked, shrink-wrapped in plastic and sold individually at exorbitant prices to those same dog owners as "natural treats" for those same dogs. Go figure.

Anyhow, it's been a real windfall for the slaughterhouse industry, which just goes to prove once again that it's an ill wind that blows nobody good. Let's look at our options here:

- **Pig's ears** (and the even less-appealing **pig snouts,** both of which big dogs merrily crunch up like large overpriced potato chips) *will* last awhile for puppies, and puppies adore them. On the other hand, they are, not surprisingly, greasy and "piggy-smelling" and have a tendency to stain everything they come in contact with.

- **Lamb's ears**, which are dry, white, and odorless, are a cleaner choice and being less fatty are less likely to cause stomach upset. *In the customer review department, pig's ears and snouts probably average 3.5 stars while lamb's ears average 4-5 stars, with the 5 star ratings mostly from owners of puppies and small dogs, because they are very expensive potato chips for the big guys.*

- **Rawhide.** Even though most dogs adore it, giving dogs rawhide in any shape is pretty controversial— although independent research has shown ingestion of rawhide is safe, large chunks of rawhide CAN be bitten off and swallowed, presenting the same choking hazard found in chopped compressed bones, so a lot of vets advise against it. (*Of course, if you ask a vet, they'll tell you nothing is really safe for a dog to chew on, because the only time vets see a lot of this stuff is when they're surgically removing it from a dog's digestive tract.*) In spite of that, America's dog population probably consumes untold tons of rawhide on an annual basis. The key to rawhide chews for puppies if you choose to give it is to stick to big knotted rawhide bones and toss them as soon as the puppy starts to untie the ends into slimy strips he could ultimately swallow. Depending on the puppy, this can take anywhere from days to weeks, by which time it's probably pretty disgusting anyway. *Rawhide products rate 3.5-.4.5 stars*

- **Cow's hooves** are another chew toy option for puppies. Once again, they all like them and will chew away merrily for hours. Although they're not greasy like pig parts, they do have an odor and some people find them unappealing to have lying around the house, since they look a lot like, well…hooves. Totally unprocessed and pretty safe for young puppies, older dogs who are strong chewers can break chunks off if they work at it for awhile. *Hooves average an Amazon customer rating of 3.5-4.5 stars.*

- **Bully sticks** are universally loved by dogs, and are about as natural as you can get, since they are in reality simply raw bull or steer penises which are hung and dried without any cooking, processing or chemicals. They do have a fair amount of nutritional value, and because they are low in fat, they are unlikely to cause stomach upset. (*Many owners feel bully sticks have a "calming" effect on their dogs, most likely related to the fact that they're high in taurine, an amino acid known to be protective against glutamate excitotoxicity in the brain – in fact, taurine is used to treat both seizures and head tremors in dogs.*) They're considered safer than rawhide from a choking standpoint, especially if you buy the thickest ones. In fact, if it weren't for the "yuck" factor, and the fact that they all smell pretty awful (even the so-called "odorless" ones), bully sticks would probably rate 5 stars based on safety, palatability and nutritional value. But what can you say about a product where one of the 5 star reviews actually starts out with "Gross, but worth it"? *Overall, 4 stars.*

OK, assuming you haven't fallen off your chair in a coma by now, you've probably figured out that a "5 star chew" would be 100% natural, nontoxic, nutritious *and* incapable of splintering or breaking off into chunks so you could leave it in his crate with him when no one's around, as well as odorless, not greasy, messy, or disgusting to look at or pick up, and hopefully not something you'll have a hard time explaining to Aunt Eleanor when she comes over at Christmas and asks what the dog is chewing on. "Sustainably harvested" seems like too much too ask, but what the heck, let's throw it in there anyway. Oh yeah, and dogs should actually *like* it.

Well, Mick, it might not happen often, but if you try sometimes, you just might find you get what you want...*and* what you need.

The absolute BEST puppy chew toy at any price is a good-sized chunk of antler.

Elk, whitetail, mulie or moose, doesn't matter, good quality antler meets all of the above criteria, *and is probably the only thing on God's green earth that's actually safe enough to leave with an unattended puppy.*

And unlike bones, rawhide and hooves, the majority of antler is harvested in the most sustainable manner one can possibly imagine, because **no animals need be killed in the process.**

In case you're not from Wisconsin, Minnesota, or one of those big square states out west and consequently didn't know this, antlers are not the same as the horns on a cow, who is stuck with the same set for life.
Although antler is also made of bone, bucks of all of the above species actually shed their antlers, or "racks", every year, and pretty much abandon them where they fall, after which they promptly begin to acquire a new and usually more impressive set. Sort of like iphones.

"Harvesting" these discarded racks consists mostly of wandering around the woods until you find a set, which is not as easy as it sounds. In fact, it is so difficult that some people are now training "shed dogs" to assist in the hunt.

In order to get there before the local rodentia do, shed gathering (also known as "clinting" for no good reason) is done between December and February, and often requires tromping around in sub-zero weather on snowshoes, which is not everyone's idea of a fun time.

Because harvesting is so labor-intensive, antler dog chews are absurdly expensive, but when you factor in how long they last and how clean, odor-free and safe they are, they really are a great bargain.

In fact, one could make a strong argument for dispensing with the nylon and rawhide and pig parts and dried penises altogether and making antler pieces the *only* chewing option available for your puppy right from the get-go, in which case you'll want to buy a couple, because, like snowflakes, no two are identical and variety is good for puppies as well as people.

You do need to toss them when they finally are gnawed down to a size that could be swallowed whole, but it will take a long time, especially if the puppy is working on several at once.

Antler chews get 5 stars from Amazon's dog owning customers, with the exception of those who thought that for eighteen bucks they were getting a whole bag of them instead of just one.

Soft Toys

Unfortunately, there are no really "natural" alternatives in the soft toy department short of picking up actual roadkill, which is a little more natural than most of us are comfortable with.

There is an argument, however, for choosing stuffed toys that at least vaguely resemble what might actually be found in nature, though— in addition to being more "culturally respectful", dogs often innately prefer them. The best are animal- or bird-shaped, made of sturdy material, well-sewn, and have few appendages to be chewed off and swallowed. (Tags should be cut off with a scissors.)

But you do need to bear in mind that no matter how well-made, stuffed toys are not designed as chew toys by definition—they should always be used in an interactive manner to some degree, and under supervision.

When a puppy starts to seriously chew on or rip into a stuffed toy instead of playing with it, common sense should dictate that it's time to pick it up and replace it with a "real" chew toy like a bone or an antler – failure to do this teaches the puppy that destroying items made of cloth and stuffing is acceptable behavior, and it's *not*… unless of course you want your couch cushions to meet a similar end.

Toys that suffer small "accidental" tears caused by sharp puppy teeth should also be picked up immediately. (At the risk of pointing out the obvious, using a needle and thread to sew up a small hole before the first irresistible-to-puppies wisps of polyester stuffing appear will stop the process in its tracks and extend the life of the toy significantly. Your sewing skills really don't matter here, and it only takes a minute.)

That said, buying well-designed stuffed toys right from the get-go will actually lessen the chances that they will be destroyed.

In addition to durability, the best dog toys are designed with an understanding of the canine instinct to eviscerate small fuzzy animals.

And the manufacturer that literally *owns* this market is Kygen. They make several lines of plush toys designed with smaller stuffed squeaky toys that fit *inside* bigger stuffed toys, and they are nothing short of brilliant. The little toys may be easily removed, leaving the big one intact, by all but the dumbest of dogs after a little helpful instruction from the owner, who will then spend the rest of his life sticking them back in so that his dog can pull them out again. No matter, Cockapoo puppies adore them…in fact, puppies and dogs of nearly all breeds and ages adore them.

The undisputed winner here is surely **Kygen's Hide-a-Squirrel**. Essentially a fuzzy gray tree stump with three removable squeaky stuffed squirrels inside, it is Amazon's #1 best-selling dog toy and yes, Virginia, it is indeed the one boasting 676 reviews and counting. Even *more* astonishing is the fact that over 80% of reviewers gave it 5 stars, which is probably some sort of record. And because it speaks directly to their DNA, dogs just universally love it. It actually comes in 4 sizes, but since most people ultimately upgrade to the "ginormous" size (which boasts no less than *five* removable squirrels) you might just want to start there.

If a Cockapoo puppy could only have three personal possessions, two good-sized chunks of antler and a Hide-a-Squirrel would probably serve him well.

Since that's clearly not gonna happen, the next toy worth buying is **Kygen's Platypus**, another Amazon best-seller and part of its Egg Baby series.

Using the same principle as Hide-a-Squirrel, the squeaky eggs (which are remarkably sturdy) are gleefully removed from the Platypus by the puppy, then tossed around and played with until you put them back in, after which the whole process is repeated endlessly until the puppy gets tired, at which point you trade it for a chew bone so he'll go lay down and leave you in peace for awhile.

There are actually several toys in the Egg Baby series, and Harvey the Hedgehog is another good choice. *These are all 4 star toys.*

If you get tired of stuffing little toys back into big toys and want to add a couple of less-interactive ones, **Ethical's Skinneeez** line is pretty cool.

Because the bodies of these plush critters have no actual stuffing, the "eviscerating gene" doesn't automatically kick in, and the long skinny shape is extremely attractive to puppies, who'll immediately toss them around and shake them. (This is obviously another DNA-based thing…as anyone who's watched a dog destroy a stuffed animal knows, the "tossing and shaking" behavior naturally appears *after* the toy is gutted.)

There's a Skinneeez skunk, a squirrel, a fox and a raccoon among others, all fairly realistic – unfortunately this realism coupled with their flat shape may cause the uninitiated to mistake them for roadkill, but that's really their only downside. They're also all under ten bucks. *Skinneeez get 4 stars from Amazon's customers across the board, although apparently somebody's dog actually managed to swallow one whole and had to have it surgically removed, after which the owner posted warnings all over the internet. (This should not be a problem for Cockapoos.)*

A couple more stuffed toys worth adding to the pile are all made by Coleman, the sporting goods company. All exhibit the "durability at a reasonable price" that's Coleman's stock in trade.

The **Coleman pheasant** is popular with dogs mostly because of its cool squawky squeaker, as is the **Coleman duck**, which actually quacks. (Cockapoos probably like them because they have sporting dog ancestry, but even toy breeds are attracted to these "game birds", which is a little surprising.)

Their neoprene **Water Sport Duck** is great for teaching puppies to retrieve out of water in a lake or backyard pool.

Last but not least, **Coleman's Super-Sized Trophy Bear** is a sturdy and immensely popular "cuddle toy" for puppies of all ages with a good track record for longevity. *This last one is another dog toy with over a hundred Amazon reviews, and over two thirds of them are 5 stars. For some reason Coleman just got it right, and dogs instinctively love this bear. All of Coleman's stuffed dog toys are rated highly by customers, though—usually rating 4-5 stars across the board.*

Interactive Treat Toys

There is a last category of interactive toys which are fairly new to the market, and these are "treat toys". Unlike the interactive stuffed toys, the owner doesn't have to do much here— once it's filled, the dog simply interacts with the toy without a lot of input from anyone else. They are based on the premise that, unlike a grazing animal that just needs to put his head down, a canid is hard-wired to *work* for his food.

The fact that dogs think these toys are lots of fun and will often choose their food ball over a dish of food indicates the designers may be on to something. (Some trainers are now recommending these as the primary "dog dish", and many suggest their use to prevent or alleviate separation anxiety as well as food-bolting.)

Usually designed in the shape of a ball or cube with a hole for the food to fall out of when rolled, these will keep dogs entertained for anywhere from 10 minutes to an hour.

Two of the most popular are the **OurPets IQ Treat ball**, and **Kong's Wobbler**. Both are dishwasher -safe, which is good.

Kong's Stuff-a-Ball is one of the few made of rubber, which is harder to clean but quiet enough to allow you to watch TV in the same room.

The **Buster Food Cube** is another popular one, but its squarish shape makes it even louder than the hard plastic balls, especially on tile or hardwood floors. It's probably worth it to get a couple different shapes and switch them out just to keep things interesting. ***Overall, this bunch rates 4-5 stars from Amazon customers.***

In Summary...

Obviously there are tons of dog toys out there, and while this will get you started, you'll no doubt keep adding to your puppy's collection as you go along. If you try to remember that he's a full-fledged card-carrying member of the genus *Canidae* and not a little person in a dog suit, and always read the customer reviews to check for safety and durability before you bring anything into the house, you'll do fine.

The most important thing to keep in mind, though, is that there is no amount of dog toys, no matter how "interactive", that can take the place of human attention.

Dog toys are all meant to be used by people as a fun way to interact with their dogs, NOT to entertain dogs left alone.

Because of the way they're hard-wired, any dog would rather play fetch with a plain old stick in the company of one of his human pack members than be left alone with a boxful of expensive dog toys.

Collars, leads and tags

The collar and tag is part of a dog's basic "wardrobe" – in fact, unless he's wearing a life jacket or a service dog jacket it's probably his *whole* wardrobe, and he should wear it at all times unless he's in the tub. Some experts advise against leaving a dog unattended in a crate with a collar on, but if you actually examine any modern crate you'll be hard-pressed to figure out how a dog can get his collar stuck anywhere in there, so this may just be outdated advice. Show dog owners never leave collars on their dogs, but that's really mostly about saving coat.

Puppy Collars

To start out, you'll want a **flat nylon puppy-sized collar with a matching 6-foot lead**. (Your breeder should be able to tell you which size is appropriate for your puppy.)

The choice between a traditional "buckle" collar and the kind with a plastic snap is entirely up to you, but bear in mind this is a temporary collar, because your puppy is going to outgrow it in short order. Just pick a bright color that complements his coat.

You'll also need a tag with his phone number on it, and these can (and should) be made up on the spot at any major pet supply store like Petsmart *before your puppy arrives.* (In fact, if you are picking up your puppy, which you should do if at all possible, you should bring it along and attach it to his collar before he leaves the breeder's property.)

Some people are paranoid about putting the dog's name on the tag as well, but if a puppy is lost, it's probably less traumatic for him if the person who finds him can actually call him by name. Even if he's microchipped, a simple phone number (your cell phone is probably best) is most likely to get him home the fastest.

.When shopping for collars you'll notice a dizzying array of "training" collars out there on the same rack—martingales, slip collars (referred to as "choke" collars by people who don't like them), prong collars and head collars (the ubiquitous Gentle Leader is the best known), but if your puppy is reasonably tractable (as most Cockapoos are) and you actually take the time to train him to heel early he may never need any of them, and they'll all be the wrong size anyway.

Another handy item is one of those little plastic bag-holders that attaches to his lead—that way you'll never have to scrounge around in your pocket for a bag or Kleenex.

Check cord

In addition to the 6 foot nylon lead, what you will also absolutely need right out the gate is a 5/8 inch 20-foot, 5/8 inch **cotton web training lead**, also called a "check cord" or "drop lead", depending on the trainer's area of expertise.

This will allow your puppy some freedom to romp in areas that are open but not entirely fenced, like parks and beaches, as well as being a critical tool for teaching him to recall in your backyard. (Actually, with a check cord, you can practice the recall lots of different places, which is a very good idea.).

Check cords are infinitely safer than the ubiquitous "retractable" lead, which appeared like a nasty virus back in the 1980s and which too many pet owners now use and all experienced trainers wish would vanish from the earth.
Besides literally *teaching dogs to pull*, which is stupid, these leads are downright dangerous.

(The manufacturer of the FlexiLead actually suggests that to "reduce the risk of finger amputation" you remove your rings and wear sturdy gloves…it's right on their website.)

As if *that* isn't bad enough, if a retractable lead is accidentally dropped (which it will be sooner or later), it will immediately and loudly retract, and then the poor puppy will find himself being chased by a noisy chunk of plastic banging along right behind him no matter how fast he runs! Nine out of ten puppies will panic in this situation, for which you can hardly blame them, and the results can be lethal. Even if you can manage to get to the puppy and the damned leash before he gets hit by a car, the damage to his leash-training will be extensive, to say the least.

(By comparison, if you drop the check cord, you can casually scoop it back up, and odds are good the puppy won't even notice.)

To avoid these and other possible disasters, here's my advice:

- **DO NOT BUY A RETRACTABLE LEASH FOR YOUR PUPPY.**
- **DO NOT ACCEPT ONE AS A GIFT.**
- **DO NOT PUT ONE ON YOUR PUPPY UNLESS SOMEONE ACTUALLY HAS A GUN POINTED AT YOUR HEAD.**
- **DO NOT STAND ANYWHERE NEAR A DOG WHO'S ATTACHED TO ONE.**

Is everyone clear on that? The retractable leash is probably the *worst* thing that ever happened to dog training, and the second-worst idea to come out of Germany in the last hundred years.

Once your puppy gets bigger, you might need to replace the 5/8 inch cotton web lead with a stronger nylon one (LL Bean makes the best ones), and you can buy them in lengths up to 50 feet. They are a great investment.

Books

If Amazon's *"Customers who bought this item also bought..."* is any sort of a guide, most people buy a handful of books on puppy-training and general dog ownership while they are killing time waiting for their puppy by ordering crates and dog beds and antlers and Hide-a-Squirrels. *But which ones should you buy?*

This can be extremely confusing, especially for the poor novice dog owner, as the various philosophies of dog training rival maybe only organized religion in both sheer number and intolerance for opposing opinions among their respective adherents. (For that reason alone, reading the reviews will only confuse you more.)

So let's make it easy:
If you are only going to buy one book on dog training, that book should **be *Mother Knows Best: the Natural Way to Train Your Dog* by Carl Lea Benjamin.**
Written back in 1985, it's been selling steadily ever since and it's now also available on Kindle.

What sets this book apart? Simply put, *Mother Knows Best* is to dog training what *The Art of French Cooking* is to cooking, and Carol Lea Benjamin is no less than the Julia Child of dog training— the person who first introduced dog owners to the idea of "natural training" nearly thirty years ago. **No one does it better.**

In addition to teaching you in clear and simple steps how to actually train your dog, Carol Benjamin teaches you to *enjoy* him. She makes natural training *fun* for both the dog and his owner, rather than an unnatural chore.

Mercifully lacking the endless autobiographical material and "case histories" that seem to plague nearly all training books, Ms Benjamin spends a little time explaining her philosophy and then jumps right into a practical "curriculum" for a typical 8 week old puppy. The section on Etiquette for Puppies includes a housebreaking schedule, broken down hour-by-hour.

It really is the only training book you will ever need, unless you want to add **How to Survive Your Puppy's Adolescence,** which you might as well break down and buy at the same time, since you'll need it in only a few short months, anyway. Not surprisingly, it's written by the same author.

Assuming you want to keep your dog as healthy as you possibly can (and who doesn't?) the other book worth buying right out the gate is **Dr Pitcairn's New Guide to Natural Dog Care.**

Written by the world's foremost authority on natural and alternative veterinary medicine, this book offers some important insights into why modern dogs now suffer from so many chronic health issues and what you can do to avoid them. Newly revised, it now includes a chapter on environmental toxins and dogs that's a real eye-opener. Read it with an open mind and try to incorporate as much of it as you realistically can into your dog's care, even if you don't plan to make him home-cooked organic meals. The section on homeopathic and herbal remedies for minor problems will save you enough to pay for the book several times over…and you'll have avoided giving your dog a lot of unnecessary antibiotics to boot.

Another book worth buying, especially if you're thinking of cooking for your dog rather than feeding commercial dog food, is **Home-Prepared Dog & Cat Diets: the Healthful Alternative by Donald R Strombeck DVM PhD.**

The recipes are surprisingly EASY, inexpensive and backed by a lot of hard science. If you find the idea of home-cooked food for your dog appealing but are at all worried that it may result in nutritional deficiencies, this book is a must-have.
Dr Strombeck is Professor Emeritus at UC Davis School of Veterinary Medicine and is a recognized authority in canine nutrition. At 366 pages, it's packed with information; it's also *very* expensive, but you can usually buy a used copy on Amazon. It's worth knowing that much of the information in the book, including a lot of the recipes, can also be found online at http://dogcathomeprepareddiet.com.

Another good book on cooking for your dog is **_Dinner Pawsible_**

If you're a compulsive reader, another book you might want to consider adding to your library is Stanley Coren's **_How to Speak Dog_**, which expands upon the guide to understanding dog language introduced in _Mother Knows Best._

In the DVD department, **Cesar Millan's _People Training for Dogs_** is available on Amazon and worth owning. Like most of his books, this is not a "training manual" (by his own admission, Cesar Millan is not a dog "trainer" per se), but rather explains the psychology behind effective dog training.

Anyhow, this list should be enough to get you headed in the right direction, so you might as well pull out the plastic and start ordering so you'll have everything disinterred from its annoying packaging and assembled by the time you get your puppy.

And when the bills for all this stuff start coming in at the end of the month you'll immediately understand why the initial cost of the puppy really doesn't matter much.

CHAPTER SIX:

Off to a Good Start
(or...surviving the first few days and nights and beyond)

The most important year of any dog's life is without doubt the first one. In fact, much of his future success in life depends upon what he learns not only in the first year, *but in the first 4 months*. Puppies start learning very early from their mothers. If you want a well-balanced and well-trained dog (and who doesn't?) you'll want to continue this learning process puppy right away, rather than waiting until he's old enough to go to training classes, by which time you'll already have problems to "fix".

Cockapoos are highly intelligent and if *you* do not train your puppy he will train *himself*, which rarely works out well for anybody. Virtually all the "problems" with which professional trainers have to deal really involve *retraining* the poor dog who was forced to train himself due to a lack of leadership on his owner's part when he was little and cute. For example,

The dog who jumps on everyone was simply never taught how to appropriately greet a human when he was little, so he came up with his OWN greeting.

As with children and spouses, it's a lot easier and more effective to teach a dog what we DO want him to do than to only try to teach him what we DON'T, because in the latter case he won't have an appropriate alternative behavior with which to replace the unwanted one

If you don't want a dog to jump up on you to greet you when you walk into a room, exactly what *DO* you want him to do —-sit, lie down, roll over, stand on his head? I mean, think about it...he's got to do SOMETHING.

Dog training is not rocket science—- it's common sense. All you really have to remember is that no command should start with "don't" or "no" (as in "no jumping!") **because "not doing something" is not a *behavior*, and therefore can't really be rewarded**. And negative commands are also less effective than positive ones— probably why we have "Stop" signs instead of "Don't Go" signs.

Now, it takes a total of maybe 20 minutes to teach even the most dim-witted 8 week old puppy a good *sit/stay.* Then as soon as he even starts to *think* about jumping up, he can be given the sit-stay command and be *rewarded* with praise and a pat on the head instead of a knee in the chest and yelling… or even worse, his best-beloved person *ignoring* him while he gets more and more desperate to have his existence acknowledged, because **whoever came up with the breathtakingly stupid idea that *ignoring* an unwanted behavior will cause it to disappear obviously never had children.**

It's also kinder. The saddest cartoon ever is the one where two dogs meet and one says "My name is No No Bad Dog—what's yours?"

So the training begun by his mother should be continued seamlessly by you the minute you have your hands on your new puppy. Reading *Mother Knows Best* all the way through before you bring him home will give you all the confidence and tools you need to do it right. The clock starts ticking the minute you actually pick up your puppy, so let's start with that.

When is the best time to pick up your puppy?

Odds are you won't have a lot of leeway here—most breeders have a "pick-up weekend" based on what they feel is the optimal age for the pups to go their new homes. Usually with Cockapoos, this is between 8 and 9 weeks. So you need to find out when you're supposed to pick him up and clear your calendar well in advance.

But under NO circumstances should you buy a puppy from a breeder who will let them go before 7 weeks. Puppies taken from their litters before this time will often have problems getting along with other dogs and in addition often lack "bite inhibition", which they learn from their mothers and siblings.

98

Is it Really Safe to Have a Puppy Shipped?

At the risk of alienating a lot of well-intentioned breeders, the short answer is NO. Convenient for breeder and buyer, yes. **But really safe? Not so much.**

For the better part of the last hundred years, buying a puppy meant looking for breeders pretty close to home, finding one you were comfortable with, and then driving over to pick up the puppy as soon as it was old enough to leave its mom and littermates. (*For a wealth of reasons, this "buying local" method is still by far the best.*) But the idea of flying a puppy across country was unheard of.

But in the internet world we now live in, buyers more often select a puppy online from a breeder halfway across the country whom they've never met, purchase the puppy without ever visiting the breeder's home and/or meeting the puppy or his parents, and then have the poor little guy shipped cross-country when he turns eight weeks old as if he were a cappuccino maker. We're now all so used to online purchasing and having everything delivered that no one seems to think twice about this whole process, or whether or not it is actually in the best interest of the puppy himself. **IT IS NOT.**

For a multitude of reasons it is far better for a puppy to be picked up rather than shipped. The first, of course, is that it's far safer for the puppy. ***Think about this for a minute— you're willing to trust your puppy's very LIFE to the same idiots who regularly lose your luggage???***

It should not come as much of a surprise to learn that the airlines lose *puppies* as well as luggage. In fact, according to the US Dept of Transportation, between 2005 (when airlines were required to actually turn in reports for the first time *ever*) and 2011, US airlines killed, injured or lost 224 pets. Here's the breakdown:

- Delta —70
- Continental—69,
- Alaska Airlines—50,
- American Airlines —45
- United —24.

Close to 90% of the deaths reported were dogs. And lest you think that these were perhaps all elderly animals or bulldogs (which is what the airlines would like us to believe) the 2000 Samoyed National Specialty Winner, a four year-old prime specimen of a dog, died in the cargo hold of a flight from Orlando to CA *while his owners were in the cabin of the same plane.*)
And as awful as that sounds, it's actually much WORSE than that….

Those figures only include dogs traveling as excess baggage when their owners are in the cabin. They DO NOT include "incidents" involving any of the thousands of unaccompanied puppies shipped each year as cargo from breeders to their new owners —like yours! — *because the airlines are not required to report those.*

How many of these puppies shipped "unaccompanied" are killed or injured? Because they do not need to be reported, no one knows the exact number, but according to the ASPCA, Air Transportation Association data puts the estimate at around *5,000 per year*, or roughly one in every 100 puppy shipped. This would include the 7 puppies that died of apparent overheating on a single American Airlines flight from Oklahoma to Chicago O'Hare in August 2010, as well as Maggie May, the Westie pup who was crushed to death in 2008 by a baggage cart on the tarmac at Atlanta's Hartsfield enroute to her new owner.

Although the airlines claim that the baggage holds are pressurized and air-conditioned, temperatures ranging from below freezing to 115 degrees have been recorded in the crates of shipped dogs, often because the plane was delayed on the tarmac. (When a Continental flight bound for Denver was delayed for 3 hours in Philadelphia, 3 Samoyeds in the cargo hold were found dead on arrival.)

What sorts of injuries are recorded? United was recently sued when a dog's eardrums were punctured during transport—the owner received $410.50 in compensation, based on the weight of the dog. And any dog that dies enroute to or at the vets' office rather than being found dead in its crate when they take it off the plane is listed as an "injury" rather than a death in the incident report.

So why do breeders assure puppy buyers that shipping puppies is perfectly safe, when the numbers indicate pretty clearly that it is NOT?

That's easy....*you* didn't know any of this until right now, did you?

Odds are, neither does your breeder. Ask them exactly how many dogs died flying the friendly skies in the last five years— *I guarantee they will not know. Unfortunately, hardly anyone does.*

Because they make a lot of money shipping dogs, the *airlines themselves* obviously don't advertise the risks, or the number of dogs and puppies lost each year, so most breeders remain blissfully ignorant until the awful day when one of their own puppies dies enroute.

The commercial breeders DO know, but for them, it's simply part of the cost of doing business online. Shipping puppies sold via the internet is the best thing that ever happened to puppy mills—instead of selling them wholesale to brokers, they can now sell them at retail directly to the consumer, who thinks he's buying from a responsible breeder. *They're making more money than ever.* What's the loss of a couple of puppies compared to that? They simply write them off as business losses.

In fact, puppy mills would be out of business in short order
if the airlines simply banned the shipping of puppies under the age of a year,
because it is absolutely critical to their continued existence.

Aside from the very real physical risks, there is also a lot less *psychological stress* if you pick up your puppy yourself directly from the breeder, because he will know he has "permission" to be with you – his care is simply being transferred from one higher-ranking pack member than himself to another, which happens in the wild all the time.

On the other hand, there's really no natural equivalent to a puppy being put in a crate and driven to an airport by one person, shifted around innumerable times, subjected to highly toxic lead-laden jet fumes and a noise level that requires ear protection for humans, and then ultimately taken out of the crate after all this by a person *he's never seen before* at the other end. He has nothing in his DNA to cope with the stress of that.

Besides being the most popular week to ship puppies, the eighth week also marks the beginning of the first "fear" period in canine development.

The period between 8 to 12 weeks is when fear of loud noises develops,
and *anything associated with fear at this stage* will be a fear stimulus throughout the dog's life.

If a puppy is subjected to shipping when he is going through the first fear period, the potential for long-lasting trauma is extremely high. Because no one has any idea exactly what may have frightened the puppy during shipping, there is no way to "undo" it with a program of desensitization.
Some trainers believe that the fact so many puppies are now routinely shipped to their new homes explains a lot of the noise fears (hence the exploding popularity of "thunder shirts") and separation anxiety problems as well as the free-floating anxiety they now see in dogs.

If you think about these problems in terms of what a puppy may have experienced being shipped in the cargo hold on an airline during the first fear period, the theory has merit. How do you think your luggage gets so scuffed up???

The fact that many puppies apparently handle being shipped as well as they do is a credit to the adaptability of the canine psyche, but that's hardly an excuse for putting a puppy through the experience simply because it's more "convenient" for the new owner.

So if you want to keep your puppy safe, give him the best possible start in life and avoid creating any phobias you'll have to identify and figure out how to deal with later, **arrange to pick him up yourself** …your personal convenience is really *not* the most important factor here. Being responsible for a dog for the next 15-20 years is going to be pretty inconvenient at times, and this is as good a time as any to get used to it.

Does this limit you to breeders near your home? *Of course not.*

If you've selected a responsible breeder six states away, talked at length with the breeder via phone, seen photos and videos of the parents and litter in their environment (not just cute "posed" puppy shots!), and it's just too far to drive, *just fly in and pick him up.* This is the twenty-first century, for Heaven's sake!

Flying in an underseat pet carrier is not stressful for a puppy at all because the cabin is pressurized, air-conditioned and he is never more than 3 inches from human feet— most will sleep the whole way, even on a cross-country flight, with no need for sedation.

In fact, for reasons unknown, puppies are less likely to get airsick than carsick, assuming they're inside the cabin. (If he gets squirmy mid-flight, he probably needs to relieve himself. Simply carry him to the loo right in his bag and spread out a piddle pad on the floor, which you'll of course have tucked into the pocket of the bag. When he's done, pop him back into the bag and go back to your seat. If you forgot the piddle pad use paper towels.)

If you use air miles or shop around for a deal, you can often pick up your puppy for less than the average cost of shipping, which is usually between $350 and $400. And some breeders will meet you at the airport so you can do it as a "turnaround".

Most airlines charge a fee of around $100 to bring the puppy into the cabin with you, which is irritating on principle but a great deal when you consider the alternatives.

On the other hand, if the breeder does not WANT you to fly in
or drive to their home to pick up your new puppy,
but insists on shipping,
find yourself a new breeder, because that's the hallmark of a puppy mill.

Substandard breeders actually count on the fact that you will find it more "convenient" to have the puppy shipped, because that way, you won't see the God-awful conditions under which he was raised, or how many dogs they have or how many puppies they are cranking out.

Planning Your Pick-Up Trip

Whether you drive or fly, try to arrange it so that the puppy spends his first night away from his littermates in his new home rather than in a Holiday Inn somewhere along the way.

As everyone who remembers *Lady and the Tramp* is aware, the first night is going to set the tone for what follows, and what you'll have to do to keep a homesick puppy quiet in a hotel room probably won't make the next night any easier.

If you have a long drive it's best to stay at a hotel close to the breeder the night before. That way you can pick up the puppy early enough the next morning to make it home that evening, where his new setup will be waiting for him. (If you can't make the drive home in one day, it's really better to fly in and pick him up— less stress all the way around.)

In addition to a crate, you'll want to pack a "puppy pick-up bag" with the emergency supplies you will almost certainly need for the trip. This should include:

- His collar (with tag attached) and a leash
- A baggie of whatever food he's used to
- A bottle of water and a small bowl
- A big roll of paper towels
- Several plastic grocery bags
- Bonine (half a tab will help a lot if he's carsick)
- An antler to chew on
- A soft toy or towel you can rub on his littermates and/or mom

If you can manage the trip without an extraordinary number of small children and elderly relatives the whole thing will be easier, but two people are better than one— it's best to have a person sitting *next* to him on the ride home rather than sticking him in the back all by himself, where he's much more likely to put up a racket. You're also much more likely to know when he wakes up and has to go so you'll be able to pull into the nearest gas station or rest stop ASAP.

In that regard, if you have to stop to let the puppy out, do try to avoid the "official" dog-walking areas at a rest stop if you can – that's where all the dog germs are! It's far safer to find a less-used grassy area at a service plaza.

Housetraining

Once you've arrived at home, begin your housetraining routine immediately.

Take the puppy out of the car directly to the area of the yard (or sidewalk if your in the city) that you plan to use to for him to relieve himself, tell him to "hurry up". It's good to choose a not-too-stupid phrase and stick to it so your puppy will learn to relieve himself on command—and for Heaven's sake don't use "good boy!" or it will come back to haunt you!

Praise him lavishly when he goes, and then *walk him around a little to sniff and explore afterwards.*

And try to remember that unlike an adult, a puppy rarely empties his bladder all at once, and he's been in the car awhile, so let him squat a couple times so he doesn't have to finish emptying his bladder the first time he sets foot in the house, which is not an auspicious start.

Now, once you're pretty sure he's empty, bring him into the house and directly into his rendezvous area, where he can get a drink of water and a meal. A small meal is best if it's late, but no matter how late it is, you don't want to put him to bed hungry.

Give him time to explore and play a little inside, and as soon as he looks like he needs to go again, take his paw and ring the bell and then take him right out the door that you intend him to use directly to the area you want him to use (this will now be the second time he's been there), and praise lavishly again when he goes.

If he actually starts to relieve himself in the house, you missed the signals, because there always are some and you better figure out what they are—circling, sniffing the floor, whatever. (It varies from

104

puppy to puppy.) But until you do, just say *"Oops, out-SIDE!"* with sufficient volume to stop the flow, scoop him up quickly and take him out to the appointed area to finish (using his paw to quickly hit the bell on the way out), so you can praise him again.

Here's the magic key to housebreaking:

The more times the puppy does it right,
the faster he'll "get it" and let you know he has to go.
The more mistakes he's allowed to make because you're not paying attention
the longer it will take. It's that simple.

It's also good to keep in mind that the average age for a puppy to be really reliably housetrained is 6 months or so, although most Cockapoos are reliable way before then. ("Reliably housetrained", by the way, means the dog understands that he is not to eliminate inside, and will hold it until someone lets him out.)

Assuming you're feeding him at the same times each day, actually *writing down* the times when your puppy has a bowel movement and urinates for a couple of days can help a lot, because it allows you to be proactive.

Although this sounds a little OCD, it really *does* help—once you realize that your pup always has a bowel movement 20 minutes after he eats, you can get him outside at the right time; if you have no idea, you're going to have more accidents.

You'll also realize how many times in a single day a puppy pees, which is illuminating, to say the least. Use this information to make up a schedule. (If you're *really* OCD, you'll no doubt design a nifty spreadsheet, but a pen and paper will work just fine.)

Having a bell hanging from the door speeds housebreaking
because a puppy will learn to ring a bell way before he'll learn to bark at the door.

This will avoid puddles in front of the door, which are a good indication that the puppy is learning faster than you are.

This is also a good time to reiterate that you'll get farther faster if you always let the puppy explore and play outside for a little bit *after* he has relieved himself in his designated area, as you did the first time.. If he is always brought inside immediately after he goes, he'll figure that out in a hurry, and it will take him longer and longer to relieve himself so as to stretch out his time outside.

Also, DO remember that young puppies do not generally completely empty their bladders all at once, which is why so many people complain that the puppy went outside and "did his business" and then came inside and promptly made another puddle on the floor. A puppy may have to squat twice or even three times before he's done, so it pays not to be in a huge hurry when he's outside.

Anyhow, continue this "playing-exploring-going outside" routine until it's time for the humans to cash it in and go to bed, remembering to cut off his water supply after 7PM.
(Giving him unlimited access to a big bowl of water 24/7 is not a great idea, by the way—young puppies will drink until they are tired, not until their thirst is satiated, and a puppy can drink a *lot* of water before he gets tired!)

Tuck the puppy in for the night in his little crate in your room (right next to the bed is best at first) with his blanket that smells like home, a stuffed toy for company and his antler chew in case he needs to relieve some stress by chewing a little, and try to get some sleep. He should settle in after some cursory whining, which you will respond to by cheerfully telling him to "go to sleep" rather than by letting him out.
If he's tired out and hasn't had water after 7 PM, he may sleep all night, or he may have to get up at 2 AM. If he does, take him outside (don't forget to ring the bell!), let him relieve himself but not play, and tuck him right back in his crate. (Note: *don't* turn on all the lights or he'll think it's morning and he'll want to play. Nightlights are good if you don't want to run into furniture on the way out.)

As soon as he makes any noise in the morning, take him directly outside, ringing the bell on the way. (If he walks well on a leash, there is an advantage to snapping it on and leading him quickly out the door, because he'll learn the route to the door with his feet. If he's not leash-trained, it's best to carry him, because he can't learn two things at once.) Have your slippers and robe next to the bed and your jacket and snow boots right by the door if need be. DO NOT STOP to go the bathroom yourself— you're a grown-up and should be able to hold it for a couple minutes, while your puppy surely cannot.

The week following should be more of the same, except he'll use his "big crate" for naps during the day, and assuming you don't let him "tank up" on water in the evening he should start making it through the night. This is the week when you want to be sure someone is home pretty much 24/7.

Crate-training

Although a necessary skill to learn (among other things, the desire to keep his bed dry will teach a puppy that he can actually *hold it* for awhile if he needs to) being alone in a crate is not "natural" for a puppy, nor is it self-rewarding behavior, so you'll want to use treats for this.

Crate-training is best started when he's tired out from 10 or 15 minutes of running around outside and ready for a nap. Pop him into his crate, using a little treat as "bait" if you need to bribe him in there, give him an antler chew, close the door, and leave the room. If he falls asleep, leave him in there undisturbed until he wakes up, then take him immediately out to his exercise area.

If he's clearly not tired and barks and howls — and you're sure his bladder is empty, *tell him to "settle" (or whatever word you prefer,), and ignore him until he stops.* Immediately letting him out of his crate when he kicks up a fuss is a bad idea, because that rewards the behavior, and even the most dim-witted puppy will quickly learn that barking and whining is the way to avoid staying in his crate.

Once he's quiet for a while (even a minute or two will do it if that's all you can get between tantrums), you can praise him and let him out, because now you've rewarded him for *not* fussing. Run him around until he's really tired this time and try again.

Needless to say, crate-training is much easier if the puppy was already familiarized with the crate by the breeder. (Breeders who take the time to do this are worth their weight in gold. It also makes the ride home a lot easier.)

And NEVER leave a young puppy home alone in a crate so he is forced to eliminate in it, because you will lose ground in the housebreaking department. Until he's housetrained, an expen with a piddle pad or litter is the best choice if he needs to be left alone.

Giving Him Time to Recharge

It's not uncommon for the puppy to spend a lot of Day One or Day Two sleeping quite a bit and maybe seeming a little "off" – if he's eating OK and doesn't have diarrhea or a fever, odds are it's just a stress reaction and he needs the time to recharge his little batteries. (Not surprisingly, this is more common in puppies who've been shipped, which is a lot more stress than being picked up.)

On that note, you will want to take your puppy's temperature on his first full day home, so you have a baseline for what's "normal". (It'll probably be somewhere around 100.5—101.5, but like people, there is natural variance from dog to dog.) That way, if you need to take his temperature because he's throwing up or seems ill, you'll have something to compare it to. And it's often the first question the vet will ask if you call, so it's good to be prepared.

Once your puppy has settled in (which should take no more than a couple of days), you're ready to begin the training program laid out in Chapter 3 of *Mother Knows Best*. Hopefully, you will have read the whole book while waiting for your puppy, so you'll understand the basic philosophy of natural training. And do try to remember that for a puppy, praise is a better reward than food, and correction (which is critical to training a dog or a child) is not he same as "punishment", no matter what the dolphin trainers say. If you want to train a dolphin, get a dolphin.

One last caveat – although all your friends and relatives will be anxious to meet the new puppy, it's best to wait a few days until he's had time to decompress and recharge his batteries before introducing lots more new people into his life. No matter how much the puppy enjoys the attention, being charming is a lot of work and innately stressful, and you'll want to make sure his immune system is up to the task.

Taking Him Out in the Big World

In order to have a well-socialized Cockapoo, it is absolutely *imperative* that he be exposed to new people, places and dogs within the first four months of his life. Without it, he can become shy of strangers and fearful of strange dogs and new places. Cockapoo breeders all agree that in this breed it is especially important, and failure to get these puppies out in the big world is the main cause of "shyness problems".

On the other hand, your veterinarian will no doubt warn you that it is unsafe to expose your puppy to new places, people and dogs before he has "completed his puppy vaccination schedule", which probably won't happen until he is 4-5 months old, when he gets his rabies shot. And that's *way* too late to start taking your puppy out in the big world for the first time.

This leaves the poor owner, who understands the critical need for socialization but certainly doesn't want his puppy to contract a potentially deadly infectious disease in order to get socialized, caught in the middle, not knowing what to do. Luckily, there is a simple solution here.

When you take your puppy to the vet for his puppy check-up,
simply ask to have a "serum antibody titer" run.

Vets can now buy in-house titer kits very reasonably, and these will tell you within minutes if your puppy is protected against Distemper and Parvo. The average price for having them run is about $30. (If your vet is not aware of this in-house option, a blood sample will need to be sent to an outside lab. Hemopet, which is the best lab to send it to, charges $45 for a parvo and distemper titer, and your vet will probably tack on a few dollars more for the blood draw.)

With MLV (modified live virus) vaccines like those in puppy shots, immunity begins about 5 days after vaccination, so if it's been at least a week since his last vaccination, the titer should accurately reflect his immunity level. If the results show your puppy has adequate immunity, he's good to go pretty much anywhere.

It's interesting to note that in England, puppies are generally vaccinated only twice rather than 3 times as is done here—once at 8 weeks and then again at 10 weeks, after which they are considered immunized and safe to go out and about in the world for socialization. (This abbreviated schedule is recommended by the RSPCA, in fact.) And they use the *exact same vaccines* used in the US!

Now, as your vet is legally bound to point out, your puppy still won't be protected against rabies, which is admittedly deadly to man and beast. But in all honesty a puppy's risk of exposure is just about nonexistent because the US has been free of canine rabies for years, and the only way dogs in the US now contract rabies is from direct contact with rabid skunks or raccoons. Statistically, your puppy is probably more likely to be eaten by an alligator (don't laugh— this is a real risk in some parts of the country!) than he is to contract rabies at Petsmart before he's had his first rabies vaccination.

Where to take your puppy?

A well-trained puppy, especially one as cute as a Cockapoo, can go *lots* of places as long as they're on a leash. They can go to soccer games, art fairs, and many outdoor markets. Most parks and downtown "pedestrian" areas are dog-friendly, and some outdoor cafes allow them. Petsmart welcomes leashed dogs, as do many other pet shops. In Florida, dogs are often seen riding in carts in Lowe's and wandering around the garden section.

And then, of course, there are dog parks. These large fenced areas give dogs a place to run and play and socialize with other dogs, and most well-socialized dogs love the experience. For many urban dogs, it's the only place they can safely burn off energy. Although some trainers don't recommend them for puppies, dog parks can be a great experience as long as the owner exercises some common sense. Most dog parks now have a "big dog" area and a "little dog" area, and a Cockapoo belongs in the small dog area. And of course you should be taking him for walks around the neighborhood on a leash from Day One even if you have a fenced-in back yard.

Dogs familiar with their own neighborhood who know their human and canine neighbors are much less likely to panic and get hopelessly lost if they find themselves accidentally loose, which will happen sooner or later no matter how careful you are.

The important thing is not *where* you take your puppy, but that you *do* take him lots of different places, because it's absolutely critical for his socialization. Dogs who are not exposed to what animal behavioralists call "novel stimuli" in the first 3-6 months of life will never be really comfortable away from home as adults, and this can be crippling for the dog and a pain in the butt for the owner.

So take him as many places as you can, and practice some basic on-leash obedience work in as many different places as you can, so he learns to be well-mannered everywhere he goes. And remember to bring clean-up bags!

The other thing you want to do with your puppy in the first 4 months is take him on lots of car rides. If the first and only car trips a puppy experiences in the first 8-11 week "fear" period are to and from the airport, the odds of his developing chronic "car anxiety" and carsickness go way up, because that is the only association he'll make with riding in the car.

Because of this, it's *really* important to take him for short little car trips to somewhere *fun* during this period so he will make positive associations *and* realize that he'll get to come back home again. If you live in Manhattan, take him for short cab rides in a carrier bag for as long as he'll fit in one.

Have Crate, Will Travel...

Dogs like vacations, too. A well-trained Cockapoo with a folding wire crate can be taken on most family vacations and is welcomed by many hotels, B&Bs, National and State parks, private campgrounds and more. To find out which ones, check online before you make your reservations— a Google search for "pet-friendly travel" will bring up lots of helpful websites.

When vacationing with your dog, you might also want to consider vacation rental properties (which rent by the night or week) instead of hotels, as many are pet-friendly and come with fenced yards. And because they come with kitchens, you don't have to worry about the dog barking in a strange hotel room every time you go out for meals.

For lots of reasons, pet-friendly vacation rental properties are the best thing that ever happened to dog owners. VRBO is a great website to check in this regard – all listings with a paw print are pet-friendly. Even if they only accept pets under 20 pounds, you can often get around that by explaining that your dog is crate-trained and will be left in his crate any time he is left alone.

And if you are staying with family or friends, a well-behaved crate-trained dog is much more likely to be welcome than one who isn't.

And When He Just Can't Go Along...

However, no matter how well-behaved your Cockapoo may be, there are bound to be some times he just can't go along.

For example, if you are flying and your dog doesn't fit under the seat in a soft-side carrier, it's really safer and less stressful for him to leave him home than to check him as baggage and hope he ends up in the same city you do. (If this is important to you, look for a breeder who specializes in smaller Cockapoos.)
And even if you're driving, funerals are another event where even the best-trained dog might not be welcome. Weddings can go either way, but destination weddings in exotic locations are usually not dog -friendly.

In those cases, you have three options—you can A) leave him with friends, B) hire a pet sitter, or C) take him to a boarding kennel. Each has its advantages and disadvantages.

If your puppy is young (like less than 4 months or so), you may want to consider leaving him with friends he knows, because a boarding kennel will be pretty traumatic and he'll be lonely staying home alone with a pet sitter, unless you can find someone to stay at your house full-time.
Geriatric dogs (who sleep a lot anyway), or dogs who live in a multiple-dog household, may prefer to be left at home with a sitter coming in a few times a day, especially if it's only for the weekend. Young energetic dogs will probably be safest (and have the most fun!) at a boarding kennel.

If you choose option C), be sure and do your homework first. Most boarding kennels now have web-sites, and you can see what their rates are and if you like the place before you even call. Some even have webcams so you can check on your dog.

It's still a good idea to physically visit the kennel before you commit to it, though. As with breeders, you want to steer clear of any place that does not encourage you to visit, or won't let you get past the office to see where the dogs are actually kenneled.

If you find a kennel you like and use it exclusively, you may find your dog is actually happy to go there—luckily, dogs often have a very different idea of what constitutes a "vacation" than people do, and social dogs like Cockapoos (and Cockapoos are *very* social!) can find a kennel situation, where there are lots of new dogs to run and play with, pretty exciting.

One of the things you want to find out is whether the kennel has secure "play areas" and scheduled exercise periods as well as individual runs. If it does not, your dog will be safe, but he'll be bored silly.

Also check to make sure the kennel accepts titers in lieu of annual vaccinations. Some do and some don't. Most will still require bordatella (kennel cough) vaccination, and all will require an up-to-date rabies certificate.

What to Expect in the First Year

It's important to remember that for a canine, most of their physical and psychological growth takes place in the first year. The old "dog years" rule does not apply to the first year, because a year old dog is not the equivalent of a seven year old— he's usually achieved his adult height, he's sexually mature, and he's mentally well into adolescence by 12 months.

And although Cockapoos do not grow with the blinding speed of their larger hybrid cousins (which is probably why there are few if any orthopedic problems reported in the breed) in the space of 12 short months, he will grow from a blind and helpless little slug weighing half a pound to a physically and sexually mature animal that may weigh 25 pounds.
Even the smallest Cockapoo will go from half-a-pound at birth to maybe 10 pounds...if you think about it, that means at a year he will weigh *20 times* more than what he started at. Compared to human growth in the first year of life, that is still phenomenal.

This rapid mental and physical growth is biologically "expensive", and not surprisingly during this period his brain and his immune system may not always be able to keep up. This REALLY needs to be taken into consideration, in both training and *especially* in regards to vaccinations given and toxic anti-parasitics used in the first year.

Within a space of a few months your adorable puppy dashes headlong from roly-poly toddlerhood (that's usually when you pick him up) to gangly puberty and then without even stopping for breath charges into full-blown adolescence, at which point he appears to have forgotten everything he knew a few months earlier.

Virtually all of the critical phases of canine development take place within the first year.

These phases (which include the development of the fear response) are like so much else, hard-wired into his DNA and were necessary to survival in the wild, even if they seem less critical (and often counterproductive) in a domesticated suburban companion. Knowing what is occurring at various stages will help a lot in maintaining your sense of humor.

The Good News is, as long as you are consistent and firm in your training, and willing to correct and reinforce when needed as adolescence strikes, both you and your most excellent Cockapoo will make it through just fine. It's also good to remember that if you can just get through the first two years, the next ten or twelve are pretty easy sledding.

CHAPTER SEVEN:

Feeding Your Cockapoo

Like a whole lot of other things, feeding the family dog is a LOT more complicated than it used to be. Even a decade ago, most people did *no research at all* before they bought dog food—they either fed the food the breeder recommended, or the same food they fed their previous dog. All in all, these both appear to be sensible approaches, and it in fact would be...*except for one thing*:

The INGREDIENTS in all dog foods have changed so radically in the last few years, they're not really the "same foods" at all.

What most people do not realize about pet food is that it's become a lot like people food—in other words, it's now Really Big Business. In 2010 alone, pet food sales in the US amounted to around 18 BILLION DOLLARS. And although most of them didn't start out that way, the majority of the well -known dog food brands out there are now owned by only FIVE giant multinational corporations.

Some of these giants own their own dog food manufacturing facilities, and some subcontract production out to large "contract manufacturers" you've probably never heard of. And a lot of small "independent" companies use these same contract manufacturers, which means they really have no guarantee that the ingredients they list on the bag are actually in the food itself.

115

Welcome to Dog Food Inc.

Here's a rundown of who currently owns which well-known dog food brands, admittedly incomplete and subject to change at any given moment due to new acquisitions and corporate mergers:

Mars, Inc. *Owns the Pedigree, Royal Canin, Kal Kan, Waltham and Nutro brands.*
Products in the US are manufactured in 16 Mars-owned plants around the country. It also contract manufactures the O' Roy brand for Walmart. (And, yes, this is the same Mars that makes M&Ms. *Mars also bought the Wm. Wrigley Jr. Co in 2008 for $23 billion in a cash deal.* That's a lot of chewing gum.)

Nestle Purina Inc. *Owns the ProPlan, ProPlan Selects, Purina ONE, Purina ONE Beyond, Purina Dog Chow, Puppy Chow, Mighty Dog, Beneful and Alpo brands.*
In the US, Purina products are all produced in one of Purina's 13 company-owned and managed manufacturing plants. Purina does not contract manufacture for other companies Ralston Purina, founded in 1894, merged with Swiss-based Nestle (another chocolate company) back in 2003, although the Nestle Purina Pet Care Division is still based near St Louis, MO.

Proctor and Gamble Inc. *Owns the Iams and Eukanuba brands, and Natura's Innova, Evo, California Natural, Healthwise, Mother Nature, and Karma brands.*
Some products are manufactured at company-owned facilities (Natura products are produced at the P & G-owned Natura plant in Nebraska), while most are contracted out. P&G also makes many well-known cleaning products.

Colgate-Palmolive Inc. *Owns the Hill's Science Diet, Prescription Diet and Nature's Best brands, which are all contract-manufactured.*
Longtime makers of toothpaste, dish soap and a gazillion other personal care products, these guys now own the well-known Hill's dog food line sold by thousands of vets nationwide.

Del Monte Inc. *Owns the Nature's Recipe, Milk-Bone and Kibbles N Bits brands. Del Monte also does contract manufacturing of canned dog foods.*
Other than pet foods, canning giant Del Monte mostly produces canned fruits and vegetables.

In addition to the Big Five, there are two other less well-known major players in the dog food game:

Diamond Pet Foods Inc. *Owns the Diamond, Diamond Naturals, Chicken Soup for the Dog Lover's Soul, Kirkland, and Taste of the Wild brands. Contract manufactures Dick Van Patton's Natural Balance, Wellness, 4Health Pet Food, Canidae and Solid Gold.*

Diamond only manufactures dry food; it contracts out its canned foods, so some of these brands also offer products produced by *other* contract manufacturers. Foods produced by Diamond have been involved in several recalls in past years and at least one of its plants has been repeatedly cited by FDA.

Simmons Pet Foods Inc. – *A giant in the poultry processing industry, Simmons is the second-largest employer in the state of Arkansas after Tyson. Its pet food division is probably now the largest contract manufacturer and private label producer of dog food in the country and produces canned foods for most of the dog food industry, with the exception of Purina.*

In fact, Simmons bought contract manufacturer Menu Foods in 2010 for $239 million after Menu was caught up in the "tainted wheat gluten" scandal. As their website states: **"In a world obsessed with brand names, ours is conspicuously absent. Your brand is our brand, and we wouldn't have it any other way."** (Which foods do they make? Who knows…)

Other contract manufacturers of both canned and dry dog foods include the following:

CJ Foods *—makes Blue Buffalo and Burns Pet Health canned foods*

Ohio Pet Foods *—makes Blue Buffalo and Life's Abundance dry foods*

Chenango Valley Pet Foods *—makes Drs Foster & Smith, Back to Basics*

Blue Sky *– makes Solid Gold.*

Crosswinds Industries *—makes Nature's Logic*

American Nutrition *—makes Natural Balance*

Ainsworth *—makes Dad's, VF, Rachel Ray's Nutrish*

(As with brand ownership, this list changes constantly as companies switch contract manufacturers.)

Clearly, with very few exceptions, dog food branding has become a sort of "shell game", and it's pretty hard for the average consumer to figure out where their dog food is actually made, or who actually owns the brand. **So too often consumers believe they're buying from small, caring companies that use only "carefully hand-selected wholesome ingredients", when in reality that may not be the case at all.**

Instead, they're paying a premium price for the *illusion* that their dog food is made in a sunny kitchen full of cheerful elves mixing up vats of healthy meats and fresh colorful veggies from the local health food store, when odds are pretty good it's being churned out in ten-ton runs in a humongous totally mechanized factory (some of which are state-of-the-art and some of which are pretty awful) that may also manufacture much cheaper brands, using many of *the exact same raw ingredients*. Here's why....

It is the *contract manufacturer* who purchases the ingredients,
NOT the company whose brand name is on the bag.

For example, "chicken meal" is found in many high-end, supposedly "natural" dog foods. What is it? According to the Association of Animal Feed Control Officials (aka AAFCO), chicken meal is "***the dry rendered product from a clean combination of chicken flesh and skin with or without accompanying bone, derived from whole carcasses of chicken, exclusive of feathers, heads, feet and entrails***".

This stuff is all purchased by the TON by the contract manufacturer from rendering plants and trucked in. Although high in protein, it is frankly unlikely to be "carefully hand-selected", no matter what the bags or the company websites (with their attractive photos of farm-fresh chicken and veggies) claim. And every company these guys contract manufacture for is getting *the exact same chicken meal.*

Meat meals and poultry meals ALL come from rendering plants, no matter how dog food companies try to hide that unappetizing fact. Although rendering lard can actually be done in one's kitchen (assuming you have a big pot, access to the fat of a freshly slaughtered hog and don't mind the smell), rendering whole animal *carcass*es into safe and usable meal requires millions of dollars in high-tech equipment if one does not wish to run afoul of the EPA. Even organic farmers don't render their own chicken meal—they can't.

So what about "real chicken"… as in "real fresh chicken is the first ingredient"? The average consumer is going to perceive that a food "made with real meat" or has "real chicken" as the first ingredient" is a higher quality product, and the dog food companies' marketing guys know this. *But is it?*

To answer this question we need to determine exactly what legally constitutes "chicken" in dog food. The best place to look is the AAFCO manual again wherein chicken (or actually any poultry) is defined as "***the clean combination of flesh and skin with or without accompanying bone, derived*** *from the parts of whole carcasses of poultry or a combination thereof, exclusive of feathers, heads, feet and entrails".*

And these are not the "parts" that you'll find in the grocery store either. Think about it— chicken meal currently sells at around 45 cent a pound, and even the "lesser cuts" (like wings and feet) cost several times that. Purchasing "real" chicken for pet food applications occurs primarily in the same supply chain as that of hot dog or "nugget" meat. (In other words—MSM, more commonly known as "pink slime".) **So basically, it looks like the main difference between "chicken meal" and "real" chicken is whether or not it's rendered**.

The truth is, making dog food today is a lot like making any other modern highly processed meat product like chicken nuggets, hamburger, sausage and hot dogs—decidedly unappetizing. This is because commercial dog food is essentially "fast food" for dogs. Synthetic vitamins and minerals are added to make it "100% nutritionally balanced", and since pet owners have been brainwashed into believing that adding any fresh food to the mix will destroy that critical balance, most dogs eat nothing but this highly processed "fast food" *every single day of their lives*.

If you think about it, convincing millions of otherwise intelligent people that eating *no fresh food at all* is somehow *healthier* for dogs represents some seriously successful marketing. But is it logical? Why on earth did ever we buy into this idiocy? *Would we feed our kids this way?*

If you try to eat more organically yourself and want the same for your dog, you need to know that the word "organic" is used pretty loosely in the dog food world.

One of the most alarming trends in dog food is what's called ***green-washing,*** which is no more than a marketing ploy to make the ingredients (which are often the exact same ingredients found in less-expensive foods) simply *sound* more "green".

There are no 100% USDA certified organic complete dog foods—in fact, there are really even no rules for terms like "all-natural", "organic", or "holistic", which represent the fastest-growing segment of the dog food market. Basically, you can call your dog food "***Good Earth's Holistic All-Natural Organic Formula***" even if it's made from recycled Twinkies and there's no law against it, honest to God. This loophole allows the manufacturers to charge a lot more for their "green-washed" brands, although most are still loaded with the same processed meat scraps and pesticide-laden genetically modified grains and other GMO ingredients.

Genetically modified ingredients in ***dog food?*** Unfortunately, yes.

119

Although a growing number of Americans are becoming concerned about GMO ingredients in the human food chain and try to avoid eating them, most people are unaware of the fact that their *pets* have been eating GMOs for the past 15 years as well.

Genetically modified crops were first approved in the US in 1996 with little fanfare, and now most of the corn, soybeans, canola, cotton and sugar beets produced in this country are genetically modified. **These plants find their way into a LOT of commercial dog foods, even the "grain-free" ones.** For example, several high-end so-called "grain-free" dog foods use oils from GMO grains (i.e. soy, canola, corn and cottonseed oils) as a fat source.

Can GMOs adversely affect a dog's health? Politics aside, the real answer is....
no one really knows for sure.

And the *reason* no one knows is because NO toxicology testing on these GMO foods has ever been performed on dogs. (Or people, for that matter.)

Huhhh????? What about our taxpayer-funded Federal regulatory agencies??? Isn't it their JOB to ensure the safety of food? After all, the Biotech Industry Organization (the main lobbying group for the biotech industry) says right on its website that *"Federal regulatory agencies ensure the safety of biotechnology foods, and biotech plants and foods are among the most tested in history"*.

One can only assume they are referring to some *other* country's Federal regulatory agencies, because here in the US, the FDA and the USDA apply the rule of "substantial equivalence" to the approval of all new GMO crops.

This means that if the new genetically modified plant is determined to be
"substantially equivalent" to its non-GMO counterpart,
absolutely NO safety testing is required.

(I swear I am not making this up....go check it out yourself on the FDA's own website if you feel so inclined.)

Now, it's also very important to understand at this point that in spite of the promise of "drought and disease resistance", "increased yields", and "feeding a hungry planet", all of which are highly laudable goals and may well exist *sometime in the future*, nearly all the genetically-modified crops being produced TODAY are simply designed to withstand the applications of toxic herbicides like Monsanto's Round-Up, which then remains on (and in) the food as it works its way through the food chain and into us and our animals. (This is Monsanto's famously patented "Roundup-Ready" trait.)

And so far, the FDA has determined to their satisfaction that corn, soy, canola, alfalfa and sugar beets which have been genetically altered to withstand repeated drenching with RoundUp without dying like all the plants around them (as well as corn and cotton that have been genetically modified *to produce their own Bt pesticides* in addition to being RoundUp-resistant) are in fact "substantially equivalent" to corn, soy, canola, alfalfa and sugar beets which have *not* been genetically altered in similar fashions. Go figure.

Consequently, FDA has to date approved them *all* without ANY safety testing other than industry-provided "animal performance assessments", which consists of the following, at least according to Monsanto's website:

42-Day Broiler Study on Chickens — *At this stage, Monsanto scientists study the development and size of the animal as it's fed the product with the new gene inserted.*

90-Day Rat Feeding Study — *In addition to the growth and development testing in the broiler chicken study, Monsanto scientists also conduct a 90-day rat feeding study with most products, which is a toxicology study. A toxicology study determines if a new product has undesirable effects on the health or physiology of the animals that might predict adverse effects for humans.*

That's it. Ninety days.

So although these biotech plants may well be "the most tested in history", that statement is a little disingenuous at best. Aside from the 90 day toxicology study described above, all this "testing" is NOT safety testing— it's actually "field-testing" of the crops themselves by the manufacturer *prior to applying for approval,* in order to make sure that they are indeed resistant to the target pests and to the various herbicides they are engineered to be resistant to when doused with them at various stages of growth. (And in at least **three separate instances over the last 10 years**, these unapproved crops planted in USDA-approved "test plots" scattered around the country have managed to show up in non-GMO fields and ultimately ended up in the human food chain.)

Now, *most* other countries in the world apply what's called the "precautionary principle" when it comes to GMOs, mainly because their citizens are simply more suspicious of genetically-modified food than Americans have traditionally been. All the countries that signed the Cartagena Protocol for Biosafety (which the US not surprisingly did *not)* require all GMO crops to be labeled prior to export. Another 60 countries require labeling of all human foods containing GMOs, while another dozen or so ban them altogether.

And although few long-term animal feeding studies have been done in the US, they *have* been done in several other countries— at universities in Austria, Italy, Russia, France, Brazil, Argentina, and Norway, among others. Within the last year or two, the results of several of these long-term studies have been published, although they haven't been widely reported in the US press.

And these GMO animal-feeding studies have produced some fairly alarming results.

A **Norwegian** study published in 2012 showed that *in every species tested*, animals fed GMO corn ended up fatter, showed immune system changes and were less able to digest proteins due to changes in their digestive systems when compared to the control animals.

A **Brazilian** study on rats showed adverse effects to the reproductive system as well as unexpected changes in sexual preference in the offspring.

An **Italian** study showed changes to hepatic (liver) structure.

Studies in both **Austria and Russia** revealed infertility— in fact, in the Russian study, the third generation produced animals that were *totally infertile.*

And a recent study in **France** showed significant damage to the kidneys and liver, along with an unexpected increase in tumor development and overall reduction in lifespan.

This last one was the first to examine the LIFETIME effects of GMOs on rats, rather than the effect of eating it for only 9 weeks, using the same protocols and the same breed of rat.
(The study was published in the *September 2012* issue of *the Food & Chemical Toxicology Journal* and can be accessed at **www.gmoseralini.org** for anyone interested in learning more about it.)

Obviously, none of these studies were done on dogs—most used rats, mice, hamsters and rabbits. But we *do* know that in the last 10 years, obesity, autoimmune disease, liver and kidney disease, reproductive problems and cancers have all increased significantly in America's pet population, so the "precautionary principle" might be a good idea when it comes to our dogs. How do we do that?

It's really not as difficult as one might think. The primary GMO crops include corn, soy, cotton, canola, and sugar beets. Most fruits, vegetables, and nuts, as well as rice, oats, barley, potatoes, sweet potatoes and wheat are currently NOT genetically modified.

This gives dog food makers quite a bit to work with, nutritionally, and several companies are now introducing "GMO free" formulas. However, since there is no USDA "GMO-free" certification or even testing protocols in the US at present, you'll have to pretty much take the company's word for it.

And although any food product that's "USDA certified organic" is by definition GMO-free, under present industry standards no "complete" dog food can be USDA certified as 100% organic because many of the vitamin supplements (like Vitamin E!) required to meet these standards are now derived from GMO corn or soy.

The following companies both manufacture their own dog foods *and* offer several formulas made without GM grains and oils, at least::

Nutrisource— *a family-owned company based in Minnesota that owns its own production facilities, their Natural Planet line has several dry products made without GMO grains or fats*

Fromm's— *another longtime family owned company based in Wisconsin, they also offer several products free of GMO grains and fats. Their dry foods are also produced in their own plant.*

Champion Pet Foods—- *based in Alberta, Canada, they produce the Acana and Orijin brands of dry dog food in their own facilities without GMO grains. (According to the company, the only grain used is steel-cut oats.)*

PetFresh— *this New Jersey-based company produces fresh cooked ready-to-feed (rather than dry, canned or dehydrated), which is now sold in refrigerated cases at grocery and pet stores around the country.*

There are more options appearing all the time, as dog food manufacturers respond to consumer demand, so it's worth checking around. But it's ALSO important to remember that if the company does not *manufacture its own product,* they really cannot guarantee its ingredients, no matter how good their intentions!
The easiest way to find out if a company manufactures its own foods or not is to simply ASK them. (Every company has an email address and usually a phone number on both its website and packaging.) The same is true of GMO ingredients– if you *ask,* they pretty much have to answer.

Making Your Own Dog Food

One alternative that more and more owners are considering is cooking for their dogs at home, using *really* "fresh, wholesome ingredients" that anybody can purchase in their local grocery store.

And if you cook for your dog, besides being able to purchase non-GMO ingredients yourself so you don't have to take anyone else's word for what's actually in there, you won't have to worry about whether or not your dog food has been recalled because of possibly deadly contamination by salmonella or e-Coli or aflatoxin, which happens a LOT more than people think. Thousands of dogs are sickened by this stuff every year, and it's getting worse and worse as the industry becomes more consolidated and fewer and fewer plants are producing more and more brands.

These recalls due to food-borne pathogens have become at least as common in dog food as they have in the human food chain, and for the same reason— *Agribusiness*. Because of the way our food supply is now designed, when you eat a hamburger, you are no longer eating the meat of one cow— **the meat of *hundreds* of cows can end up in a single pound of ground beef.** Remember the old "one bad apple can spoil the bushel" adage? That's what's happening with meat and poultry.

And it's even worse in dog food- how many chickens contribute to a bag of dog food containing chicken meal? Since rendering plants process literally *millions* of chickens a day, the answer is: *"More than you can possibly imagine"*. And the possibility of eColi or salmonella contamination exists in every stage of the complicated dog food manufacturing process if the temperatures are off by a few degrees anywhere along the way.

When it comes to food-borne pathogens, you're statistically *way* better off simply buying and cooking *one* chicken to an internal temperature of at least 160 degrees, which is what the USDA says is needed to kill pathogens like eColi and Salmonella.
How hot is that? Remember, water boils at *212 degrees*, so if you simply boil chicken in a pot on the stove until it's cooked through, you're way over the required 160 degrees...no scientific training required. Which brings us to the next topic….

Home-cooked vs Raw Feeding

There's a lot on the internet about the health advantages of eating only raw food for both dogs and people. Its proponents are an inarguably enthusiastic lot, although at this point in time, there have been no controlled studies to either back or refute their claims. Several companies are now selling commercially-prepared raw foods for dogs, and business is brisk.

But is raw feeding dogs SAFE? Not so much. Although many dogs clearly thrive on it, the danger from food-borne pathogens like eColi and salmonella is why raw feeding is not recommended by the USDA or the FDA— recent studies have shown that a high percentage of the meat and poultry we buy from the grocery store is carrying these pathogens, and it's not exactly listed on the package label.

In addition to possibly making *dogs* sick, **raw feeding can pose a very real danger to humans,** especially babies, the elderly, and those with compromised immune systems, because raw-fed dogs have been shown to carry these pathogens in their saliva as well as in their urine and feces. Neither freezing nor dehydrating will kill most food-borne pathogens, by the way—it takes 160 degrees internal temperature. Vegetables pose less of a pathogen risk, but research has shown that the availability of nutrients in many vegetables is actually increased by cooking. (That said, many dogs enjoy a washed raw carrot as a chew toy!)

What About Nutritional Balance?

Most of the world's dog breeds were developed prior to the availability of commercial dog food, which wasn't even *invented* until around 1900 and then really didn't catch on until after World War II, especially in rural America. Dogs ate what people ate— or more often what people *didn't* eat, because dogs got a lot of "table scraps". (In many parts of the world, they still do.) In the history of man's relationship with dogs over the millennia, commercial processed food made especially for dogs is really a pretty new concept.

And aside from convenience, the main marketing ploy used to sell Americans on this new (and financially lucrative) idea was by stressing the need for "100% balanced nutrition" in a dog's diet every day.

In fact, post-WW II owners were warned that should their dogs not receive the correct "scientifically formulated nutritional balance" as well as 100% of the minimum daily requirement of every vitamin and mineral necessary to his well-being each and every day without fail, that dog was going to be in BIG TROUBLE. (Remember, this was right around the same that time modern "scientifically formulated" commercial baby formula was considered vastly superior to nursing...)

Fifty years later, many vets still learn this silliness in vet school and pass it on to their clients, which is why vets have long stressed that feeding your dog any "table food" at all makes you a BAD OWNER.

Of course, what the client *doesn't* know is that virtually all the "nutrition" courses taught at America's vet schools are underwritten to the tune of millions of dollars annually by the Dog

Food Industry… go look it up if you don't believe me. (This is a little alarming, because a recent survey revealed that when choosing pet food, *69.4 % of owners trusted their veterinarians.* Another 36.3 % turned to the internet, while 20.6 % decided at the pet store, 4.4 % utilized a breeder and 1.3 % trusted a groomer.)

Bottom line is this— *the need for 100% balanced nutrition daily is just not scientifically supported in man or beast.* For example, we now know that Vitamin B12 (which like most B vitamins is found in abundance in meat, dairy and eggs) can be stored in the liver for up to *5 years or more*—— with the exception of vegans, Vitamin B12 deficiencies in developed countries are usually a side effect of a *pathological condition* rather than a dietary deficiency. And dogs, like most animals except man and guinea pigs, manufacture their own Vitamin C. Like humans, *dogs were designed to get all the Vitamin D they need from the sun and to store it in the liver for cloudy days*— in fact, Vitamin D was originally discovered and studied in dogs!

What both humans and dogs have relied on for millennia is what's called "balance over time". This method, designed by Mother Nature, allowed us to get all the nutrition we needed from a *variety* of foods that were only available seasonally and locally before food could be shipped around the planet in a matter of days. This "variety" thing works for dogs, too— if a dog's diet includes a variety of meats, eggs, fish, and a variety of plant-based products (vegetables, GMO-free grains and even some fruits) on a weekly basis, odds are good he's going to end up getting all the nutrition he needs.

With the exception of extra calcium (which can be easily provided by ground eggshells if your dog doesn't get a lot of bones to chew on) this sort of varied diet will provide all the vitamins and minerals a dog needs in the form Nature intended—- as part of food. **The only reason commercial dog food adds all that stuff is to cover what's lost in processing.** And because many supplements are now synthetic and either derived from GMO corn or, like calcium supplements contain added GMO fillers, what's found naturally in fresh food are probably a better bet all the way around.

Finding GMO-free dog food recipes

Now, although there are *tons* of "cooking for your dog" cookbooks of varying quality out there, few if any are specifically GMO-free. But this is something you can easily do on your own with any recipe you like, by simply substituting a non-GMO ingredient for a GMO one. Here's what's currently MOST likely to contain genetically-modified organisms:

- *Corn* **and corn products like** *cornstarch* **and** *maltodextrin*

- *High-fructose corn syrup* (hard to imagine putting this in dog food but you never know)

- *Soy* and all Soy products, including most *Lecithin*

- *Sugar beets,* including *beet pulp* and any "sugars" not labeled as "pure cane sugar"

- *Cottonseed, Canola and Corn oils,* most of which are made from GM plants

- *Papayas, zucchini and yellow squash.* (The genetic modification in this group has nothing to do with pesticides and herbicides but rather to resist a mosaic virus that attacks a lot of these crops. On the other hand, if that makes you uncomfortable, the average dog, like the average human, can probably get through life just fine without ever eating any of them.)

- *Vitamin and mineral supplements* that are not specifically certified as GMO-free or USDA certified as 100% organic. Some, like Vitamin E, are usually made from GMO corn, and some have GMO-containing fillers like cornstarch or maltodextrin.

Simply avoiding these few ingredients will allow your dog (and you!) to eat GMO-free. Most of them are used in processed foods only because they're *cheap*— none are critical to good human or canine nutrition, or even to good *livestock* nutrition. After all, cows existed on this planet for thousands of years without eating soybeans, and were probably healthier for it.

Which brings up another point— in human food (unlike dog food) the term "organic" is highly regulated, and 100% *USDA Certified Organic* automatically means that the product does not contain any genetically modified organisms. **In the case of meat, dairy products and eggs, it also means the animal from whence it came was not *fed* any genetically modified ingredients**.

Is that important? Frankly, *no one knows,* although there's a growing body of evidence that GMOs can indeed move up through the food chain. It's safest to buy organic meat (cheaper cuts are fine) if you can afford to, and just do the best you can if you can't— even meat from GMO-fed animals is going to be better quality that what's in commercial dog food. There are lots of inexpensive wild-caught fish that are not GMO-fed, and like eggs, fish is also a terrific protein source for dogs. Smaller fish tend to be "cleaner" than larger fish in terms of PCBs and mercury— canned sardines (in tomato sauce rather than GMO soybean oil) and canned mackerel are great choices, and cheap. Grass-fed meat is unlikely to be GMO-fed, as is wild game if you have a hunter in the family.

Anyhow, cooking for your dog is nutritious, easier than you think, and actually *less expensive* than buying good high-end dog food. A big pot of it can be cooked up once a week (which will take about an hour of actual prep time) and divided into containers and refrigerated or frozen.

Owners who've made the switch invariably report their dogs are less itchy, have fewer ear infections, and are less inclined to obesity. Breeders often see an improvement in reproductive fitness, with larger, healthier litters. Perhaps most amazing, many owners notice "standoffish dogs" switched to a non-GMO home-cooked diet undergo an actual personality change, and become more affectionate.

AND cooking nutritious food for a dog is really a lot more *gratifying* than cooking nutritious food for children, because dogs are not nearly as picky! Once they get used to the change, they'll snarf down vegetables your kids probably won't touch. Go figure. Which brings us to …

Actually *feeding* your Cockapoo

In addition to *what* you should (or maybe shouldn't!) be feeding your Cockapoo to keep him at his healthiest, many new owners also want to know *how much* and *how often* their dog should eat. These are also really important questions. Here's why….

As with their American owners, there has been an alarming increase in obesity in America's cats and dogs, and it's getting worse by the minute.

In 2007, roughly 19% of cats were found to be obese. *By 2011 it was up to 24.8%.* For dogs, obesity rates were just over 10% in 2007. *By 2011 they were 21.6%*

In fact, by 2011, over 50% of all dogs and cats were classified as either overweight or obese.

Is this because we've been overfeeding them? Maybe, but surprisingly, it turns out humans (both children and adults) **have been eating steadily FEWER calories for almost a decade, despite the continued increase in obesity rates,** at least according to survey data from the CDC. (Among children aged 6 through 19 years in 1999-2002, 16.0% were overweight or obese. Ten years later, it was one in 3.) Common sense tells us same thing may well be happening in our pets.

Is it because they are getting less exercise? That would make sense for dogs, but the same thing is happening in *cats,* and there's no indication that the average housecat is getting less exercise than he did ten years ago— *how exactly does one exercise a cat?*

Leanness is especially critical in Cockapoos, because he is descended from two breeds both prone to **canine hip dysplasia** (CHD). And it now appears that *how lean your dog is* has a lot to do with whether or not he develops it— in fact, it probably matters more than his genetics.

The groundbreaking study on this was led by researchers at Nestlé Purina and included scientists at Cornell, the University of Illinois, Michigan State University and the University of Pennsylvania, published in the *Journal of the American Veterinary Medical Association* back in May 2002 if you want to read it.

For the study, 24 pairs of Labrador retriever siblings between 6 and 8 weeks of age -- matched by sex and weight-- were selected, with one of each pair assigned to eat *25 percent less of the same food* than its sibling. That's 25% less calories.

The dogs were a part of the study from the time they were weaned until they died, and their health was closely monitored throughout their lives. The study lasted 14 years. The median age of dogs in the reduced-diet group, the researchers found, was 13 years -- almost two years longer than the median age of dogs fed a "normal" diet.

When it came to hip dysplasia, 16 dogs in the "well-fed" control group developed CHD at 2 years of age, while 8 were normal. **However, of the 24 dogs in the "lean" group, only 8 developed CHD, while 16 were normal!**

The reduced diet was also found to reduce the risk of developing osteoarthritis, which generally is one of the most common sources of chronic pain in dogs.

Only SIX of the 24 dogs on the reduced diet developed osteoarthritis of the hip by age 10, while NINETEEN of the 24 control group dogs did. And for the dogs on reduced rations who *did* develop CHD, the odds of developing concurrent osteoarthritis decreased by a whopping 57%.

Although many owners (and vets!) still believe canine hip dysplasia is a "genetic disease",
the newest research from Cornell's Baker Institute puts the heritability at only 25-48%.

That means more than half (and actually up to 75%) of the causative factors are environmental rather than genetic, and within the *owner's* control rather than the *breeder's*. (This also goes a long way toward explaining why, after 50 years of responsible breeders selecting only animals OFA-certified free of hip dysplasia for breeding, the Baker Institute now tells us that on average, **25% of the offspring of two parents free of hip dysplasia will still develop the disease.)**

Obviously, what the Labrador study revealed was that from 6-8 weeks on, consuming less calories significantly reduces the dog's chances of developing hip dysplasia AND osteoarthritis. Does this mean dogs have to go hungry?   OF COURSE NOT.

According to the nutrition guys at the UC Davis vet school, a 14 pound, moderately-active adult dog requires around 500 calories a day. For a 20 pound dog, it's around 650. (And let's face it, most dogs are NOT "moderately active", so probably need less to stay lean.)

Those are the number of calories found in the average SINGLE CUP of a lot of "high-quality" commercial dog foods! In fact, the most expensive dog foods often have twice the calories per cup as the "grocery store brands".

So that means, assuming you feed a high-end food twice a day, to stay lean, a 14-20 pound dog probably needs *a half-cup of dry kibble in the morning and a half-cup in the evening, and nothing else.* If he's less active or overweight, he going to have to eat *less* than that.

Now, by comparison, here's a recipe for *Meat Loaf Dog Food* from the *Dinner PAWsible* cookbook, adding up to 550 calories:

1/2 lean ground beef
1 cup cooked brown rice
2 cups mixed vegetables, frozen or fresh
1 raw egg
1/2 broth (optional)
1 tsp cod liver oil (dogs like this a lot more than people do!)
500 mg calcium or slightly more than 1/4 tsp finely ground egg shell

Combine ingredients in a large bowl; mix well. Place in loaf pan and bake at 350 for an hour. Allow to cool and serve.

You don't have to be a rocket scientist to figure out that the average dog is going to be a lot happier with half this meatloaf (maybe two cups by volume) in his bowl for dinner than he will be with a measly half-cup of dried kibble! Yet, depending on the dog food brand, he could easily be talking the same number of calories.

Even if you don't want to make all of your dog's meals from scratch, replacing maybe a third of his kibble with "fresh food calories" will allow you to up the volume quite a bit while lowering the calorie count— a half cup of cooked sweet potato is only 90 calories, while a *whole* cup of cooked carrots only adds around 50 calories, and a cup of cabbage or green beans only adds around 40.

Adding fresh foods will also add tons of enzymes and phytonutrients —like the glucosinolates found in cruciferous vegetables like broccoli, cabbage and kale. Glucosinolates turn into chemicals during the cooking process and digestion that can actually hold in check the development and growth of cancer. Pretty good bargain at under 50 calories a cup!

Clearly, cooking real fresh food for your dog has a lot of advantages. Probably the main reason people *don't* do it is a simple lack of confidence, which is not really surprising considering the millions of advertising dollars the Dog Food Industry (and the vets they've trained) have spent over the last 50 years convincing us that our dogs can only thrive on commercial dog food. Thankfully, the tide is now beginning to turn, and vets like UC Davis's Dr. Strombeck and the always-holistic Dr. Pitcairn, longtime proponents of home-cooked dog food, are getting more press.

If you want to try cooking for your Cockapoo, probably the best book to start with is *Dinner PAWsible* by Cathy Alinovi DVM and Susan Thixton, available on Amazon. It' well-written, the nutrition chapter is easy to understand, and the recipes are simple and well-within the capabilities of even those who can't cook. (And unlike many dog cookbooks, which read like a chemistry text, the ingredients needed are those you may actually have in your pantry.)

So how often should you feed your Cockapoo?

Young puppies (under 4 months or so) of any small breed really need to eat three times a day. After that, twice a day for life is really a lot kinder than only once. (I mean, seriously— would *you* want to go all day without eating?)

And from a practical standpoint, dogs who get breakfast prior to be left alone are often less inclined to be destructive than those who do not. Hunger in a predator is a great motivator, while a full stomach usually encourages napping. (You've probably noticed the same thing yourself, because of course we're also descended from pack-hunting predators…) The main thing to remember is that the total calorie count needs to be divided into those two meals– if you double it, you're going to end up with a fat dog!

On a final note, many owners who feed fresh-cooked food report that their dogs are easier to housebreak— this may be because dogs who eat fresh foods (which naturally has a lot of water in it) don't need to drink as much water (or pee as often) as dogs who eat only bone-dry desiccated kibble.

CHAPTER EIGHT:

Cockapoo Health Basics
(what you need to know BEFORE you buy a puppy)

Much has been written about the wonders of hybrid vigor, and indeed, recognition by the dog-buying public about the advantages it produces in health and longevity are in large part responsible for the soaring rise in popularity of many of the new "designer breeds". By simply combining two different breeds with multiple health issues, you produce puppies with none....How cool is THAT?

It's pretty cool. Too bad it's not true.

Because this model has actually worked well for breeds like the Puggle and the Goldendoodle, an awful lot of enthusiastic but inexperienced breeders assumed it would work for *all* hybrid crosses. Instead of having to spend all kinds of money health-screening and gene-testing, one could just combine *any two different breeds* and not have to worry about all that stuff any more. (This is why so many hybrids come from breeding stock that's had no health-screening done.)

Unfortunately, whether this works or not depends entirely on the disease in question. For things like autoimmune disorders and cancers, hybrid vigor really does appear to help. For other diseases that may either be congenital (like deafness) or which may develop later in life (like PRA/pcd) hybrid vigor *will not reduce the risk at all.*

*And there are several possible genetic problems in Cockapoos
that are not affected in the least by hybrid vigor.*

THE GOOD NEWS IS: These problems can now ALL be avoided through relatively inexpensive and non-invasive gene-testing of breeding dogs or by simply making informed breeding decisions.

THE BAD NEWS IS: Way too many Cockapoo breeders *don't even know some of these health problems even exist,* which means they're probably not screening their breeding stock.

Understanding Disease and Heritability

There are basically five different kinds of diseases (or *disorders)* in dogs. Some are totally heritable, others are far less so, and some are not heritable at all. **This is important to know because in general, hybrid vigor has the greatest positive effect on traits with LOW rather than HIGH heritability.**
Some diseases can be avoided by wise decisions on the *owner's* part, while others are entirely dependent on choices the *breeder* made prior to the conception of the puppies, either knowingly or unknowingly. This latter group includes what are called *classical genetic disorders.*

Classical genetic disorders.

Although a whole lot of diseases are heritable to some degree and tend to "run in families", classical *genetic disorders* are actually rarer. Caused entirely by the action of a genetic mutation inherited from one or both parents, there are no environmental factors involved here at all– the presence of the mutation is enough to cause the disease no matter *what* you do. They are 100% heritable.

Despite media hype about some new "cancer" or "autism" gene, *genes do not cause diseases.*

Mother Nature is not a nihilist—genes are simply the recipes for specific proteins or enzymes needed for an organism to survive and reproduce.
It is when a particular gene *mutates* (usually through a random error in copying during meiosis which alters the "recipe" for that gene) and the mutated form of that gene is passed to the next generation that a genetic disease may result.

Now, the mutation may also be totally benign or even advantageous—gene mutations are responsible for evolution, after all, and without them we'd all still be swimming around in the ocean, breathing through our gills.

In the wild, mutations that provide some evolutionary advantage tend to be carried forward, because the animal displaying them usually exhibits "reproductive fitness", which really means he lives long enough to produce offspring, while those with none do not. (Color variations that allow an animal to blend in with his environment fall into this category– although they may occasionally occur, most pie-bald rabbits would probably not live long enough to reproduce in the wild.)

Of course, with domesticated animals, it is *humans* who decide if a gene variant that happens to pop up is beneficial or not, and whether or not the animal displaying it should reproduce.

Sometimes a particular genetic mutation might make an animal uniquely qualified for a job that some human decided dogs needed to do— like herding sheep, or in the case of the FGF4 gene that produces short-legged dwarfism, allowing the Dachshund to fit into holes to dispatch badgers, which is a bit of a problem for a longer-legged dog.

And sometimes, as is the case with a gene like merle, humans just decided it looked cool.

Now, if the mutated gene is ***dominant,*** inheriting one copy from either parent is all it takes for the dog to display the trait. (Those showing variable expression are considered "dominant with incomplete penetrance." Those showing weaker expression in the presence of a single allele and stronger expression in the presence of two are considered "incompletely dominant." or "co-dominant".)

A mutation that produces no change unless a copy is inherited from each parent is traditionally called a ***recessive*** gene. But there is often overlap here, too– it's now recognized that some "carriers" of a recessive disease can display subtler symptoms, so this whole dominant/recessive thing is not as cut-and-dried as we once believed.

Because of this, instead of using the term "carriers" at all, many geneticists now simply use the terms "heterozygote" for a dog carrying one copy of a genetic mutation and "homozygote" for a dog carrying two.

Here's a rundown of *classical genetic disorders* that can occur in the Cockapoo::

Prcd/PRA

PRA refers to a group of diseases that cause the retina of the eye to degenerate slowly over time. The result is declining vision and eventual blindness. "*prcd*" stands for "progressive rod-cone degeneration" which is the type of PRA known in over twenty breeds, including American and English Cockers and

Poodles. (This indicates that the mutation has probably been around a long time.)

In the prcd/PRA form, the "rod" cells (which operate in low light levels) are the first to lose normal function, resulting in night blindness. Then the "cone" cells gradually lose their normal function in full light situations. Most affected dogs will eventually be blind. Typically, the clinical disease is recognized first in early adolescence or early adulthood, but age of onset varies among breeds and even among dogs of the same breed. Unfortunately, at this time there is no treatment or cure for PRA.

Prcd-PRA is inherited as a recessive trait. A mutated gene must be inherited from each parent in order to cause disease in an offspring. A carrier has one disease gene and one normal gene, and is termed "heterozygous" for the disease. A normal dog has no disease gene and is termed "homozygous normal" – both copies he inherited are the normal "wild type" gene. And a dog with two disease genes is termed "homozygous affected" – both copies of the gene are abnormal. Sooner or later, this unlucky dog will go irreversibly blind.

All breeds tested for prcd-PRA have the same disease, *caused by the same single mutated gene,* even though the disease might develop at different ages or with differing severity from one breed to another. The same gene mutation causes prcd/PRA in American Cockers, English Cockers and Miniature and Toy Poodles. This means that an F1 litter of Cockapoos out of two "carrier" parents will likely contain some affected pups. Although prcd-PRA is a classical genetic disorder, it can be avoided in future generations by testing dogs before breeding.

Identification of dogs that do *not* carry disease genes is the key. These "clear" dogs can safely be bred to any mate - even if the other parent turns out to be affected, no affected pups will be produced. Because these tests are reasonably expensive (currently $180 in the US) many breeders only use clear males (Poodle or Cockapoo) for breeding.

A dog whose parents have *both* tested clear (or "homozygous normal") is called "clear by parentage". This dog *cannot* be carrying any copies of the mutated gene, because neither his sire nor dam was carrying a copy to pass on. In fact, every puppy in his litter is clear by parentage. These dogs do not require gene-testing prior to breeding as long as both parents' "clear" status is verifiable.

Puppy buyers who purchase a puppy from breeders whose breeding dogs (or at least their sires) have been tested "clear" for prcd/PRA do not have to worry about their Cockapoo going blind from this devastating disease. For the rest, it's really a crapshoot. Because it's incurable, this is one of those cases where it's *really worth it* to pay a couple hundred dollars more at the outset from a breeder who can guarantee against it.

136

Familial Nephropathy

This is an autosomal recessive disease causing juvenile onset renal failure in the English Cocker Spaniel. This devastating and fatal disease has plagued the English Cocker Spaniel breed for over 50 years.

Very similar to Alport syndrome in humans, Familial Nephropathy is an autosomal recessive disease in the English Cocker Spaniel. Born with normal kidneys (it is different than renal dysplasia), affected dogs have two copies of a mutation in a *type IV collagen gene* which cause glomerular thickening and splitting and which eventually leads to renal failure. This causes death within the first few years of life, and can appear as early as 6 months. There is no cure for FN, and a kidney transplant is the only treatment.

The mutation which causes this disease in the English Cocker was identified in 2006, and a genetic test has been developed to identify not only affected puppies (it can be used diagnostically in English Cockers and their hybrid offspring) but will also identify carriers and homozygous normals.

Because there is no evidence to date that this gene mutation occurs in Poodles or in American Cockers, the Cockapoos at risk for FN would be multigenerational dogs with English Cocker ancestry on both sides. Because the disease is so devastating, *all* F1 and Multigen Cockapoos with English Cocker ancestry should ideally be tested prior to breeding unless they are verifiably clear by parentage.

Phosphofructokinase (PFK) Deficiency

Canine Phosphofructokinase (PFK) Deficiency is an autosomal recessive genetic disease in which an enzyme deficiency prevents the metabolism of glucose into available energy. Symptoms range from mild to life-threatening and can include exercise intolerance, fever, muscle wasting, intermittent dark urine and jaundice. PFK deficiency also destroys red blood cells in affected dogs, leading to anemia.

As with the two previous genetic disorders, there are no effective treatments for PFK deficiency, but the symptoms typically resolve within hours to days. If situations that induce hyperventilation (excitement, exercise and warm temperatures) are avoided, affected dogs have a relatively normal life expectancy. (*Exactly how one would do that* is not explained by any of the experts on PFK Deficiency, unfortunately…)

The causative gene for this disease was recently identified in Cockers (both English and American) and a gene test is now available. The PFK deficiency gene frequency in Cockers is estimated to be 10% of the population, *or one out of every ten Cockers*, which is unfortunately a little higher than was expected. The incidence in Cockapoos is not known, but it does exist.

Because the mutation causing PFK in Cockers hasn't been found in Poodles and *two copies* are needed to produce an affected dog, F1 Cockapoos should not be at risk for it themselves. (However, if they *did* inherit a copy from their Cocker parent, they will pass the mutation on to half their offspring if bred, so this is one test multigen breeders might want to consider, at least for their sires.)

Ocular Dysgenesis

Ocular Dysgenesis (also called Merle Ocular Dysgenesis) is a collection of vision-impairing congenital eye abnormalities entirely associated with mutations on the MITF and SILV genes, most often in combination. It is most common and generally most severe in homozygous merles displaying excessive white.

These abnormalities include Microphthalmia, coloboma, eccentric, dropped and starburst pupils, lens luxation, congenital cataracts, retinal detachment, and lack of tapetum. Some abnormalities can be easily seen with the naked eye, and some require examination by a canine ophthalmologist for diagnosis. Sometimes there is minimal visual impairment, and sometimes the dog is functionally blind.

Along with congenital deafness, the possibility of producing pups with Ocular dysgenesis is why responsible breeders *never deliberately breed two merle dogs together*. Because in Cockapoos the e/e buff/gold/red phenotype can effectively "mask" the merle gene, pups of those colors with a merle parent should ideally be gene-tested for merle before being bred to a merle dog.

Hereditary Congenital Sensineural Deafness

This is also a classical genetic disorder— although deafness can be acquired later in life due to environmental factors such as a virus, **there is no indication that environment plays a part in HCSD at all—it's entirely due to genes**. Dogs with HCSD are functionally deaf all their lives.

HCSD is a "color-related" form of deafness— it is associated with a lack of melanocyte function in the hair follicles of the cochlea, or inner ear. And although it is yet unknown whether or not there are other gene mutations involved besides those that affect melanocyte function (such as piebald and merle), it is pretty obvious at this point that the MITF and SILV mutations are major players.

In English Cockers, HCSD is estimated to be 7 times more prevalent in parti-colored dogs than solids. It has also been identified in American Cockers and Poodles, and although the prevalence in these breeds has not been established, it is most often found in parti-colored dogs, often with a lot of white, especially on the head, and often when combined with one or two copies of the merle gene. (Mostly-white dogs with blue eyes are often more likely to be affected, while mostly-white dogs with a lot of

Pathogenic disorders.

Also called *infectious diseases*, these are caused by invading pathogens, most commonly viruses and bacteria. Lyme disease, Leptospirosis, Parvo and Distemper would all be examples of pathogenic diseases—the first two are caused by invading bacteria, while the last two are viral.

A dog's resistance to these "bugs" (many of which are pretty ubiquitous in the environment) is largely dependent on the ability of his immune system to identify them and mount an appropriate response after exposure.

On the surface, the heritability of infectious diseases is pretty much 0%, because whether or not you get one is entirely dependent on environmental exposure. In other words, no matter what his genetic makeup, if a dog never crosses paths with the distemper virus, he simply cannot contract the disease we call Distemper.

On the other hand, the immune system has a LOT to do with how well the body deals with foreign pathogens when they do cross paths.

This is because although the two terms are often used interchangeably, *infection* and *disease* are two different things from an immunological standpoint. Infection, which is the invasion by and multiplication of a foreign pathogen upon exposure, may or may not progress to disease, depending upon the body's ability to halt that multiplication before it gets out of hand and causes damage to the host.

This ability to halt the proliferation of foreign pathogens is what we generally refer to as *disease resistance*.

Innumerable studies in both plants and animals in recent years have demonstrated that diversity in the immune-regulating genes of both the Major Histocompatability Complex (the DLA complex in dogs) and the various cytokine loci confer resistance to everything from potato blight to HIV.

In fact, this theory of *heterozygote advantage*, which won a Nobel Prize for Doherty and Zinkernagel back in 1996, has become a cornerstone of modern immunology.

Not surprisingly then, resistance to infectious disease is one area where F1 hybrids have a huge advantage, because hybridization produces genetic diversity in the offspring.

Environmental disorders.

This bunch, which has gotten a fair amount of press in recent years, are not influenced by genetics much at all, because diseases caused by exposure to environmental toxins both natural and manmade are pretty dose-dependent. In other words, *no matter what your genetics,* exposure above one level will cause sickness, while exposure above another level will result in certain death. (Lead and mercury poisoning famously fall into this category, as well as exposure to radiation and most chemical herbicides and pesticides.)

This occurs because the immune system is primarily designed to recognize live pathogens—it has little or no ability to mount an immune defense against toxins or inorganic "toxicants". **Essentially, we're talking about poisons here.**

And because the body's ability to excrete toxins the effects of most are cumulative – in other words, exposure to small amounts over a long period of time can have the same effect on the body in the end as a lot of exposure all at once. In general, the less exposure to toxins an organism is exposed to, the better its chances of long-term survival. The greater the exposure, the greater the chance of serious illness and death.

What falls into this category? *A LOT of stuff, unfortunately.*
In the "naturally-occurring" department we have toxic heavy metals like mercury and aluminum (which are used as preservatives and adjuvants in many canine vaccines), uranium and lead, as well as the "true" toxins (such as the post-synaptic neurotoxin *a-Cobratoxin* unique to cobras) produced by various snakes, insects, and plants and the icky little microorganisms called *endotoxins*.

In the "man-made" department we have ionic radiation (most commonly from x-rays) and somewhere in the neighborhood of around 60,000 man-made chemicals, most of which are toxic at some level of exposure.
These range from ethylene glycol, the killer ingredient in antifreeze, to BPA found in plastics, to synthetic neurotoxins like those found in flea and heartworm preventatives. In fact, according to the EPA, of the 3,000 high-volume production chemicals (meaning over a million pounds of each is produced in or imported to the US each year) *over 40% of them have never even been TESTED for toxicity.*

Environmental disorders manifest in many ways, the most well-known of which are cancers.
So this one is the exception to the rule— although the heritability is pretty much zilch, hybrid vigor cannot help much here, either. The only real defense is to avoid unnecessary exposure to toxins insofar as possible in the first place, which is the owner's responsibility.

Nutritional disorders.

Nutritional disorders arise when the dog's diet is deficient in one or more essential amino acids, vitamins, or minerals. In general, people probably obsess a lot more about possible nutritional deficiencies than they really need to, given that close to 50% of America's dogs now suffer from *obesity* rather than malnutrition.

Because all commercial dog food is formulated to contain the minimum daily requirement of nutrients, nutritional deficiencies in American dogs are now pretty rare, with the possible exception of Vitamin D, which can be "cooked off" in processing if the manufacturing plant is not careful about temperature. (The good news is that dogs, like people, can manufacture all the Vitamin D they need if they're simply exposed to sunlight. The bad news is that dogs, like their owners, are spending a lot more time indoors than Mother Nature had ever imagined they would, but this is clearly something the owner can control. And when there is no sun to be found, it's worth knowing that a teaspoon of cod liver oil will provide over 400 IUs.)

With the exception of actual genetic diseases like Cobalamin Malabsorption Syndrome (where a mutated gene prevents absorption of Vitamin B12) most nutritional disorders rank pretty low in the heritability department, and so it's probably not surprising that the ability to utilize nutrients is increased with hybridization—what are called *feed conversion rates* are increased in hybrid offspring.

This means hybrids both grow faster and pack on fat easier than purebreds eating the same amount and type of food. This is a real advantage if you're raising beef cattle, but when it comes to dogs…*not so much.*
Since lean dogs live longer and are significantly less susceptible to orthopedic problems, the average Cockapoo owner really needs to worry more about overfeeding and excess nutrition resulting in too-fast growth and weight gain than to worry about nutritional deficiencies.

If you're cooking for your dog, it's good to remember that although we've all been told that dogs need 100% of their required nutrients every day or they'll get beriberi or something, it's really not true. Few if any critical nutrients (except glucose) are metabolized in a day. Many hang around for *months.*

Like humans, dogs are essentially "stuff or starve predators" and like all predators are nutritionally designed for "balance over time". In fact, prior to the invention of commercial dog food, they managed to thrive for probably 50,000 years without eating a "100% complete and balanced diet" every day! So no matter what the dog food companies say, home-cooked food will *not* put your dog in danger of nutritional deficiencies.

Immune System Disorders.

This group, which comprises the last category, are probably the most complex of the bunch, but they all share the same common cause—*dysregulation of the immune system.* To quote the National Cancer Institute, from whence most of this information originated: "When the immune system malfunctions, it can release a veritable torrent of diseases and disorders." This torrent can be broken down into three major categories, according to the nice folks at the NCI:

Allergies:

An "allergy" is an inappropriate or exaggerated immune response to common substances that are not generally harmful. The most common allergies in dogs are flea bite dermatitis (caused by an exaggerated reaction to flea saliva) and atopia, which is caused by a reaction to environmental allergens. Together these account for about 90% of itching and skin problems seen in dogs.

Atopic dermatitis in dogs is actually the canine version of hay fever, and is often triggered by the same things.

In both species, IgE antibodies (whose original function is protection against parasites) coat *mast cells*, where they consequently sit waiting for contact with the parasite proteins for which they are sensitized. If encountered, the mast cell releases histamines which will attempt to destroy the invader. (This is why dogs with healthy immune systems are rarely bothered much by fleas, by the way.)

In allergic animals, the whole system is oversensitive and histamines are released inappropriately in response to innocuous substances such as pollen, mold, and dust mites. *In dogs, however, rather than being concentrated in the linings of the respiratory system, these mast cells are concentrated in the skin, with the greatest number found in the face and feet.* This is why dogs respond to allergens by scratching, rubbing their faces on furniture and chewing on their feet, rather than wheezing and sneezing like people.

It's worth noting (again!) that food allergies, which is usually the *first* thing owners suspect when a dog is itchy, actually account for only 10% of allergies in dogs. And about 80% of dogs with food allergies also have *atopy,* which accounts for the high failure rate in treating food allergies by diet manipulation alone.

As with autoimmune disease, susceptibility to allergies, which tend to run in both human and canine families, is linked to genes that control immune function. What causes the oversensitivity in some genetically susceptible individuals and not others ? Environmental triggers.

It is now pretty well understood that *over-vaccinating a puppy* can over-stimulate the immune system, and the AVMA does not recommend it for that reason.

Autoimmune Disorders

These disorders are the result of the immune system's inability to distinguish between antigens produced by foreign pathogens and healthy tissue. Unable to determine the difference between "self" and "non-self", the immune system begins to attack its own tissue, resulting in what we call autoimmune disease.

Autoimmune disorders are the fastest-growing group of diseases in dogs, especially among purebreds.

All autoimmune diseases recognized to date in dogs and humans have one thing in common—they all are associated with genes that regulate the immune response. In dogs, these genes are gathered in a distinct region on canine chromosome 12. An identical region exists in all species of mammals and birds and is known as the major Histocompatibility Complex (MHC).

The MHC of the dog has been designated the "dog leukocyte antigen' (DLA) complex. The DLA complex is divided into four regions, containing Class I,II, III, and IV genes.

A strong association between autoimmune disorders and the DLA class II genes has been shown for a number of canine disorders to date, including diabetes, hypothyroidism, Addison's disease, autoimmune arthritis, immune-mediated hemolytic anemia, chronic granulomatous meningoencephalitis and most recently chronic canine inflammatory liver disease.

Particular DLA haplotypes have been shown to have significantly increased *susceptibility* to these autoimmune diseases, especially when they have inherited the haplotype in a "double dose".

This is because the main function of the DLA genes is self/non-self recognition. The immune system must be able to identify every foreign protein that invades the body, whether it is on a bacteria, virus, fungi parasite, etc, as being "non-self", and to recognize every protein that is part of itself and *not* react to it.

As genetic variability is lost in the DLA, not only does the immune system lose the ability to mount an appropriate response, but the ability to differentiate between what is "self" and what is "non-self" becomes more and more tenuous.

Although there are well over 140 different haplotypes spread across the canine world, most breeds have now been reduced to only a very few, many of which are unique to each particular breed.

143

F1 hybrids are likely to inherit an entirely different haplotype from each parent, and are therefore less susceptible to the autoimmune diseases that plague their parent breeds. In succeeding hybrid generations, this diversity is best maintained primarily through the avoidance of inbreeding and the introduction of new foundation stock as needed.

Cancer

In the final analysis, cancer really represents a catastrophic breakdown of the immune system. As cells constantly reproduce, errors naturally occur, and it is the job of specific cells of the immune system to constantly seek and destroy these aberrant cells by recognizing the antigens they produce as "non-self" invaders.

When this surveillance system fails, tumors form and cancer results.

It has long been recognized that genetic susceptibility to cancer may be due in part to inherited variation on MHC genes. In fact, in recent years, several specific HLA gene alleles have been associated with either susceptibility to, or protection from, various types of cancers in humans, including breast cancer.

The fact that different breeds of dogs are predisposed to different cancers pretty much reinforces the theory that cancers have a genetic component. By some estimates, purebreds have a cancer incidence rate nearly twice that of mixed breeds — fully 60% of Golden Retrievers now die of cancer, for example, mostly hemangiosarcomas and lymphosarcomas. This indicates that genetic diversity is probably advantageous here as well.

Since even cancer susceptibility appears polygenic rather than caused by single gene mutations, a dog whose genes are a blend of two breeds is simply less likely to inherit all the genes (including those in the DLA complex) necessary for susceptibility to a cancer that may plague one of its parent breeds.

But the key word here is *susceptibility*. Cancer, like all disorders of the immune system, clearly has a genetic component, but the heritability is nowhere near 100% on any of them, even where a specific DLA haplotype has been identified that clearly increases risk.

Like allergies and autoimmune disorders, cancer is primarily a disease of the developed world, and that indicates some fairly strong environmental factors at work, which act as "triggers". For example, it is known that rabies vaccination can trigger a particularly lethal form of sarcoma at the injection site in both cats and dog, although we don't know which ones are susceptible until the cancer develops.

In other words, with all diseases involving the immune system,

genetics loads the gun....

but environment pulls the trigger.

By virtue of its genetic diversity, the immune system of a hybrid dog should be in pretty good shape genetically, but even the best immune system can be overwhelmed by environmental factors *that are totally within the owner's control.* In addition to providing the cleanest and most nutritional diet, which is within any owner's control, things like vaccination protocols and the insecticides you use both on your dog and in your home and yard can all adversely affect immune function.

Keeping your Cockapoo healthy is not only the job of your vet....

It's also yours.

The more you know the better decisions you can make, and the healthier your Cockapoo is going to end up.

CHAPTER NINE:

Keeping Your Cockapoo Healthy

The time to find a vet is *before* you bring your puppy home. Since this will be your puppy's Primary Care Provider, you want to put some effort into finding the best one you can, not just the one who's closest or recommended by a dog-owning friend. You'll need to check out websites, make some phone calls and ask some questions.

Why Choosing the Right Vet is Critical

In addition to the decisions you make, the decisions made by your vet can also affect your dog's overall health and longevity, and unfortunately not always for the best. As with breeders, all vets are *not* created equal —common sense should tell us that *somebody* graduated dead-last in class back at vet school, and also that the lucky recipient of that dubious distinction is unlikely to have a plaque displayed in his office commemorating it. Some vets keep up with current research in their field while others appear to have never cracked a book or read a scientific journal since the day they left vet school.

In order to keep your dog healthy, you'll need to shop around to find one from the first category. But how can you tell who's who?

The easiest way to tell if a veterinary practice is up-to-date
is by simply asking about their vaccination protocols.

For many years, vaccinations were administered annually whether the dog needed them or not, and no one thought much about it. (Odds are your previous dogs were vaccinated annually, and a lot of "expert" advice on the internet still recommends this.)

All this changed back in 2003, when the American Animal Hospital Association, the American Veterinary Medical Association, and most veterinary teaching hospitals changed their vaccination protocols based on new research. All now recommend only "core" vaccines for all dogs, with others added only where necessary, based on a dog's individual risk. And none recommend annual vaccination.

However, it is absolutely amazing how many vets in clinical practice around the country seemed to have missed that memo ten years ago. You do NOT want to take your puppy to one of those guys, because we now know this sort of vaccination regime can compromise his long-term health and well-being.

Although necessary to protect a puppy against infectious disease, vaccines can also be one of the triggers for autoimmune disorders.

So let's talk about vaccination here, because unless you're well-informed yourself, it's going to be pretty hard to figure out if a prospective vet is!

ALL the statements in boldface below were copied *verbatim* from the **American Veterinary Medical Association's 2011 Vaccine Policy Statement**, just so you know…you might want to be wary of any vet who finds them totally unfamiliar.

Revaccination of patients with sufficient immunity does not necessarily add to their disease protection and may increase the potential risk of post-vaccination adverse events."

Exactly what are these adverse events?

"Possible adverse events include, but are not necessarily limited to, failure to immunize, anaphylaxis, immuno-suppression, autoimmune disorders, transient infections, long-term infected carrier states, and local development of tumors."

And when it comes to triggering autoimmune disorders, over-vaccination is clearly one trigger you do not *need* to pull. Here's why:

"Unnecessary stimulation of the immune system does not necessarily result in enhanced disease resistance, and may increase the potential risk of post-vaccination adverse events."

But how do you and your vet figure out if your dog actually *needs* another vaccination in order to be protected? Here's the AVMA again, with the answer:

"Due to the emergence of newer and improved antibody tests, serological assays are being used to determine immune status and establish vaccination protocols for animal patients."

These are called "titer tests" (pronounced like "tighter" just so you don't embarrass yourself) and they use a simple blood sample. The cost of in-house titer testing currently runs between $30 and $50 in most parts of the country, and is worth every penny. So *"Do you routinely run titers in your practice?"* is also a good question to ask.

What about "booster shots"?

Aside from rabies, the "core" vaccines your dog needs are now all *modified live or recombinant vaccines* and according to all scientific evidence do *not* need to be boosted in order to be effective. (*Killed vaccines*, which do require a "booster", have not been used in decades for these diseases.)

According to the 2011 AAHA Guidelines (which any vet should have read) *a single dose* of a **modified live vaccine administered to a dog over 14 weeks of age will both "prime" the immune system** *and* **provide immunity for several years.**

You cannot make an already immune dog *more* immune by "boosting" it— the dog either has immunity against a disease or he does not. And a dog with an adequate antibody titer is considered immune. (Actually, because of what's called "cell memory", a lot of dogs who display an inadequate titer have demonstrated immunity when challenged, but most vets and owners prefer to err on the side of caution here.)

The ONLY reason puppies get a series of puppy shots is because of possible interference from maternally derived antibodies, not because the vaccines themselves need "boosting".

Here's what happens: Puppies display "passive immunity" for those diseases to which their mothers were exposed—either naturally or through vaccination. These maternally derived antibodies, passed primarily through colostrum in the first 48 hours of life, can last anywhere from 5 to 16 weeks, depending on the puppy. Puppies under 5 weeks are usually completely protected.

However, for each puppy, there is about a week when there are still sufficient maternal antibodies to destroy the attenuated antigens in the vaccine, but not enough to fight off the disease itself if the puppy is exposed. This period is called the "window of vulnerability".

At 6 weeks, only 37% of puppies are protected by a vaccination given at that time—the other 63% still carry enough maternal antibodies to prevent the vaccine from working.

Some of those puppies may have high enough maternal antibody levels to protect them if they are exposed to the disease itself over the next couple of weeks, while others may not.

Because the vet does not know which puppies are protected, a second vaccination is generally given to all puppies only because it is frankly cheaper than running titers on all of them.

Now, if you read the stuff from the AVMA carefully, you don't need more than three functioning brain cells to figure out that the poor guys in the 37% who *were* protected by the first vaccine are the ones at risk for adverse effects from over-stimulation of the immune system when they get the second round.

This is why many breeders and vets now believe that where the risk of parvo and distemper is not high, the first shot not be given until 8-9 weeks, when around 80% of puppies will be protected by it. By 12 weeks, over 95% of the puppies in a litter will have outgrown their maternal immunity to the point where they will be protected by vaccination. (In fact, research in the UK indicates that the new "high-titer" vaccines *now used both there and in the US* provide protection for nearly all puppies by 10 weeks.)

By 16 weeks, maternal immunity is no longer a factor, and every puppy who can seroconvert will do so and be protected by a single vaccination given at that time, even if it's the first one he's had.

So it should be pretty clear that if a puppy misses one of the shots in the series for some reason, there is no earthly reason to give him "extra" shots to get to some magic number *as long as the last one given produced a titer or was administered at 16 weeks or later.*

Once the puppy goes to his new home, the owner can elect

to have titers run BEFORE any subsequent shots are automatically administered.

Because this is hands-down the SAFEST approach for the puppy from both a "short-term protection" and a "long-term immune function" standpoint, all vets should offer this option, although few actually do.

To be on the safe side, titers should be run 5-7 days after the last vaccination. If the puppy does *not* have a positive titer, it means he was one of the puppies with a high level of maternal antibodies at the time the vaccination was given and the shot "didn't take." In that case, the vaccines can be re-administered to protect him.

On the other hand, if he *does* have a positive titer, the 8-week shot "took" and there is no logical reason to increase his risk of adverse reaction by giving him vaccines he does not need. (Remember, immunity is a lot like pregnancy— there is no such thing as "more immune"!!)

And if your puppy has a positive titer at 10 or 12 weeks, you can take him out and about for socialization without worrying about waiting until he's "completed his puppy shots" at 16 weeks.

How cool is THAT?

And that way his vaccination protocol is designed *for his individual immune response,* rather than representing a "one-size-fits-all" approach that can lead to autoimmune problems down the road. The vet you choose should be on board with that philosophy.

A Case for Making a Couple of Extra Trips to the Vet...

Many vets assume all pet owners are unwilling to schedule more than one vet appointment a year, so they try to stuff everything into one visit. This is often not a great idea, especially when it comes to vaccination.

Aside from unnecessary revaccination, the other danger to a puppy's immune system and overall future health is from the sheer NUMBER of different vaccines given, especially if they are given all at the same time, or in a combination (*polyvalent*) vaccine.

In fact, here's the AVMA's advice on the subject:

"Vaccines, including polyvalent products, should be selected to include only those antigens appropriate for the specific risk of the patient, thereby eliminating unnecessary immune system stimulation and thus lowering potential risks of adverse events.

Veterinarians should be aware of the risk of "endotoxin stacking" with the use of multiple Gram -negative vaccines."

What does this mean? The more vaccines given at one time, the greater the risk of over-stimulating and thus damaging the immune system. This includes a single shot that contains multiple antigens – the above-mentioned "polyvalent products". Here's why:

Endotoxins are intracellular toxins found in gram-negative bacteria, and are found in all vaccines (although they are generally present in highest numbers in vaccines that protect against bacterial diseases like leptospirosis). When released, endotoxins produce a powerful inflammatory response in the system, and "endotoxin stacking" by combining vaccines makes it worse. Common symptoms of what is essentially "toxic shock" can include both fever and lethargy, which are all too common in puppies after vaccination.

In a recent large study on adverse vaccine reactions in dogs published in the JAVMA, the two greatest risk factors were found to be **the size of the dog** and **the number of vaccines given at one time**. In fact….

Research showed *each additional vaccine* given to a dog weighing less than 22 pounds increased the risk of adverse reaction by 27%!!!!

The size part makes perfect sense because *all dogs get the same vaccines*, no matter what their size or age. That's right— your 5 pound Cockapoo puppy will receive *exactly the same vaccine* as an adult Newfoundland weighing 150 pounds! It's amazing how many people logically assume there are different vaccines for different sized dogs, but unfortunately, that is just not the case.

This means that proportionally, a puppy's immature little system has to deal with 30 times the amount of antigen (that's the viral or bacteria component) as well as 30 times the *endotoxins, adjuvants, carriers and preservatives* as a large adult dog. These include a fair number of toxic substances including (but certainly not limited to) aluminum, formaldehyde, and mercury. And obviously, the more vaccines a puppy is given at one time, the more of these toxic substances he is exposed to at one time.

And the worst part of this is that many of these vaccines protect against diseases for which the dog is at little or no risk in the first place.

Plain old common sense should tell us that an animal would never experience this sort of "all-at-once" exposure in nature, and no immune system is designed to handle it. Sort of like flying in the cargo hold of a 727, the possibility of vaccination as it is now too often practiced just never occurred to Mother Nature when she was designing the canine immune system.

Not to put too fine a point on it, but if the vet you are considering using as your puppy's primary health provider doesn't know any of this, he needs to take a brush-up course in Immunology 101 *and you need to find a different vet.*

The days when being a responsible dog owner meant taking your dog in to the vet for his "yearly shots" without even knowing what on earth the dog was being vaccinated against or whether he even needed another vaccination at all are OVER. *Keeping your puppy healthy means you have to do your homework.*

No state, county or city in the US actually requires vaccination for anything other than rabies. *It's amazing how many people do not know this.* Now, most training classes, boarding kennels, day care facilities and even groomers require more than that, but it's not the "law". So let's see what shots he actually needs to be both protected from life-threatening diseases *and* welcome in most canine establishments.

Understanding "Puppy Shots"

The most important thing to understand is that all so-called "puppy shots" are not the same. Depending on the vet, if you do not specify, a "puppy shot" may be a DP, a DHP, a DHPP, a DA2PPVL, a DA2PPV+CV, or the mother of all combos— the dazzling DA2PPVL+CV, which many vaccine experts wish would simply vanish from this earth.

And those are just from *Merck's* personal Vaccine Buffet. If you throw in the various offerings of Pfizer and Merial (which is really the animal products line of pharmaceutical giant Sanofi), you are pretty much guaranteed to be lost in the Alphabet Soup of canine vaccines forever.

The whole thing is further complicated by the fact that in the last few years there have been a rash of mergers in the pharmaceutical world— for example, Intervet became part of Shering Plough, which then merged with industry giant Merck, and all animal vaccines formerly made by those three companies (including the Galaxy and Proguard vaccines) are being relabeled under the Nobivac brand.

Fort Dodge was bought out by pharmaceutical giant Weyeth, which recently merged with Pfizer, which markets the Vanguard line of animal vaccines, but then Pfizer announced in 2011 that it planned to sell off its Animal Health division completely, so who knows where they will end up.

What all this means is you can't just assume your new dog is getting the same vaccinations your last dog got, or that your vet is using the same vaccines he used to use.

(And if this is starting to remind you forcibly of the Wonderful World of Dog Food, you're not alone….)

So let's try to sort this mess out so you'll know what your puppy needs and what he really doesn't need so you'll know what to ask for…and remember, YOU can specify which vaccines you want your dog to get.

The Four "Core" Vaccines

Back in 2003, after years of study, the Association of Animal Hospitals came up with a new vaccination protocol for veterinarians. At that time they decided to recommend only FOUR vaccines for all dogs, which they designated "core vaccines".

Certain other vaccines could be given only as necessary if a dog is at particular risk, while some are not recommended at all. (Some combination vaccines routinely given to puppies actually include these "non-core" and "not recommended" vaccines, which is why you need to read this part carefully.) Presumably all vets got this memo.

All 4 core vaccines can be covered in two "shots" – the DHP and the Rabies shot.

Although the core vaccines can be given separately, three of them are usually combined in the puppy shots, while rabies vaccine is always administered as a single shot. Here's the breakdown of the DHP and what's in it:

Distemper (that's the "D")

First described by Edward Jenner (the smallpox guy) back in the 18th century, distemper is an old disease. Primarily affecting puppies under 6 months of age, canine distemper is rarely seen in the US today outside of shelter populations, and many vets in practice today have never seen a single case. But prior to the 1960s, when widespread vaccination of dogs really took off, it killed roughly *half the puppies* born in the US in any given year.

Distemper begins with an upper respiratory infection (often characterized by a thick greenish discharge from the nose and eyes) before progressing to the nervous system, where it can cause seizures and even death. Because it is caused by a virus, the only treatment for distemper is supportive. And it's a pretty horrific disease—without supportive treatment, close to 90% of puppies who contract it will die. Even *with* supportive treatment, a puppy's odds of survival are not all that hot, and those who do survive often have lifelong neurological and ocular damage.

The reason all dogs still need to be vaccinated for what is now a pretty rare disease is because both wild animals (in 1994, a third of the lions in the Serengeti died from canine distemper) and shelter populations provide a constant "reservoir" for the virus. The virus is spread primarily through direct contact and is not particularly hardy in the environment. For this reason, puppies from shelters and commercial breeding operations (i.e. purchased through pet stores and online brokers) are at higher risk than puppies from small private breeders. But dogs adopted or purchased from these places can shed the virus for weeks if they've been exposed, putting all unvaccinated dogs who come in contact with them at risk.

The distemper virus, which is a close cousin of the human measles virus, has been shown to deplete the body's store of Vitamin A – in fact, the symptoms of distemper closely resemble the symptoms of serious Vitamin A deficiency. In one study, ferrets who were Vitamin A replete were shown to be completely resistant to challenge with the distemper virus. For this reason, a teaspoonful of old-fashioned cod liver oil a couple days before a dog is scheduled for a distemper vaccine to boost his Vitamin A levels might lessen the chance of reaction and certainly can't hurt.

Canine Infectious Hepatitis (that's the "H")

This is another disease that's rare in the US since widespread vaccination began in the 1960s—in fact, it's so rare *there hasn't been a single case of it* recorded in dogs in this country in the last 20 years at least and probably longer. (Why it was included as a Core Vaccine is frankly a total mystery.)

Caused by the CAV-1 (Canine Adenovirus- type 1) virus, infectious hepatitis primarily attacks the liver, kidneys, spleen and eyes- symptoms can range anywhere from relatively mild with spontaneous recovery to death within hours, with mortality most likely in puppies. The CAV1 virus is highly contagious and is spread primarily through ingestion of urine, feces and saliva of infected dogs. The virus is considered hardy and can survive in the environment for 6 months or more.

Somewhat oddly, modern vaccines do not actually contain the CAV-1 antigen, as early vaccines using it produced pretty severe side effects like corneal opacity (blue eye), which is also one of the symptoms of the disease. However, it was discovered that vaccination against CAV-2 (a similar virus but which only causes a mild self-limiting respiratory infection) also protected dogs against the more serious CAV1, and that antigen is now used instead.

So, if your dog is given a "3-way", he's actually protected against both canine infectious hepatitis (CAV1) and the milder CAV2, which means the DHP "3-way" actually protects against 4 diseases. Since the risk for puppies in the US contracting canine hepatitis is low to non-existent and the risk of adverse reaction is statistically higher than the risk of contracting the disease (especially if the puppy weighs under 22 pounds at the time of vaccination), the CAV2 antigen is usually the one that is left out of the initial puppy shots by many holistic vets and breeders, who opt for the DP combination instead.

Parvovirus (that's the "P")

"Parvo" is a word that strikes terror in the hearts of breeders everywhere, and with good reason. The parvovirus attacks the rapidly dividing cells in the digestive tract, which is where the virus does the most damage, causing vomiting and bloody diarrhea. Untreated, 80% of affected puppies will die usually of dehydration. With the best supportive treatment, maybe 75% will survive, but it's going to cost a breeder untold thousands of dollars to try and save a litter, and a quarter of them probably won't make it no matter what they do. *Fear of parvo is the reason so many breeders limit visitors when they have a litter.*

The virus first appeared in dogs back in the 1970s, and prior to development of a vaccine, thousands of dogs of all ages across the US died a pretty horrific death. Today, because of widespread vaccination and because the virus is ubiquitous in the environment, parvo is primarily a disease of puppies between 6 weeks and 6 months of age.

The *bad news* about parvo is that unlike distemper, the virus is extremely hardy in the environment, spread through the feces of infected dogs and picked up by human shoes. Once in the soil, it can live for up to 9 months outdoors, and actually longer if the ground freezes during that time.

The *good news* is parvo is actually pretty easy to kill indoors. A simple solution of water and chlorine bleach at a ratio of 30:1 will effectively kill it. (And anyone who bred dogs back in the 1970s probably still remembers that 30:1 translates to a quarter of a cup of bleach to a gallon of water.)

The truth is, out of the whole bunch, parvo is really the virus a puppy in the US is most likely to come in contact with. Unlike distemper, it is not confined to shelters, pet shops and puppy mills. Because it is so ubiquitous in the soil, unprotected puppies are at risk anytime they leave their own fenced yard.

Until you know for sure that your puppy is protected by running a titer, his feet really shouldn't touch the ground off your property, *even in the vet's office*. Bring him in his crate and keep him in it except when he's on a newly disinfected examining table, because the last dog who walked through the waiting room may have tracked it in on his paws. That dog may be vaccinated and therefore immune, but your puppy may not be. Remember, parvo is not an airborne virus – it is spread through feces, and clings to surfaces that it comes in contact with, like paws and shoes.

Now, since the 3-way DHP combination vaccine will take care of all the recommended core vaccines except rabies, one would logically think all vets would administer it. They don't.

For some unfathomable reason, many clinics in the US routinely use the CHPP combination instead, which includes parainfluenza, a non-core vaccine that protects against a second mild self-limiting respiratory infection. This would be fine except that each added vaccine increases the risk of adverse reaction in a dog under 22 pounds by 27%! (And virtually all Cockapoo puppies are under 22 pounds when they are getting vaccinated.)
So, assuming your vet does not even carry the DP (which most do not), be sure and ask for the 3-way DHP instead of the 4-way DHPP.

Rabies

The last of the 4 "Core Vaccines", this one is always given as a single shot and is never a component of a combination vaccine. Because rabies poses a public health risk to humans, it is the only canine vaccination required by law in all 50 states.

However, because it is a killed vaccine and has a higher level of adjuvants and endotoxins than an MLV, it is also the cause of a LOT of serious vaccine reactions in dogs, so what we want to do is vaccinate our dogs to protect both them and us and to comply with state laws, but not over-vaccinate or vaccinate earlier than needed for protection and thereby increase the risk of adverse reactions.

Unfortunately, most people have little or no knowledge about the rabies virus, the disease it causes, actual risk to their dog or the laws in their state, and so there is an appalling tendency to over-vaccinate for rabies. Understanding both the disease and the relative risks of contracting it will help you make better decisions for your Dood.

Rabies is a particularly nasty viral disease first described back in 2000 BC. It can technically infect any warm-blooded vertebrate, although it is common in some (like canines) and virtually unheard of in others (like rodents).

Rabies is *zoonotic* and is passed from animals to other animals or humans through saliva (or rarely through actual tissue in the case of organ transplants), but *cannot* be transmitted through feces, urine, or blood. The virus is not hardy in the environment and becomes noninfectious when it dries out or is exposed to sunlight, usually within minutes or at most a few hours. (Simply petting or handling a rabid animal does not automatically constitute exposure, at least according to the CDC…who knew?)

Once it enters a new host, usually through a bite, the virus travels through the peripheral nerves (which can take weeks or even several months depending on where the bite occurred) until it reaches the central nervous system, at which point it causes acute encephalitis and is almost always 100% fatal, usually within days of symptoms appearing. In humans who've been exposed, the rabies vaccine can be successfully administered as a prophylactic prior to the appearance of symptoms, usually in a series of 5 shots. Unvaccinated dogs who have been exposed are generally euthanized.

How prevalent is it? Rabies kills around 55,000 people a year, mostly contracted from dog bites, with the overwhelming majority of rabies cases occurring in Africa and Asia. A hundred years ago, the US averaged about 100 human deaths from rabies every year, and nearly all were the result of dog bites.

Once widespread vaccination, that changed radically, and in 2007 the CDC declared the US to be offi-cially free of canine rabies, a "vaccine success story" by any measure. But in spite of that, there were 59 cases of rabies in dogs and 2 rabies cases in humans reported to the CDC in the Continental US in 2010. *This is because there are several OTHER STRAINS of rabies besides the canine one.*

Carried by wild animals, these strains can be transmitted to both animals and humans, and until we figure out how to eradicate those strains, dogs will continue to need rabies shots. (It's worth noting that there are almost *five times* more cases of rabies reported in (free-roaming) cats than in dogs every year, the only species for which incidence is actually rising. So what are the risks of your puppy contracting a "wild animal" strain of rabies before he's had his first rabies shot? It all depends upon where you live.

The following map (which changes little from year to year) shows the incidence of confirmed rabies cases in dogs in the US in 2010....all 59 of them. Each dot represents one case.

In people, virtually *all cases* of rabies contracted in the US are caused by bites from infected bats, and rabid bats have been identified in most states, making rabies pretty much of an equal opportunity disease for humans from a geographical standpoint. *(It's also good to know that your odds of contracting rabies from a bat in the US are somewhere in the neighborhood of one in 155 million- you actually have a better chance of winning the lottery. Or being elected President.)*

Dogs, on the other hand, are unlikely to contract rabies from bat bites— in fact, there are exactly ZE-RO "bat-to-dog" rabies cases recorded by the CDC over the years. Go figure.

159

Instead, both dogs and cats are nearly always infected by bites from rabid skunks, raccoons and foxes, with skunks leading raccoons by a margin of two to one and foxes barely in the money.

And for unknown reasons, the incidence of rabies in raccoons is limited almost entirely to states along the Eastern seaboard and Texas, while the incidence in skunks is greatest in the Eastern states from Maine to Georgia and in a vertical band through the Midwest extending from Minnesota down to Texas, with a few scattered on the Pacific coast. Not surprisingly, if you look at the map, you'll notice the incidence of rabies in dogs and cats occurs primarily in those areas as well.

Contrary to popular belief, squirrels, chipmunks, rabbits, rats and mice are NOT carriers of rabies in the US, and pose no rabies risk to an unvaccinated puppy. (Good to know that we've been worrying unnecessarily about backyard squirrels and chipmunks all these years, huh?)

Now, that pretty much confines his risk to areas where these skunks, raccoons and foxes are found (in other words, *outdoors*) and then only in those parts of the country where they carry the rabies virus.

A dog cannot "catch" rabies from casual contact.

The only way a puppy *could* conceivably contract rabies is if he were allowed out unsupervised (in other words off-leash) in a state where rabid animals are found and happens to get bitten by a rabid one in the "furious" late stage of the disease, so it makes sense to avoid letting your puppy run loose in parks, landfills and around dumpsters prior to vaccination if you live in one of those states.

But you'd have to be a total *dunce* to do that anyway for a wealth of other reasons...I mean, just *think* about it— statistically, a loose puppy is about a million times more likely to get hit by a car than he is to contract rabies from being bitten by a rabid skunk or raccoon that just happened by *at that very moment.*
And even if you *are* a total dunce, the statistics are still weighted heavily in a dog's favor— remember, there are over 75 million dogs in America, and between 50-70 total cases of rabies in dogs per year.

Given all this, it's pretty obvious that although rabies vaccination is necessary, there is no reason your puppy needs to get his first rabies shot on the same day as his other puppy shots at 12 or 14 weeks, because his risk of contracting rabies is so low. *It is simply not necessary and will seriously increase his chances of an immediate or delayed vaccine reaction, so don't let anyone talk you into it.*

What About the Law?

Ah....*the Law*. Now that you understand the actual risks or lack thereof, you can probably wait the recommended 3-4 weeks needed to give his immune system time to recover after his last puppy vaccines before getting him his first rabies shot and still not run afoul of most state and municipal rabies laws.

And extensive research has failed to turn up anyone who's ever gone to jail (or even been fined) for waiting until their puppy was 6 months old before having him vaccinated for rabies. He just can't get a dog license until he has proof of rabies vaccination.

In most states the first vaccine is a "one-year vaccine", so a second will need to be given a year after the first in order to comply with most licensing laws, although according to the CDC, a dog is considered immune to rabies 28 days after a single rabies vaccine. (That's a year after the first, not when the dog turns a year old , by the way.)
And thanks to a lot of lobbying by concerned vets and owners, **all subsequent rabies vaccinations are now good for three years in every single state.** This is an improvement over the old "annual rabies vaccine" laws, but it's still probably overkill—most immunologists and vaccine experts agree that a rabies vaccination provides immunity for at least 5 and probably 7 years.
(In fact, there is an ongoing research study at the University of Wisconsin designed to prove exactly that, so that state rabies laws can be changed. For more information on it, Google the Rabies Challenge Fund. And feel free to donate while you're on the website, because as one might imagine, the entire study is being funded by private donations rather than by the pharmaceutical companies that manufacture and sell rabies vaccines.)

So let's sum up here:
- **The risk of your puppy contracting rabies from a wild animal is statistically very, very low.**
- **NO state requires annual rabies vaccination any more, so do not allow your vet to do so..**
- **NEVER allow the rabies shot to be given within 3-4 weeks of any other vaccination.**

It's just not worth the risk to your dog. Other suggestions from vaccine experts for decreasing the chance of a rabies vaccine reaction include:

- *Using a "clean" (i.e. containing the least number of adjuvants) vaccine*
- *Giving the homeopathic remedy lyssin 30c (anyone can purchase this online) the day before and within 2 hours after vaccination may lessen the risk of reaction.*

- *Always delaying vaccination on a dog who is, or has recently been, ill, especially with GI problems.*
- *Delaying vaccination when the dog is under stress or has recently changed homes.*
- *Adding probiotics to the dog's diet for a week or two before and after vaccination*

Many vets erroneously assume the only adverse reactions to rabies vaccine are immediate acute reactions (anaphylaxis), but delayed reactions to rabies vaccines (vaccinosis) may occur up to 45 days later, and so no one associates them with the recent vaccine given, especially seizures, which are often misdiagnosed as "idiopathic epilepsy".

Delayed reactions to rabies vaccine may include:

- *Behavior changes such as aggression and separation anxiety*
- *Obsessive behavior, self-mutilation, tail-chewing, shredding bedding*
- *Pica- eating wood, stones, earth, stool*
- *Destructive behavior, shredding bedding*
- *Seizures, epilepsy*
- *Fibrosarcomas (cancer) at injection site*
- *Autoimmune disease (like immune-mediated hemolytic anemia)*
- *Chronic gastrointestinal problems*

(If any of these problems appear after a rabies vaccine, your best bet is to locate a holistic or homeopathic vet who can prescribe specific remedies that can actually help a lot. Most "conventional" vets are frankly not much use when dealing with vaccinosis, especially if they administered the vaccines. Or as a last resort, contact Dr Jean Dodds at Hemopet for advice.)

In fact, many holistic vets suggest that any previously unseen behaviors or health problems occurring within a month or two of rabies vaccination should probably be viewed with suspicion.

If your puppy reacts adversely to the rabies vaccine in spite of all efforts to be careful, it's good to know that in the following states at least, he can get a Medical Rabies Waiver from his vet. This is *critical* because if a dog has reacted adversely to rabies vaccine once, odds are the next time will be worse.

<h1 style="text-align:center">States with Medical Rabies Waivers</h1>
(as of 2012)

Alabama, California, Colorado, Connecticut, Florida, Illinois, Maine, Massachusetts, Missouri, Oregon, New Hampshire, New Jersey, New York, Vermont, Virginia, Wisconsin

If your state does *not* currently have a Medical Rabies Waiver Form, or if your county or municipality still requires annual rabies vaccination, visit the **Rabies Challenge Fund** website to see how you can help change these dangerously outdated laws.

Non-Core Vaccines

The AAHA Guidelines consider some vaccines to be "non-core vaccines", or optional, based on the individual dog's lifestyle, environment and risk of exposure. These include parainfluenza, bordatella, Leptospirosis, Lyme disease, and a rattlesnake vaccine. Because, like the rabies shot, all these vaccines are made with *killed* rather than *modified live* antigens and therefore require adjuvants, the risk of adverse reaction is by definition higher.

So before you let your puppy automatically be given one or even several of these, let's see who really needs them.

Kennel Cough (Parainfluenza and Bordatella)

Along with the CAV2 virus already used in core vaccines to protect against its Hepatitis cousin, the parainfluenza virus and bordatella bronchiseptica bacterium are primarily responsible for *Canine Infectious Tracheobronchitis*, more commonly known as "kennel cough".

Although not a life-threatening or even particularly serious disease (it's usually self-limiting even without treatment) kennel cough IS highly contagious, so training classes, groomers, doggy daycare, boarding kennels all generally require proof of vaccination.

Even though the vaccines available are not long-lasting, or effective against all the strains out there (lots of dogs who are current on the kennel cough vaccinations still end up with kennel cough), your dog is likely to need proof of vaccination against kennel cough to be welcome in most doggy venues.

The intranasal versions (which are literally squirted up the dog's nose) are the least reactive, and the most popular is probably Intra-Trac3, which includes CAV2, parainfluenza and bordatella.

Of course, if your puppy was vaccinated with the popular "4-way" DHPP vaccine instead of the 3-way DHP, he's already covered for CAV2 and parainfluenza (which is the second P) and in the interest of not over-vaccinating you should request that bordatella be administered as a single intranasal vaccine.

Lyme Disease

As anyone who's had it can attest, Lyme disease in humans is a serious and often debilitating chronic disease. Because of that, a lot of people automatically assume it's the same for dogs and that their puppy needs to be vaccinated against Lyme, especially if he lives in an endemic state. However, the most current data available indicates this may not be the case at all.

Also caused by the spirochete *borrelia bergdorferi* and transmitted primarily through the saliva of infected ticks, the symptoms of Lyme disease in dogs differ from those in people, and are for the most part far less devastating.
In addition, symptoms usually occur much later (according to Cornell's Baker Institute up to 2-5 months after a bite by an infected tick) and the classic Lyme rash is almost never seen.

Symptoms in dogs most commonly include low grade fever, lethargy, loss of appetite and shifting lameness. These usually resolve within 48 hours after treatment with oral doxycycline, which should be continued for a full 4 weeks due to the slow replication rate of *borrelia bergdorferi*.

Puppies should be treated with amoxicillin to avoid damage to the enamel on developing teeth, and probiotics should always be given after the course of antibiotics to restore normal gut flora.

But more importantly, based on nationwide test results, it is now estimated that over 95% of dogs infected with the Lyme spirochete never develop any clinical symptoms at all.

At this point, no one really knows why this is the case, but in humans, research has shown that chronic Lyme is associated with—big surprise!—a particular allele in one of the Class II HLA genes, so it's not much of a stretch to postulate that resistance to Lyme is associated with the Class II DLA genes in dogs…in other words, there's likely a genetic predisposition to susceptibility to this particular bug, and not surprisingly, some breeds appear to be particularly susceptible. In some purebreds, Lyme can cause serious kidney disease.
Most experts recommend asymptomatic dogs with a positive Lyme titer have a blood panel drawn and

an auscultation to preclude the possibility of sub clinical cardiac or kidney involvement, and because of the "lag time" between exposure and the development of symptoms, some vets feel that it is prudent to treat Lyme-positive dogs with doxycycline simply to err on the side of caution.

And much like rabies, Lyme risk is entirely geographical.

In 2010, 95% of the reported cases of Lyme came from 12 states, with another 4% coming from California. All other states combined accounted for the other 1%.

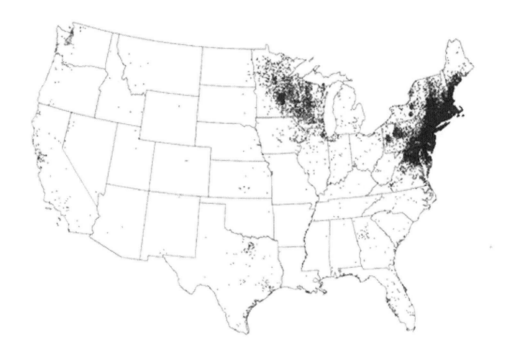

And even in Lyme endemic states like those in the Northeast, around 90% of healthy dogs have positive Lyme antibody tests. That's why those maps that show incidence of tick-borne diseases are so scary—they are not showing actual disease *incidence* so much as *exposure*. (And it's good t remember that those maps are brought to you by the manufacturers of Lyme vaccines and the companies that sell the snap-test kits....all of whom have a financial interest in selling more of their products.)

So why not vaccinate your puppy against Lyme "just to be on the safe side", in case he's one of the 5% who will develop symptoms after exposure? *Because it may not be the "safe" side at all.*

Serious questions have been raised about the safety of the Lyme Vaccine.

Testing on Lyme-vaccinated dogs with chronic inflammatory autoimmune arthritis (which does not typically occur in dogs naturally infected with Lyme) and other autoimmune diseases has revealed the presence of *vaccine-strain*, rather than wild-strain, Lyme. This raises the alarming possibility that *the vaccine itself is causing the problems.* (Not coincidentally, the human Lyme vaccine was pulled from the market when similar reports started coming in.)

At this point in time, the safest universally-recommended defense against Lyme is simply the prompt removal of ticks. After a tick attaches and begins to feed, spirochetes residing in the midgut of the tick begin to migrate into the salivary glands and from there into the host, which can take up to 12 hours. Because of that, there is actually little chance of infection during the first few hours of tick feeding, although it rises exponentially after that. So as long as you remove ticks promptly, the odds of a dog becoming infected with Lyme are pretty low.

And if you're *still* worried, you can always give your dog a single capsule of doxycycline, which is an old drug and long-proven safe for adult dogs. Why?

A large randomized double-blind placebo-controlled human study conducted in an endemic area of New York determined that a single 200 mg dose of doxycycline administered within 72 hours after a tick bite could prevent the development of Lyme disease. Efficacy was determined to be around 87%, which is coincidentally about the same as most Lyme vaccines, but without the risk of adverse vaccine reaction. How cool is that?

It's also worth knowing that currently, the University Of Wisconsin School Of Veterinary Medicine, (located in a Lyme-endemic state) neither recommends nor administers Lyme vaccinations.

Lepto

Another non-core vaccine, this is one that a lot of vets try to scare clients into buying based on a "Lepto outbreak" in their area. *This is unfortunate*, because like the rabies vaccine, the lepto vaccine is one of the most likely to cause life-threatening adverse reactions (anaphylaxis) in dogs.

Unlike rabies, however, the lepto vaccine is neither required by law nor even necessary for *any* dog, no matter what the local risk at any given point in time. **Really.**

Called Rat-Catcher's Yellows in earlier times, Leptospirosis is an old disease that's been around for a long time. It is caused by infection with the water-borne spirochete *leptospirosa*. Over 200 different strains (or *serovars*) of lepto have been identified to date, at least eight of which are known to cause Leptospirosis in dogs. The most current vaccines protect against FOUR of them.

On top of that, because it is a killed vaccine, two doses must be administered within weeks of each other to elicit an immune response (which effectively doubles the chance of reaction), and the most recent evidence suggests protection may only last 6-8 months. Combine that with the risk of adverse reaction, and the whole "lepto vaccination" picture is not particularly impressive.

So what is the real risk of your dog contracting Leptospirosis?
Probably pretty low.

A survey of the Veterinary Medical Database between 1983 and 1998 turned up a total of 340 reported cases. Even assuming that represents some serious under-reporting, putting those numbers into the framework of a canine population of maybe 50 million dogs during that 15 year period, it's not exactly what you'd call an epidemic.

Although Lepto is zoonotic, direct transfer from people to dogs or dogs to people (or even dog-to-dog) is pretty much nonexistent in the US. Instead, because the lepto spirochete is aquatic (it can survive up to 2-3 weeks in fresh (not salt) water, damp soil or mud) it is primarily transmitted through drinking or inhaling water containing the urine of an infected animal.

For this reason, lepto outbreaks tend to be clustered in small geographic areas, and are most likely to occur after flooding and overwhelmingly during September, October and November. Hunting and herding dogs, who are much more likely to drink out of stagnant ponds and such, are at highest risk.

So how serious is Lepto if the dog actually contracts it?
Like Lyme, it varies greatly from dog to dog.

Some infected dogs may be totally asymptomatic, while others become pretty violently ill within days, with high fever, and/or vomiting, excessive thirst and reduced dark-colored urine, generalized pain and often jaundice, because if not treated promptly, Lepto can attack and damage the liver and kidneys and cause death.

On the other hand, if diagnosed and treated promptly with common garden-variety antibiotics (usually a combination of amoxicillin and doxycycline) response is good and mortality in healthy adult dogs is low.

There is no data on the actual incidence of asymptomatic dogs testing positive for Lepto in the US as there is with Lyme, but a large human study in Nicaragua in 1999 revealed that over 70% of those testing positive for Lepto were totally asymptomatic; canine studies in Germany revealed a similar pattern in dogs. Once again, resistance to the disease may well be a function of the individual immune system.

So, assuming you decide not to routinely vaccinate your dog against Lepto, what do you do if your vet tells you there has been an outbreak in your area—are you stuck with vaccinating? *Luckily, the answer is no.*

At least three separate human trials have shown that 200 mg of our old friend doxycycline administered once a week will prevent Leptospirosis with over 95% efficacy.

And unlike the vaccine, which is only effective against 4 of the 240 strains, *doxycycline will protect against all of them*, and will also prevent shedding of the organism in the urine, which is a definite plus with a zoonotic pathogen. Given the fact that most vaccines—including rabies!—only have to produce an efficacy rate of 80% or better for FDA approval, doxycycline's 95% is pretty impressive.

In fact, the CDC recommends that Americans traveling to parts of the world where Leptospirosis is endemic begin a regimen of one 200 mg dose of doxycycline weekly, starting 1-2 days before arriving and continuing for the duration.

However, be apprised that most vets are not aware of the use of doxycycline as a prophylactic for Leptospirosis, and may simply think you're nuts.

To avoid this possibility, you may want to download and print the relevant information from the CDC and maybe the original NEJM publication yourself and bring it along to support your case—given the high possibility of adverse reaction to the vaccine, it's probably well-worth the effort. (Your vet may still think you're nuts, but at least you'll have some hard evidence-based medicine in your corner.)

To make that easier, links to the research on using doxycycline as a prophylactic for Lepto as well as the CDC's advice can be found in the Resources section at the end of this book.

Coronavirus, Giardia, Canine Influenza and Rattlesnake Vaccines

In the interest of not wasting anyone's time this section will be mercifully brief—the first one is another "vaccine in search of a disease" and any vet who actually recommends Corona vaccine ought to be viewed with suspicion.

The second two are not recommended by anybody except the pharmaceutical companies that manufacture and sell them. In other words, they all pretty much failed the AAHA's benefit/risk test, and there's no reason to risk overstressing any poor dog's immune system for this bunch.

The need for the last one, on the other hand, is entirely based on where you live and the number of rattlers the average Cockapoo is honestly likely to encounter, *because a rattlesnake bite can kill a dog.* Hunting dogs and Search and Rescue dogs working in rattlesnake country where the possibility of getting to a vet in a big hurry is problematic both fall into the "probably want to consider this one" category.

Because a lot of dogs do have an adverse reaction to it though, even when it's really needed the rattlesnake vaccine should always be administered by itself and never within 3-4 weeks of any other vaccines to lessen the risk.

OK, now that we've pretty much beaten the whole vaccine issue to death, let's move right on to the *other* area where you really need to educate yourself, because as with vaccination, the choices you make in this one from puppyhood on can also have a long-term influence on your Cockapoo's lifelong health and longevity. And that would be…

Parasites...Internal and External

Ok, let's face it, nobody likes parasites. We don't even like to *think* about parasites. And luckily, now that we have all these monthly pills and "topicals" we can easily protect our dogs with, we really don't have to think about them at all. *Think again.*

There's a growing body of evidence that all this stuff we've been merrily popping down our dogs' throats and squishing between their shoulder blades every month may, like over-vaccination, also be contributing to a lot of the health issues we're now seeing in dogs—everything from food allergies to autoimmune diseases to seizures. In fact, it is now pretty widely accepted than early exposure to these helminths are necessary to normal development of the IgE antibodies in the immune system, and a total lack of exposure contributes to development of allergies. (This is called the Old Friends Hypothesis.)

To begin with, way too many owners (and their vets!) erroneously view monthly heartworm (and systemic flea and tick products) as "preventative medicine" and routinely give them on a monthly basis year-round with little or no further engagement of the thought process.

This is unfortunately incorrect on several levels. **None of these products actually *prevent* fleas, ticks, heartworm or anything else from entering your environment or attacking your dog, nor are they really *medicines*, although the manufacturers certainly market them that way.**

(As their manufacturers are quick to point out, a couple of the avermectins also used as antiparasitics in humans are in fact approved as "drugs" by the FDA, but when *those exact same chemicals* are sprayed on cotton fields to kill bugs, they mysteriously become "insecticides" and are regulated as such by EPA...go figure.)

Technically, these products are heartworm and flea ***treatments,*** not preventatives, and marketing them as "meds" really borders on the unethical. **They are really just plain old *insecticides* which kill parasites that happen to be on (or in) the dog at that moment.**

Some of the flea and tick products also contain a *hormone disrupter* that prevents parasites from reproducing or maturing normally, but again, they don't *prevent* the flea or tick or worm from attacking your dog, and in clinical trials, they made close to 15% of the dogs in the study really itchy.

The most popular of these insecticides are a group of *macrolycyclic lactones* derived from the bacterium

Streptomyces avernitilis known as *avermectins,* and developed back in 1975 by scientists at Merck Laboratories from soil found on a golf course in Japan. Honest.

This group includes **ivermectin** (*Merial's Heartgard*), **selemectin** (*Pfizer's Revolution),* and **moxidectin** (*Bayer's Advantage, Fort Dodge's ProHeart*) as well as **milbemycin** (*Novartis's Interceptor and Sentinel)* .

Like most insecticides, they are all *neurotoxins*. In fact, that's how they all kill bugs—- they cause massive damage to their little bug nervous systems, resulting in seizures, coma and death.

What we count on is the fact that these neurotoxins do not readily cross the blood-brain barrier in *mammals.* But the key word here is "readily", which no one ever seems to notice.

According to their own manufacturers, "exposure at high levels" will produce all the classic symptoms of neurotoxicity (tremors, ataxia, seizures and coma) even in animals *not* carrying the MDR1 mutation (a gene found in several breeds that does not allow the dog to clear certain toxins from the brain). Gee, this would sort of indicate that they *are* indeed capable of permeating the mammalian blood-brain barrier, wouldn't it? And since researcher know that dogs with the MDR1 mutation *cannot clear these chemicals from their brains,* it's pretty obvious they're ending up there.

And unbelievably, the effects of chronic low-level exposure to avermectins has never been clinically studied in dogs *at all.*

The longest clinical trial appears to be a 24 month study on ivermectin (the active ingredient in Heartguard) performed decades ago…and that was *on rats*. No study has ever looked at the safety of monthly year-round use over a dog's lifetime. Ever.

And since these insecticides all end up in the liver sooner or later, it's probably NOT a coincidence that chronic liver problems and seizures started becoming a lot more common back in the 1980s, when dogs were suddenly exposed to these insecticides every month year-round for their entire lives.

(The incidence of seizures in dogs is inexplicably rising, and may well be linked to these chemicals.— even if they initially clear the brain, they can toxify the liver and result in seizures.)

So how do you safely protect your dog from heartworm?

Before automatically agreeing to monthly year-round treatment, it's good to know a little something about heartworms, and heartworm infestation, in dogs.

Unfortunately, most of the available information on this topic (including the brochures in your vet's office) comes from the American Heartworm Society, which is problematic.

A little casual research reveals that this organization, and its website, are in reality a marketing tool aimed at buyers and resellers of heartworm meds, and its sponsors are a *Who's Who* of drug companies. Fort Dodge (Wyeth), Merial and Pfizer are "Platinum Sponsors." Bayer merits Silver. Novartis, Schering-Plough, Virbac and Eli Lilly get Bronze. IDEXX, which is making a fortune selling heartworm tests, is also a sponsor. *Most of these companies have sales reps that regularly call on vets and show them how to sell you heartworm meds.*

Make no mistake about it, so-called "Heartworm Prevention" is Big Business, worth billions a year, and scaring pet owners is very profitable. Because of this, most information provided on heartworm by the drug companies "glosses over" some very important facts, *including what is actually required for transmission to your dog.*

So let's look first at the "natural" cycle of the heartworm, without the use of any insecticides:

- **To start the cycle, a *particular species* of female mosquito must bite a dog infected with circulating L1, which is the first larval stage in the life cycle of the heartworm, and ingest these larvae. The mosquito must then carry these larvae while they mature from the L1 stage to L2 and then L3, which takes 2-4 weeks and requires sustained day and night temperatures above 64 degrees. If the temperature drops below that at any point, the cycle is broken and the mosquito cannot infect another dog. (The manufacturers all know this— in fact, they funded the research at U.Penn. that revealed it!)**

- **Assuming the larvae (and the mosquito!) survive that long, the mosquito must then bite your dog, injecting the L3 larvae she picked up from the infected dog into the skin. If the dog has optimal immune function, the IgE antibodies on the mast cells will attack and kill all or at least most of them. (IgE antibodies were designed to deal with parasites, remember?)**

- Those that survive mature under the skin, where they will mature in 5-7 months into threadlike adults 2-3 inches long, eventually migrating to the arteries of the lungs. (In spite of their name, most heartworms are not in fact wrapped around the heart as shown in those photographs of severe infestations in the vet's office)

-

- If both male and female worms are present, they can reproduce. The larvae produced, called microfilaria, will circulate in the bloodstream, *but cannot mature into more adults within that dog.* They must complete part of their life cycle in a female mosquito.

- The adult worms will live around 2-3 years in the dog and then die of old age. Because of this, most heartworm infections are in fact self-limiting, and unless there are a whole lot of them or the dog's immune system is compromised, no symptoms will be seen in an otherwise healthy dog. (Most dogs who test positive for adult heartworms on an IDEXX test are completely asymptomatic.)

This is actually an elegant example of the symbiotic nature of the parasite/host relationship as designed by Mother Nature. Think about it...whether the designated host is a tree or an animal, there is absolutely no benefit to the parasite killing it, as that would also ensure its own demise. (As far as we know, there are no Kamikaze parasites.)

The "intermediary host" that many parasites employ— in this case the mosquito— helps keep the odds from tipping in favor of the parasite, as does the IgE "surveillance system" of a healthy host. The whole thing is a system of checks and balances, sort of like the three branches of the US Government we all learned about back in 8th grade Civics class.

In a well-functioning ecosystem, heavy parasite infestations, like infectious diseases, are generally limited to weak and old animals with compromised immune systems and serve a natural and necessary (if somewhat brutal) Darwinian function....which probably explains why parasites, like viruses, are still sharing the planet with us.

However, once the environment is out of balance,
the whole system of parasite checks and balances breaks down.

In a toxic environment, the immune systems on what would normally be healthy young animals often take the biggest hit. And without an immune system that's firing on all its cylinders, the dog is unable

Given the 60,000 made-made and mostly untested chemicals we've unleashed on the environment in the past century, this pretty much describes the situation in which most of us now live, which is why autoimmune disorders and chronic disease are rampant….and it's why very few owners (and fewer vets!) feel comfortable trusting in the natural balances designed by Mother Nature when it comes to infectious diseases and parasites.

So what we need to do is tip the odds back in favor of the host a little here, without adding to his toxic load any more than is necessary. And if the real goal of "heartworm prevention" is prevention of an *infestation of adult heartworms*, which can cause serious problems, let's look at what actual academic research shows:

- **Most adult heartworms actually reside in the pulmonary arterial system (lung arteries) for the most part, where the primary effect on the health of the animal is damage to the lung vessels and tissues caused by inflammation. They only occasionally migrate to the heart.**

- **According to the University of Pennsylvania, "If you live in the Northeast part of the USA you only need to give heartworm preventative from June 1 through November 1, since maturation of the heartworm larvae requires average daily temperature above 64° F for any one-month period. There is therefore NO need to give heartworm chemoprophylaxis year-round, unless administration between June 1 and Nov 1 is occasionally missed." (Although these dates vary given the particular area of the country one lives in, there are very *few* areas where the temperature never dips below 64 degrees at night.)**

- **Even if administration during that period is "occasionally missed", lapses of up to four months between doses of ivermectin-based products still provides 95% protection from adult worms. This is called the "reach-back effect" and is well-documented scientifically.**

- **"Reach back" is important because none of these insecticides kill 100% of the L3 larvae *even if administered monthly without lapses*—estimates actually range from 97 or 98%. And 97% effective does NOT mean 100% effective on 97% of dogs, it means the insecticide kills 97% of the larvae exposed to it. Big difference.**

It should be pretty obvious at this point that the *only* possible reason for giving dogs so-called "heartworm meds" every month year round in most of the US is a desire to bolster the coffers of the pharmaceutical giants who manufacture and sell them, and last time I looked, they didn't need much help in that department. (Vets, who buy this stuff wholesale from the pharmaceutical companies and sell it retail to pet owners are also making a boatload of money on it, which is the only possible reason for them to recommend dogs stay on it year-round, since the science just doesn't back it up as a practice.)

What About Heartworm Testing?

Heartworm testing is now recommended for dogs on year-round and seasonal heartworm programs. And since a small percentage of dogs on year-round heartworm treatment will still test positive, this would make sense —if there was an accepted heartworm treatment regimen for dogs who test positive, but currently there is not.

Immiticide (the arsenic-based treatment for heartworm infection) is currently only available for dogs with Stage 3 and 4 infection, who display symptoms of heartworm infestation. (It is generally recognized that Immiticide has a VERY low safety level, which may be why it's no longer automatically used on heartworm- positive but asymptomatic dogs.)

Weekly ivermectin will also kill adult heartworm, although more slowly, and some vets are now recommending that for asymptomatic dogs who test positive, sometimes with the addition of tetracycline. Some vets simply advise retesting in several months. Before agreeing to once or twice-a-year heartworm testing, it might be good to ask the vet what their treatment protocol is for asymptomatic dogs who test positive.

Other Internal Parasites

Since the avermectins are such effective broad-spectrum anti-helmitics, roundworms and hookworms are simply not as common as they used to be, even in puppies, and many owners will never encounter them. **Pyrantel pamoate** (Nemex) is still regularly used on young puppies, and it's been around a long time and has a pretty good safety record.

On the other hand, the one thing that the avermectins can't touch are **tapeworms.** Since the tapeworm requires the flea to complete its life cycle, any time you have even *a single flea*, a dog can end up with a tapeworm. The tapeworm will not show up in a fecal float like helminths— the ONLY way to diagnose it is to see tapeworm segments stuck to the dog's fur around his anal area or in his stool— they look like flattish grains of rice.

The insecticide of choice for getting rid of tapeworms is **praziquantel.** Until fairly recently, you had to buy it from your vet (Bayer's Droncit) and it cost a whopping $10 per tablet, but the patent must have run out or something, because you can now buy a generic version on Amazon for as little as a dollar per tablet. Praziquantel is praziquantel and there's really no sense paying ten times more than you need to.

External Parasites.... AKA .... Flea and Tick Prevention

Unlike helminths, there is no evidence at present that fleas and ticks serve any purpose other than to drive us crazy. Both are *ectoparasites*, which means they have a hard external skeleton. Both have been around longer than man and his canine buddy and both will undoubtedly be around long after we're gone, because they are both unbelievably tough and highly adaptable.

The real frustration has always been trying to find something that will poison fleas and ticks *without* poisoning us and our dogs.

For the last several years, once-a-month topical insecticides looked like the answer, but that premise is starting to be questioned—and by the EPA itself, no less, a government agency usually frustratingly slow to react when it comes to potential dangers from pesticides.

Given that, the fact that topical insecticides (this includes ALL of them rather than a particular brand) are currently under investigation by the EPA should be enough to give one pause. **This investigation began after EPA received some 44,000 (that's forty-four thousand) reports of adverse effects to topical insecticides in 2008 alone.**

And since let's face it, since hardly any of us even knew that adverse reactions to stuff like Frontline is supposed to be reported to *the Environmental Protection Agency* in the first place (or how to go about doing that), those numbers probably just represent the tip of a much bigger iceberg.

According to results of their preliminary investigation, the three systems most often affected were the skin, the intestinal tract and the central nervous system, with symptoms ranging from itching, chronic skin problems, vomiting and diarrhea all the way to seizures, coma and death.

Until they discover exactly what it is about these topical formulas that is causing these problems, owners who want to minimize risk to their dog's health might want to err on the side of caution and consider some safer alternatives.

One of the best pieces of advice from EPA (and which honestly wouldn't occur to most owners) is to bathe the dog IMMEDIATELY if he seems to be showing any adverse (or even odd) symptoms at all after his monthly treatment, using mild shampoo and lots of water. In other words, the sooner you get that stuff off the dog, the better—doing so may actually save his life. In fact, do it BEFORE you call the vet!

And in the "your tax dollar at work" department, here is some more advice from our friends at the EPA, copied pretty much verbatim from their website, with editorial comments in parentheses:

Discuss with your veterinarian whether topical flea treatments are even necessary for your dog. *(Note: If your dog doesn't actually HAVE fleas on him, the logical answer here is probably no. Killing fleas you don't have is a little like treating for malaria if you live in Duluth.)*

Vacuuming on a daily basis to remove eggs, larvae and adults is the best method for initial control of a flea infestation. It is important to vacuum the following areas: carpets, cushioned furniture, cracks and crevices on floors, along baseboards and the basement. *(Recent studies have shown that a plain old vacuum cleaner will remove around 95% of fleas in **all life stages** from the indoor environment, which is about as effective as most of the toxic insecticides currently available. Needless to say, these studies have not received a lot of press from the multi-billion-dollar Flea Industry...)*

Steam cleaning carpets may also help as the *hot steam and soap can kill fleas in all stages of the life cycle.* Pay particular attention to areas where pets sleep. *(Like vacuuming, steam cleaning is every bit as effective as the hormone-disrupting Insect Growth Regulators found in many flea products and a lot less creepy.)*

Wash all pet bedding and family bedding on which pets lie in hot, soapy water every two to three weeks. *(That's pretty self-explanatory.)*

Flea combs are very effective tools in the suppression of adult fleas. They allow hair to pass through the tines but not the fleas, removing fleas as well as flea feces and dried blood. Focus combing on those parts of the pet where the most fleas congregate, usually the neck or tail area. When fleas are caught, deposit them in hot soapy water to kill them. *(If a flea comb reveals no fleas or little black granules of dried blood called "flea dirt", odds are you have no fleas in your indoor or outdoor environment, and no need to expose your dog to unnecessary neurotoxins.)*

What the EPA clearly understands that most owners do not is that fleas and ticks are an *environmental* problem. What the monthly "preventatives" actually do is turn your dog into a four-footed toxic vacuum cleaner, gathering up any fleas or ticks that happen to jump onto him for a meal and either killing them outright or rendering them incapable of reproduction via toxins delivered through the animal's skin or bloodstream.

Unfortunately, this method by definition requires that the dog's skin or bloodstream be constantly infused with neurotoxic insecticides, some of which are harmful not only to the dog but to humans and the environment, and one of which has recently been linked to Hive Collapse, which is decimating the honeybee population in the US.

Natural Flea and Tick Repellants

Of course, the best way to prevent flea infestation in your home is to keep fleas the dog may encounter outdoors from jumping on him in the first place. That way they won't end up in the house. (The same is true of ticks, by the way.) What you need is a non-toxic flea and tick *repellant.*

The other advantage here is that you can spray down your dog when he leaves his own yard, which will help to keep your own yard flea and tick-free.

Essential Oils and Octopomine

And as it happens, Mother Nature has thoughtfully provided us with a fair number of them. They are found in many essential oils.

What these plant-based substances all do is interfere with the *octopomine neuroreceptors* of pheromone-driven insects and arthropods. Octopomine is sort of the insect version of adrenaline, and blocking the receptors for it causes quick death by CNS collapse. Insects are hard-wired to avoid these substances, all of which are aromatic. This is why they act as *repellants* as well as *insecticides*, and thus protect the plant from insect damage. It's an elegant example of Nature at her most brilliant.

And unlike most insecticides, octopomine is not toxic to people or dogs because mammals, fish and birds *don't have octopomine receptors.*

Most of these substances have been used effectively for literally thousands of years without poisoning the planet, and really only fell out of favor in the last 30 years or so, when the big chemical and pharmaceutical companies decided they could do better.
Unfortunately, as the toxicity of these made-made insecticides becomes more and more apparent, this is may well be another example of where "better is the enemy of good".

Along with others that may not smell as good (like neem oil and citronella, which a lot of people don't care for), the following more pleasantly aromatic essential oils have also been laboratory-tested and have been found to be both safe and effective in both repelling and killing both fleas and ticks:

- Cedar
- Lemongrass
- Peppermint
- Cinnamon
- Clove

All are FDA approved as human food additives, and are considered safe by the EPA when used as directed. (In other words, keep them out of the eyes and don't use them full strength on the skin)

Cedar oil, which has been used effectively for at least 3 thousand years as an insect repellant, is probably the overall winner here, as it's better than most at repelling ticks as well as fleas, although some owners claim peppermint oil is also effective on ticks. If you live in an area where ticks are a problem, that's worth knowing.

Non-toxic sprays and shampoos containing these essential oils are readily available commercially— you can find a wealth of them on Amazon if you search for "all-natural flea sprays" once you get there.

Most list their ingredients and you can sort of guess what they'll smell like based on that. Here are a few:

Barklogic—*gets good reviews, is primarily lemongrass and has a lemony aroma.*

Vet's Best— *another brand with good reviews, is peppermint and clove-y.*

PetNaturals — *this spray is a lemongrass/cinnamon combination that also gets high reviews.*

Natural Chemistry— *this whole line of shampoos and sprays work well and smell flat-out yummy.*

There are lots more to choose from— just read the reviews and choose one that fits your needs. Remember that buying a product online that *doesn't actually list its ingredients* can be a little dicey, though — neem oil, for example, is a very safe and effective natural insecticide but smells a lot like burnt peanut butter. (Most of these companies make both a shampoo and a spray. If you are going to go this "non-toxic" route, you will need both.)

In addition to these, a lot of dog owners swear by the whole line of **Cedarcide** products, which can be sprayed outside as well, and is a lot safer than most chemical insecticides people spray on their lawns.

In that regard, one of the oldest and safest products around for both inside and outside use is *20 Mule Team Borax*. Unfortunately, there appears to be a lot of confusion about it. In spite of what you often read on the internet, borax is NOT the same as boric acid, although boric acid is commercially produced from borax. Borax is a naturally occurring mineral (like salt) and is mined in California's Death Valley.
According to most chemists, borax is about as safe as table salt, and can keep fleas out of your house for up to a year. Go to Amazon and type in 20 Mule Team Borax and read the many, many reviews. (It is sold as a laundry booster and all-natural household cleaner, and works great for that, too!)

Making Your Own Flea and Tick Repellants

Of course, you can also make your own natural flea and tick repellant spray by simply adding a couple tablespoons of essential cedar oil to a spray bottle of water, and then adding a teaspoon or so of any of the other bug-repellant essential oils you happen to like….truth is, it's hardly rocket science and it's a lot cheaper that way if you're a "do-it-yourself" type. Here's a pretty easy "recipe":

Natural Flea and Tick Repellant

2 Tablespoons Cedar oil

1 Teaspoon Cinnamon oil

1 Teaspoon Clove oil

2 Teaspoons Vanilla extract

1 drop Dawn dish soap (keeps spray nozzle from clogging)

12 oz filtered or distilled water

Mix ingredients together in a plastic spray bottle and shake well before each use.

Spray head (cover eyes with your hand first), feet and legs and underside well. Lightly spray top of dog and work it into the fur with your hands, or brush through the damp coat, which is even better.

This spray can also be used on dog beds, furniture, baseboards and anywhere else you want to use it, checking upholstery fabric in an inconspicuous spot first to be sure it doesn't stain.

Remember, you want to spray the dog where fleas and ticks are going to jump on hitch a ride And adding a couple tablespoonfuls of cedar oil (along with a teaspoon or two of any other essential oils you feel like adding) to a bottle any shampoo will turn it into a safe and effective flea shampoo, although it's best to start with an unscented shampoo so you don't end up with something overwhelming. And always spray it on the inside of your arm before spraying it on your dog to make sure it's not irritating—if it is, pour some out, add more water and try again. And always keep it away from the eyes and mouth.

Now, unlike the once-a-month stuff, these sprays do have to be applied every day or two during the flea season, and you might want to spray your dog down again right before taking him for a walk in tick-heavy areas, but they really will repel fleas and ticks if used religiously, and they won't cause seizures or other weird side effects.

Besides insecticides that you actually put on or in your dog, the other major possibility for toxic exposure that the intelligent dog owner may want to consider is:

Lawn Chemicals

We all want a healthy, green lawn for our families to enjoy. But many people do not know that using synthetic lawn chemicals in your yard may increase your dog's risk of developing certain types of cancer.

A landmark 2004 study from Purdue University involving Scottish Terriers showed that dogs exposed to chemically treated lawns, specifically those treated with a chemical called **2,4-D** had a risk of transitional cell carcinoma (bladder cancer) 400% to 700% higher than that of dogs not exposed to these toxins.

An earlier study published in The Journal of the National Cancer Institute, a link was found between 2, 4-D and malignant lymphoma in dogs and non-Hodgkin's lymphoma in people, while a third study showed 2,4-D in the urine of dogs exposed to treated lawns.

This is probably not all that surprising when you consider that 2,4-D was one of the two primary components of *Agent Orange*, the jungle defoliant widely used during the Vietnam war and associated with a horrific number of immune problems, cancers, reproductive issues and birth defects in humans and animals exposed to it. Why it is approved for use on America's lawns is a total mystery.

Although most lawn care companies will try to convince you that their products are "safe for children and pets", there are a few things to consider before treating your lawn. First, they're only obligated to provide information on ***"Active Ingredients"*** in their products. This list leaves out the many ***"Inert Ingredients"*** also found in the products, many of which are known carcinogens or have documented health risks associated with them. One chemical that is often (amazingly) considered an inert ingredient is **2, 4-D** , the focus of the Purdue cancer study.

Dogs are at greater risk of exposure and potential side effects from lawn care chemicals because dogs do not generally wear clothes so chemicals get on fur and are more easily absorbed into the skin. Nor do dogs wear shoes -- lawn chemicals are absorbed through the paw pads, can be tracked into your home, and may be ingested when dogs lick their paws, as they often do. They also have a higher ratio of skin surface in relation to their body size, which gives them a proportionally larger surface area which can absorb toxins.

And dogs don't just walk on the grass— they roll in it, lay in it, sniff around in it and dig in it -- all opportunities to inhale, ingest and absorb more toxins than the average human would.

And last but certainly not least, in addition to walking on and playing in grass, Lord knows it's not uncommon for dogs to EAT grass while out in the yard, either intentionally or as part of all of the sticks

and other things that they chew on while outside. *Chemically treated grass was never meant to be eaten.* Even if you don't treat your own lawn, it's good to remember when taking him for a walk that your neighbors might treat theirs.

If you think your dog may have been exposed to "toxic grass", hose off his feet (especially the pads on the underside) after you get home. That way he won't end up tracking the toxins onto his bed or ingesting it if he licks his paws.

In summary....

OK, now you know that with the exception of classical genetic disorders over which you have no control, a whole LOT of how healthy your Cockapoo ends up is really up to you, and the decisions YOU make for him from puppyhood on.

Remember, in general, *less toxins equal better overall health*. Choosing a more "holistic" vet who is up to date on immunology and who understands the dangers of over-vaccination and automatic overuse of insecticides and antibiotics will make things a lot easier, because you won't have to argue with someone who's basically trying to sell you what are often *totally unnecessary* toxins.

That said, in spite of all efforts, your dog may find himself in need of emergency treatment at some point in his life, because of an accident or the ingestion of something not intended for ingestion. In these cases time is often of the essence, which is why you really need to do the following:

Post the phone numbers for your vet, the nearest emergency clinic
and the poison control center on the WALL instead of in your cell phone
so everyone in the house has easy access to them.

CHAPTER TEN:

The Well-groomed Cockapoo
(what you need to know to keep yours looking good!)

No matter what you may have read on the internet, the typical Cockapoo is a pretty *high-maintenance* breed, and this should be clearly understood before you commit to adding one to your household.

Breeders who "gloss over" the substantial grooming requirements of a breed in an effort to sell puppies do potential owners and the breed itself a disservice, and actually contribute to the numbers of dogs finding themselves in need of a new home.

And unfortunately, much of the well-meaning information on Cockapoo Coat Care available on the internet is pretty useless.

The main reason for this is because very few of these breeders started out showing and breeding Poodles, which have a very different coat (and very different coat-care needs) than most other breeds. Not surprisingly, a lot of these unique coat qualities are passed on to the Poodle hybrids, including the Cockapoo, which is one of the reasons people get them in the first place..

But because the very *thought* of Poodle hybrids sends experienced and knowledgeable Poodle breeders into fits of apoplexy, they are pretty disinclined to share their wealth of knowledge with the hybrid community at large, which is especially bad news for the breeders and owners of Doodles and Poos.

Here's an example;
Maintenance of the Poodle coat requires very specific combs and brushes to prevent matting, and virtually all Poodle breeders tend to swear by the same ones. But because they do not *share* this information, most Cockapoo breeders just recommend the ever-popular slicker brush, and most owners consequently use one to brush their dogs. *This is the worst possible brush for this coat.*
And because hybrid breeders rarely stress the importance of early table-training as Poodle breeders do, most Cockapoos are not table-trained at all when they get to the groomer's for their first appointment.

This inevitably causes the following all-too-common scenario:

The owner drops an adorable but shaggy Cockapoo off at the groomers in the morning, with explicit instructions for a bath, a brush-out and a trim, as well as instructions not to shave him or on any account "make him look like a Poodle", a possibility the owner has already been warned about by Cockapoo breeders and owners everywhere, and which is often construed as an insult by the groomer.

When the owner comes back to pick him up in the afternoon, she's presented with an exorbitant bill by an extremely grumpy groomer, who tersely explains that the dog was "matted to the skin", along with a shaved-down dog who looks like a cross between a naked Poodle and Mamie Eisenhower with a mustache.

The disgruntled owner, who swears the dog wasn't matted, adds her voice to the legion of owners badmouthing professional groomers.

Meanwhile the groomer, who's lost money by spending way too much time on a matted dog who's "not even table-trained", adds her voice to the legion of professional groomers badmouthing both all Poodle crosses *and* their owners, who they think are stupid people who "spent way too much money on a mutt".
(It's helpful to know that many professional groomers are purebred Poodle owners and breeders, and

many dislike Poodle hybrids on principle…so it's always good to ask how they feel about grooming hybrids before hiring the services of any groomer.)

This animosity between owners and groomers has gotten so bad that an alarming number of groomers will no longer take any new poodle crosses as clients. At any price.
And the real pity here is that this whole scenario could be easily prevented if hybrid breeders would do what all reputable purebred breeders of what we call "coated breeds" have done for years:

- Teach new owners exactly what it takes to keep the breed's coat conditioned and groomed.
- Provide a list of tools and products that work well on that specific breed.
- Explain the necessity of a thorough comb-out *at least once a week.*
- Explain the necessity for a grooming table and post.

Then professional groomers could do a great job in half the time even if the dog was only brought in once a *year* and everybody would be happy.

Since that's probably not going to happen any time in the foreseeable future, however, let's do the next best thing and honestly explain what's required to keep a typical Cockapoo looking good, and exactly what the owner needs to do and what tools are required, whether they want to keep him short, long, or anywhere in between. The same principles apply whether they plan to employ the services of a professional or want to learn how to groom their dog at home.

Since most owners are probably going to use a professional groomer, let's start there, because the basics are actually the same for both groups.

Avoid Disaster….Know the "Look" You Want

First off, if you are planning to have your Cockapoo groomed professionally, you have to decide exactly what you want the end result to look like so you can clearly communicate that. Groomers really DO want to please their clients (it's better for business and the tips are more generous), but they are *not* mind-readers, and most do not keep a resident psychic on staff.

Bring a photo to the first appointment….with a caveat.

Many websites suggest bringing a photo of the look you want along when you drop the dog off, and this is actually pretty good advice, except for one problem—*nine out of ten owners will bring a photo of a dog that (to the groomer's experienced eye) is pretty clearly several weeks out from its last grooming appointment.*

Faced with these photos, many groomers have concluded that (unlike the rest of their clients, whom they perceive as sane) what all these crazy hybrid owners really want are dogs who leave their grooming shops looking, well… *totally ungroomed*…which they simply cannot get their heads around.

I mean, *think* about it for a minute—odds are pro groomers *became* groomers in the first place because they personally *like* the looks of sculpted, plush, sort of "frou-frou" dogs. Remember… these are people who actually think little bright-colored satin bows stuck onto various parts of a dog's head with teeny-weeny rubber bands are *cute,* and photos of shaggy dogs romping on the beach just don't do anything for them.

So for Heaven's sake find a photo of a *freshly-groomed* dog that illustrates the length and overall pattern you want. Also make sure it's a dog with the same sort of coat that yours has—what works for a slightly wavy dog will be impossible to achieve with a curly one and vice-versa. **(The best thing, of course, is to take a full-body and a "face" photo of your *own* dog right after he's had a haircut you really like and bring that to all future appointments.)**

Unfortunately, unlike the Bichon or the Bedlington or the Dandie Dinmont, there is no immediately recognizable "official" trim pattern for the Cockapoo to be found in the classic grooming texts, which seriously complicates things for the self-taught groomer. (This is mostly because they have no history of being exhibited at dog shows, which is where the various trims that different breeds sport evolved over the years.) On the other hand, most grooming schools do teach students the Cockapoo "teddy bear cut".

That said, the one thing that *all* owners seem to agree on is that they do not want their Cockapoo to "look like a Poodle". So what does that mean?

In the US, all the different Poodle trims involve varying amounts of plush body coat in various (and seemingly random) places, but all of them require:

- A closely-clipped muzzle
- Closely-clipped feet
- A rounded "pompadour" on the top of the head or a topknot held with a band
- A round sculpted pompon on the tail.

Although a well-groomed Poodle is a work of art (the best groomers are really topiary sculptors whose chosen medium is hair), collectively this is *not* a look most owners seem to desire in a Cockapoo.

So what are some Better Cockapoo Trimming Options?

If you happen to like it, the clipped-down no-frills "sporting" look is far and away the easiest to maintain and probably best for people with allergies, because dogs in this clip can be bathed frequently with very little prep or finish work required. If your Cockapoo happens to be a merle, it's still going to stop traffic in this cut. (In fact, if this is the look you want for your dog, you can skip a lot of this chapter....!)

Virtually any groomer can take down a dog with a 10 blade, or you can buy a decent set of electric clippers and learn to do it yourself in no time flat, as there is not a great deal of artistry required—it's the canine version of the military buzz cut.

However, this utilitarian sporting trim is not every Cockapoo owner's cup of tea, and has reduced more than a few to tears when a dog actually comes out of the groomer's sporting it.

The "official" breed trim that actually comes the closest to what most Cockpoo owners seem to want is probably the pet trim for the Soft Coated Wheaten Terrier, with the only real difference in the trimming of the top of the head, the ears and the tail.

To see what this looks like, just Google "pet wheaten images" and you'll find lots of examples. In terms of wave and texture, the F1 Cockapoo and the Wheaten have very similar coats, and the overall squarish body proportions and angles are pretty similar as well, which is why this works. (The main anatomical differences are really in tail set and ears– although the head proportions and are pretty similar, most Cockapoos have more ear leather and the ears are set on lower on the skull.)

The basic pet Wheaten trim can vary in length, depending upon the owner's wishes, but in all cases it involves a shorter "jacket" on the body (either clipped with a 4 blade or ideally scissored) blended into slightly longer hair on the underbody and the legs, which are scissored in a column straight down to the toes, without shaving the feet.

Any professional groomer should know how to do this trim—just be sure and tell them to scissor the head into a "Benji" trim rather than a standard Wheaten show trim, and to leave a plume on the tail. Unless the groomer is completely inept, requesting a modified Wheaten trim will pretty much guarantee that your Cockapoo does not end up being mistaken for a clipped-down blonde Poodle.

Plush vs. Shaggy

Of course, what *some* owners really mean when they say they "don't want their dog to look like a Poodle" is simply that they don't want them to look overly "coiffed", because it is the shaggy, casually tousled appearance that attracted them to Cockapoos in the first place.

In reality, this is a difficult look for the majority of groomers to achieve, and virtually *impossible* to achieve with just a clipper, which is what most groomers use. Even with a snap-on comb attachment that leaves the hair up to an inch long, all the hair will be more or less the same length and the finish will be "plush" rather than shaggy.

No matter what pattern is used, the *only* way to achieve a shaggy rather than a smooth plush finish is by using a peculiar breed of scissors called a "chunker". In essence a one-sided thinning shears with very coarse teeth, they are also called a "texturing shears". Popular for some years with hairdressers for producing a "beachy" look, these are relatively new to the dog grooming world.

Although just starting to catch on, groomers who know about them love them, as do their clients, because they truly are capable of producing a more natural, shaggy-dog look while still taking off needed inches of hair. If that's really the look you want, request that the groomer use a chunker. If they don't know what you're talking about, find one who does, because the results will be worth it.

How often does a Cockapoo REALLY need to be taken to the groomer ... and what will it cost?

If you want to keep your Cockapoo in a fairly short trim (maybe between one to three inches), most groomers agree he will ideally need to be trimmed every 4-6 weeks or so, although many owners can stretch it out to 8 weeks if they are religious about brushing. The Poodle coat spends more time in the anagen, or growth, phase than most breeds— this translates to a really fast-growing coat, and most Cockapoos appear to have inherited that trait, especially the multi-generational ones.

If you do not want to brush your own dog at all but don't want to keep him really short, most groomers agree he should be taken to the groomer's *weekly*, because that's the bare minimum of how often the average one needs to be brushed out in order to avoid matting.

Currently, the cost for having a Cockapoo of typical size groomed runs between $30 and $75 per visit, depending on where you live. (Some groomers will give a discount to owners who bring their dogs in frequently, because it takes them significantly less time to groom these dogs, and groomers' fees are really based on the hours involved.) Spreading out the time between sessions rarely saves money in the long run, because the groomer will have to charge more if the coat has been neglected.

But any way you slice it, keeping your dog pretty short will quickly add up to hundreds of dollars a year and untold thousands of dollars over his lifetime if you plan to have him professionally groomed, so you need to factor that in before deciding to add one to your family.

Grooming Your Cockapoo at Home

Can you do it yourself? *Absolutely*. Anyone can learn to bathe and brush a dog. And if you have maybe two hours once every 4 to 6 weeks to put into the project, you can invest in two decent pairs of shears (one of which is the aforementioned chunkers) and learn to scissor your dog yourself to whatever length you prefer, which frankly is NOT rocket science.

Although your first efforts may produce less than stellar results, the soft wavy Cockapoo coat is both forgiving of scissoring errors and grows back with astonishing swiftness, so you'll have lots of opportunity to practice your technique. (A do-it-yourself trimming guide follows the sections on brushing and bathing because whether you have your dog trimmed professionally or do it yourself, that is the order that needs to be followed.) And all of the equipment needed to do the job will cost less than a single year's grooming bills.

The " Full Coat" Option

OR you can opt keep him in full length coat, in which case you can be prepared to literally stop traffic wherever you go. Although it also requires regular and thorough line brushing, which will take longer than brushing out a shorter coat (you can do it while you're watching TV), you will save thousands of dollars in grooming costs over the years. A dog in full coat will only need periodic "hygienic" scissoring of his feet, around his eyes and beneath his tail, which almost anyone can master.

If you have a particularly curly F1b or F2b dog, a full-length coat will tend to stand away from the body like a giant dandelion puff and probably isn't a great idea, but most F1 Cockapoos that look pretty curly cut down would only display a slight wave if kept in full coat, because the weight pulls out the wave in dogs just as it does in people. This look seems to be more popular in England for some reason.

And although no one ever believes this, a longhaired dog of any breed who's *never* had his coat trimmed will actually tangle and mat way less than one who has, because the hair is allowed to maintain its natural growth pattern of different lengths, which is lost forever as soon as it is trimmed to all one length.

Whether you decide to have your dog trimmed by a professional, or plan to do it yourself, and no matter what length you wish to keep him at, the average Cockapoo still needs frequent and thorough comb-outs *at least once a week,* and some of them (mostly F1bs) frankly need to be done daily, especially during the adolescent period when the coat is transitioning from puppy coat to adult coat. The frequency varies from dog to dog, but in general, softer coats with more curl will tangle and mat faster than straighter coarser ones, which can usually be managed with a thorough going-through once a week.

If mats never have a chance to develop, the process will be painless and relaxing and both of you will come to enjoy the grooming sessions. (A short daily grooming session will actually help to develop a strong bond between the groomer and the "groomee", and will make all other aspects of training easier.)

On the other hand, if you put it off, the combing out of snarls and mats will turn it into a long and painful chore for both of you, and *nobody* will enjoy it.

Using "the Right Stuff"

Whether or not you'll actually keep your dog mat-free depends to a large degree on how easy or difficult the job is. And that depends entirely upon having the right equipment. With "the right stuff", a thorough daily comb-out should not take more than 10 minutes tops for a well-trained puppy and *maybe* twice that long for an adult in a full coat. And if you really truly do it once a day starting from the day he arrives at your home, your dog will be well-trained in short order!

The equipment and the grooming techniques that follow are probably different than what you may have used previously, or even different than what most pet groomers use. That's because they are the tools and techniques "dog-show people" use to groom *their* dogs…you know, the ones you see floating around the ring at Westminster with flowing silky coats. (Trust me, those coats have *never* seen a slicker brush, and they've never been brushed out while the dog is standing on the floor.)

For years, the only place you could buy this stuff was from one of the big general supply booths at a dog show, but now pretty much everything else can be purchased online from Amazon and www.BBird.biz in one fell swoop. So without further ado, here it is….

The Quintessential Grooming Supply List

- **A grooming table and post.** *There is no way to overstate this: the grooming table is the single most important piece of equipment needed here. Besides saving your back and preventing your dog from up and leaving right in the middle of the grooming session, every professional groomer on the planet uses a grooming table, and they unanimously complain about the fact that "these damn designer dogs are never table-trained", which makes grooming take a whole lot longer... and for which you, dear reader, will pay dearly in hard cash. You can buy a grooming table on Amazon with a grooming post and loop for under a hundred dollars.*

- **A PSI wood-handled poodle comb.** *If this were the ONLY grooming tool you owned, your Cockapoo would be mat-free for life. Regular use of this comb from the roots to the ends will ensure a "fleece" of matted coat doesn't form at the skin, which is almost sure to happen with a slicker brush.*

- **A Chris Christensen 16mm T-brush.** *Even though a poodle comb really will suffice, most people will feel the need to "brush" their Cockapoo anyway. This brush is far and away the best one for the job. Well-made in Germany with smooth polished pins that won't damage the coat or scratch the skin like cheaper ones will, it has a smooth t-shaped wooden handle and an ergonomic shape that's far easier on the wrist than a traditional pin brush. It comes in two sizes— the large one works for most dogs, while the smaller "mini" is a better choice for their smaller cousins and puppies.*

- **A plastic spray bottle.** *As every dog-show groomer knows, brushing a dry coat is totally verboten if you want to avoid coat damage. Since damaged coats mat far more easily than coats that are not, it's well-worth the small effort involved in lightly misting the dog's coat each and every time you take a brush or comb to it— once you do get into the habit of doing this, brushing a dry dog will seem as wrong as driving off without fastening your seat belt! As far as what to* mist the coat with, plain water with a teaspoon of unscented conditioner or a couple drops of something like Silk Drops added will work just fine. Adding a couple tablespoonfuls of cedar oil will also repel fleas and ticks, so you can kill two birds with one stone here.

- **Detangler.** *A silicone-based detangler applied to mat and allowed to dry before detangling will make the job easier. Chris Christensen's Ice on Ice spray works well., as does Silk Drops , which is made for people and is available in drugstores, Walmart and Amazon.*

- **A guillotine-style nail clipper and a nail file or emery board.** *On a dog the size of a Cockapoo, the guillotine will work far better than the scissors-type with a so-called 'safety guard'. They can be purchased at any pet store or from Amazon. If used correctly (instructions are included later on) they are not scary at all, in spite of their ghastly name. A sturdy nail file or emery board will smooth the nail after clipping and avoid inadvertent scratches from an exuberant dog. It's a good idea to buy a little container of Qwik-Stop at the same time, which will stop any bleeding immediately if you accidentally do cut a nail a little too short.*

- **A box of cornstarch and a plastic parmesan cheese shaker.** *You can buy a box of cornstarch at any grocery store and the cheese shaker is another dollar store item. (You can also use cornstarch baby powder if you don't mind the scent, in which case you won't need the shaker.)*

- **Coconut oil and a bag of cotton balls.** *These will be used for cleaning the ears, which should be done every week or so. Coconut oil has great natural anti-viral, anti-bacterial and anti-fungal properties, and will actually help prevent ear infections.*

- **A good 7 or 8 inch straight hairdresser's shears or a good pair of chunkers.** *Pro-line makes a good pair of straight shears (best for curly coats) for around a hundred dollars, and if you don't use them for anything else or trim a sand-covered dog with them, they'll keep a good edge for a long time. For straighter and wavy coats, the chunker will allow you to achieve the "natural"* look most owners prefer, and is by definition very forgiving of errors as you perfect your scissoring skills. The Pro-line 7-inch chunker is a good choice. Its $139 dollar price tag might seem steep, but not when you consider you'll spend at least that amount in three grooming appointments. Don't even TRY to trim your dog with a cheap pair of scissors – a good pair will last for decades and you simply won't be able to do a good job if you try to save money here. You'll end up with a ragged-looking dog and a bad case of carpal tunnel syndrome.

- **A 5 or 6 inch straight shears with ball tips.** Breaking the rule here, this one doesn't really have to be all that good, because you're not cutting much with it, so if you need to save money, this is the place to do it. Don't go much under $15 or $20 though, or they'll get dull in a couple sessions and you'll be sorry. Even if you plan to have your dog trimmed professionally, you'll need this one for hygienic trimming around the eyes, butt and feet between times.

- **A bag of special "grooming treats", reserved for grooming only.** What's most important is that it's a treat he only gets when he's completed a grooming session, so he'll make the association and actually look forward to being groomed. It works—dogs who always get a treat after nail trimming will cheerfully offer up their paws rather than fight you.

And except for the grooming table, which folds up when not in use, all this stuff will fit in a basket that can sit on a shelf in the laundry room.

Notice that the "slicker brush" recommended on so many websites is NOT on this list.
This is not an oversight.

In fact, if you already own a slicker, *throw it out right now.* First off, it is REALLY painful….seriously, try brushing your *own* hair with one and I guarantee you that you'll feel guilty that you ever subjected your poor dog to it!
No wonder so many of America's dogs "hate being brushed" and won't hold still for it—if that's all they've ever been brushed with, you can hardly blame them. You'd run and hide, too—in fact, did you ever wonder why if it's so great they don't make a brush like this for *people*?

Unless you want to cause serious skin abrasion by really digging in, there is absolutely no way a slicker, with that stupid bend in its scratchy wire bristles, can get all the way to the root of the hair, which is why so many dogs come into the groomer's brushed on the outside and literally felted at the skin. This requires that they be sheared down like a Suffolk sheep in the spring, because that's the only way the groomer can get under the felt, and *nobody ends up happy*.

As if *that* isn't bad enough, the slicker roughs up the cuticle on the hair shaft, which damages the hair and actually *causes* future mats. Next to the retractable leash, the ubiquitous slicker brush is the worst thing to ever happen to dog ownership. Allowing a brush that looks like it was designed for scrubbing a barbeque grill anywhere near a dog just makes no sense at all.

It's probably not a coincidence that internet grooming instructions that involve the use of a slicker are invariably written by people who also misspell the word "mat", which ought to tell you some-thing...it's not a "matt", folks. It's a mat, like a doormat.

The other item intentionally missing from the list is a mat-splitter.

Another perfectly awful invention inflicted on the unsuspecting pet-owner, it's far better to learn to untangle a mat using a detangler spray, your fingers and cornstarch or baby powder. If a mat cannot be teased apart (and almost any mat can be), it's really better to just use a scissors blade as explained further on. Like slickers, mat-splitters and so-called "mat rakes" are hard on the coat and painful for the dog, and will also cause him to hate being groomed. It also makes the groomer lazy.

Line Brushing

Ok, now that you have all the right equipment, it's time to learn to *line brush*. Before you can do it, though, you need to train your puppy (or adult if you're starting late) to lie on his side on the grooming table while being brushed, because that will allow you to easily get to the parts that are most likely to mat. It's really the ONLY way to line brush, no matter what size the dog.

There are two ways to teach a dog to lie on his side on a table (or anywhere else)—the hard way and the easy way. What follows are instructions using the easy way. All that's really required is knowing right from left:

Table-Training 101

1. *Set up your table* with have your supplies close at hand.

2. *Lift your puppy onto the table* with his head to your left and his tail to your right.

3. *Now lie him on his side.* Here's the easy way: Wrap your left hand around his right foreleg about halfway up (this is the leg farthest from you!) and your right hand around his right hind leg and pull gently towards you while saying "Rufus, side" (unless of course his name isn't Rufus, in which case you'll want to use his own name so as not to confuse him) in a firm and cheery voice. Voila! In one fell swoop your dog will end up lying flat on his right side with his feet facing you. He'll also be pretty surprised if he's never done it before, so you'll want to praise him like mad for learning this new trick.

4. *Now, as soon as he's on his side and before he has a chance to scramble back up, take your left arm and lay it firmly across his body.* Put your elbow at his point of shoulder, your forearm across his ribcage and your palm flat on the point of hip.

5. *With the brush in your right hand, GENTLY brush over his feet, legs and body.* Pick up each leg and brush lightly between them. (The goal here is not to thoroughly brush him so much as to get him used to being brushed while he's lying on his side.) Be sure and tell him what a good boy he is while you're doing it, because you want the whole experience to be positive. If he starts to get up, a quick tug on both of the right legs will put him neatly back on his side without having to wrestle with him. Repeat the "side" command while you're pulling and praise him when he's back on his side.

6. *When you've gone over his left side with the brush, do the same with the other side.* The easiest way to do this is to allow him to stand, turn him all the way around so his head is facing in the other direction and repeat step 3, this time with your left hand around his left hind leg and your right hand around his right foreleg as you give the "side" command, remembering to praise him

lavishly when he's on his side once more. (This time when you lay your arm across him your elbow will be on his hip and your palm will be on his shoulder.)

7. *Once the second side is done, stand the puppy up and slide his head into the grooming loop.* Tell him to "stand" and "stay". Quickly brush his head and ears and brush the body coat down. Pick up his feet one by one, examine them, and put them back down. Finish off with his special grooming treat, praise him lavishly, tell him he's gorgeous, and lift him down.

The whole process shouldn't take more than a couple minutes, and even an 8 week old puppy can learn this in a couple lessons.

In fact, the "side" command can be used any time you want your dog to lie on his side – in case this hasn't occurred to you, it's the first step if you want to teach a dog to roll over.

"Stand" is another fairly easy command- it basically means don't go anywhere and don't sit down. Even the most dim-witted show dog learns this one with very little effort, so it should be no problem for *your* genius puppy. In both cases, it's good to practice these commands in lots of different places both indoors and out, lest the dog think they are only required on a table.

It goes without saying that even if your dog has the "stay" command down pat, no dog should EVER be left unattended on a grooming table, especially if he is attached to the grooming post— groomers don't call that loop that slides over his head a grooming "noose" for nothing!

Now, once your puppy understands the "side" command and will stay there on his own, you can actually begin line brushing.

Line Brushing Step by-Step

1. *With the dog on his side, begin by misting lightly all over.* Now brush all the hair in the opposite direction of its natural growth—in other words....up.

2. *Start with the hind foot.* Mist the whole leg lightly, then take your Poodle comb and comb a small section back down, being sure to comb all the way from the root to the end. As soon as

that layer's combed through, part off another layer maybe two inches above the first one with the last tooth on your comb (or a knitting needle if the coat is full-length) and then comb that one down, adding it to the bottom layer. Keep adding layers until the rear leg is combed through all the way to the spine.

3. **Lift the leg slightly and comb out the inside of the opposite leg.** Keep your left arm across his body with firm but gentle pressure, Any time he starts to right himself, a slight tug on the offside leg will neatly put him back on his side without a wrestling match. (This quick movement will become second nature in short order.) Comb through the tail while you're back there.

4. **Move next to the ribcage area.** Start by combing out the first layer on the tummy from elbow to the already-combed-out hindquarters, adding layers as you go until you've combed everything up.

5. **Move on to the front foot.** Using the same technique, add layers until you've combed down everything from foot to the spine, including the whole shoulder area.

6. **Lift the leg you just brushed and comb through the inside of the opposite leg, and then comb through the chest area between the front legs.** Make sure you have carefully combed out the area inside the elbow— that's a prime area for mats to form because the coat there rubs against itself with every step the dog takes. That hair can actually be trimmed short if you want.

7. **Turn the puppy around so his head is facing in the other direction, lie him down on his left side, and repeat the whole process.**

8. **Put your puppy on a sit-stay and slide the grooming loop over his head.** Adjust the slide so he can't back out of it. Now comb through his ears, neck, head and muzzle. (This is also when you'll want to clean ears, brush teeth and trim nails, all of which should be done weekly.)

9. *Stand him up (giving him the "stand" command), mist the coat lightly all over and brush the entire coat down with the pin brush.*

10. *Praise lavishly.* Give him his grooming treat, and lift him off the table. Take him outside to relieve himself, and then spend at least the next 5 minutes doing fun stuff with him.

If you actually follow the directions for line brushing on a daily basis, you will never need the following instructions, because your dog will go through life mat-free. But since life often gets in the way of our best intentions, odds are sooner or later you're going to hit a snag.

What we call "mats" are really nothing more than tangled-up hair, some of which is probably attached to the dog's skin and some of which is not. Here's how to untangle it::

Detangling a Mat Step-by-Step

1. *Don't pull. Stop combing immediately.* Spray the area lightly with detangler and let it dry while you brush somewhere else.

2. *Take your shaker and sprinkle a little cornstarch or baby powder on the tangled area and work it in well with your fingers.* This will help untangle the mat by smoothing the roughed-up hair cuticles or something. (Never mind why—it just works.)

3. *Using only the thumb and index fingers of each hand, tease the mat apart bit by bit, always pulling sideways, until it looks more like a dust bunny than a mat.* Rub in more cornstarch as needed. (For some reason, this sideways pulling is not painful for the dog at all.)

4. *Pinch the area firmly at the roots. Now take your comb and use only the very last tooth to split the mat into small sections if needed.* You can also saw through it, using the blade of your opened scissors, sawing gently out from the root to the end. Remember to keep the scissors open and SAW rather than cut (don't use your chunkers here, nor your ball-tipped scissors. A cheap scissor will do, fine here, and some groomers keep one around just for this.

5. Comb through the area with short strokes in stages, starting with the ends and working your way toward the root. Finish by brushing through it with the pin brush if needed.

NOTE: This method will painlessly remove most "garden variety" mats—you can untangle a mat the size of your fist using this method if you have the time and inclination without causing pain or losing any hair that's still attached to the dog.

However, it WILL NOT work when the dog is matted in a "fleece" all over about a half-inch from the skin, so don't even try. That condition is almost always caused by improper brushing (usually from using a slicker brush) and the only painless cure for it is an electric clipper and a ten blade. If it happens, it's not the end of the world…your Cockapoo will just look like a big shaved rat with long legs for a few weeks, and you'll know enough so that it won't ever happen again.

Bathing the Cockapoo

Many websites state that Cockapoos "don't need frequent bathing". *I guess that depends on what you want your dog to smell like.*

Besides the doggy odor, dirty dogs mat faster than clean ones, and will carry more of the *Can f* proteins that cause allergic reactions, so if you got the dog for his hypoallergenic qualities, failing to bathe him frequently will be entirely counterproductive.

Most Cockapoos who live in the house (which hopefully is all of them!) need to be bathed twice a month, although once a month may suffice. This can be done in the bathtub or shower with a handheld spray attachment or outside with the hose if it's hot enough. (Although most Cockapoos, courtesy of their sporting ancestry, like cold water well enough to swim in it, an outside hot/cold faucet will be appreciated at bath time.)

Besides a source of water and a drain, here's what you're gonna need to do the job right

- **Shampoo and cream rinse.**   *If one of the reasons you got a Cockapoo in the first place was because of allergies in the family, it's pretty dumb to cover him in shampoo and conditioner that's loaded with chemicals and artificial scents that provoke allergies.   There are now lots of brands to choose from if allergies are a problem. **Pawganics** makes a line of non-toxic hypoaller-*

genic unscented dog shampoos and conditioners that are available on Amazon. If you want to turn it into a non-toxic flea shampoo, simply add two tablespoons of cedar oil to the shampoo and shake well. If allergies are not an issue, the **Chris Christensen** line of products are hard to beat, and beloved by show people everywhere. You can buy them online from their website, chrissystems.com. (Along with their shampoos and conditioners, their **Ice on Ice Detangler** is a total winner.

- An Absorber synthetic drying chamois or two and/or a couple of old bath towels. Once you've used an Absorber to dry your dog, you'll never go back to regular towels. Way better than chamois cloths, they are more like big (like 27 x 17 inch) extraordinarily thin sponges and are the best idea to come out of Japan since the compact car. Actually made for drying cars, they will take a ton of water off a dog and can be squeezed out and used over and over until the dog is nearly dry. If you buy two, you'll think of lots of cool things to do with the second one. You may not even need the bath towels, although you can use one to finish him off if it makes you feel better. The Absorber can be purchased on –where else?– Amazon for under twelve bucks.

- A Hair dryer on a stand   Unless you live somewhere very hot and dry, air-drying your dog year-round is probably not practical, and waiting "until the weather warms up" to give him a bath isn't a great idea if you happen to live somewhere like Duluth, when that could be awhile. What everybody eventually figures out is that it takes three hands to dry even a well-trained dog, so you need a dryer on a stand.   A "table-top stand dryer" is useless for the average Cockapoo, because there's not enough room on the table for both the dryer and the dog, and it'll only dry his feet and his legs in its little stand, so you have to pick it up to get the high parts, which sort of defeats the purpose.   You need a FLOOR-stand dryer.   **The Rolls Royce here is the Oster Hi-Velocity Stand Dryer.** Rock-solid, it will last forever and adjusts to every position needed to dry every conceivable part of a dog of any size with little effort. It's as good as a dryer can get. It also retails for around six hundred dollars. If that's more than you want to

202

pay for a doggy hair dryer, all is not lost. For a mere $12.95 you can buy a "Jobar Hair Dryer Stand "from Amazon to which you can attach your very own hand-held hair dryer made for people. You'll save mucho dinero and still have both hands free.

OK, now that you have the right stuff, it's time to bathe. Although this seems like it should be pretty straightforward, the truth is 99% of people actually do it *wrong*, and cause the coat to mat.
This is why even when he's been brushed out beforehand, you'll often encounter snarls when blow-drying that seemingly *appeared out of nowhere*. They didn't…you created them your veryownself by incorrectly bathing! Here's how to do it right, start to finish, in Eight Easy Steps:

Cockapoo bathing 101

1. **Wet the dog thoroughly and pour the shampoo down the spine from head to tail.** Re-spray the shampooed part lightly and comb the shampoo through the dripping coat with your fingers only in the direction that the hair grows. Do NOT mash the hair around every which way to spread the shampoo – that's what causes matting, because the cuticles of each hair are softened and open at this point and will snag on each other when you do all that mashing around.

2. **Add more shampoo to the legs,** applying some at the top of each leg and combing it down the leg with your fingers from top to bottom, again without smooshing the hair up and down like you're scrubbing socks on a washboard.

3. **Do basically the same thing on the head, ears and neck,** finger-combing the shampoo through in the direction the hair naturally falls, and then shampoo the tail, adding the shampoo along the top and finger-combing it down through the feathering.

4. **Rinse thoroughly and apply the conditioner** using the exact same technique.

5. **Squeegee off the excess water with your hands and then use your Absorber to remove as much water as possible,** again wiping firmly in the direction the coat grows rather than "against

the grain" or around in circles. As soon as the absorber is pretty wet, wring it out and go over the dog again as many times as needed. Run it down each leg from top to bottom several times, wringing it out as needed. You can do this while he's still in the laundry tub or shower, which will keep everything (including you) a lot drier.

6. Once you have him at least halfway dry, cover him with the dry towel and BLOT, don't rub. If you're going to let him air-dry, run the Poodle comb through and set him free. Otherwise go to Step 7.

7. Spread the other towel on the grooming table and lift the dog onto it, sliding the grooming loop over his head. Turn on the dryer to low and use your pin brush or comb to fluff the coat as you dry it in sections, rather than all over. A lot of it can be done while he's sitting, or even lying down. Give him the "stand" command to finish the underside.

8. Reward with his special "grooming treat" and take him outside to play for a couple of minutes. Be sure and tell him how gorgeous he is!

Drying a dog under a dryer will pull out some of the wave, and it will produce a "fluffy" finish, at least for a day or so. Air-drying a dog will leave in a lot more wave; many "wavy" Cockapoos will look pretty curly if they're trimmed down to a couple of inches and air-dried.

Cockapoos in full coat who are air-dried often display the "rick-rack" effect you get from a crimping iron, but at least the coat will lie flat rather than looking like an overgrown dandelion puff. (To get that "show dog" look with a dryer on a long-coated dog you need to lay him on his side and line-brush as you dry, blowing *down* on the coat, rather than *up,* and brushing down rather than fluffing as you go.)

If it's breezy and warm, most dogs will be fine air-dried. If it's cool and/or damp out, using a dryer really is kinder. One compromise is "cage-drying"— you can set up your dryer, and maybe a fan, to blow on the dog in his crate (this only really works with a wire crate!) which will speed things along. When he's mostly dry, finish him with a brush on the table. You *really* need to be around when you do this, however, for safety reasons— never, *ever* leave an unattended dog in a crate with a dryer!

Trimming Your Own Dog

One of the main advantages of trimming your dog yourself is that you can scissor the coat to *whatever length you like* as often as you like, instead of the dog spending a third of his life much *shorter* than you like and another third much *longer* than you like! You can take an inch or so off whenever needed in an hour or less, which will keep him pretty much looking the same all the time.

These instructions are for scissoring only. Using a clipper is an entirely different technique. It's best to learn to scissor first, and then, once you're comfortable, reasonably proficient and committed to grooming your dog yourself, invest in a good clipper IF you decide you need to do a faster job, or want to keep your dog in a really short sporting clip.

(The reason professional pet groomers mostly use an electric clipper is because it's *faster*, and for a pro groomer, time is money. It's *not* because it does a *better job* than a scissors, which is what the "perfection-oriented" show groomers use.)

And if you decide to buy a clipper to try it, a fifty-dollar "home pet clipper set" is just not going to do it— you'll be lucky to get through halfway down the back before it heats up and bogs down. You'll need a decent professional-quality 2-speed clipper like the Oster Golden A-5 or the Andis AGC, and then you'll need a couple of extra blades (like a 4 F and a 7F) and maybe a set of steel combs because the 10-blade that comes with them will only leave 1/16 of an inch of hair, so by the time you're done you'll have well over $200 in the project.

Contrary to popular belief, unless to plan to keep him in a buzz cut, learning to use a clipper is actually *harder* than learning to scissor, because you can make really big holes in the coat in a heartbeat if the dog moves at the wrong time, and clipper burns (the mark of the inept) are downright painful for the dog. Besides, scissoring is much quieter and way more fun!

Now, until pretty recently, unless he was pretty curly, scissoring any dog took a fair amount of skill and practice if you didn't want him to look like it had been trimmed by a first-grader. That changed with the scissors known as a "chunker". By definition, this scissors will leave a feathered edge that looks natural (unlike the "plush" look an electric clipper produces) and it's very forgiving of mistakes. It is the PERFECT scissors for the slightly wavy coat typical of the F1 Cockapoo. (Curly dogs really do not need a chunker, although it works fine on them too.)

Using a Scissors...the Right Way

Before you start cutting on your dog, it's best to take a minute to practice with your scissors because nine out of ten people hold a scissors wrong, and unless you are a professional hairdresser, odds are pretty good you're one of 'em.

Here's how to use a grooming scissors correctly, assuming you're going to cut with your right hand:

- *Slide your right thumb in the hole that does NOT have a finger rest attached to it.*

- *Put your RING finger through the other hole, resting your pinkie on the finger rest.*

- *Turn your wrist so that the blade controlled by your thumb is on the bottom.*

- *Now move your thumb (and only your thumb!) to open and close the lower blade ALL THE WAY, while keeping the top blade still.*

Holding the scissors correctly will keep you from dipping into the coat and making choppy little cuts with the last two inches of the blade (which is what happens when you use your thumb and index finger the way your kindergarten teacher taught you) instead of making long smooth cuts with the whole blade. Practice doing this until the motion becomes both comfortable and second nature.

If you're using a chunker, there's actually a video by grooming maven Barbara Bird demonstrating the use of a chunker on a dog that's well-worth watching before you start—just go to YouTube, type in "GroomClassroom" and scroll down until you get to the video titled "Cool Tools for Pet Grooming". A picture is truly worth a thousand words here.

(Barbara's grooming blog also has lots of wonderful information and photos on it, including stuff on grooming hybrids, including Cockapoos.)

Until you and your dog are more experienced, it's good to have an extra person (a spouse or a large child works well) to help hold him, otherwise you'll just have to use your grooming post and the "stand" command, which you WILL have practiced beforehand if you're smart.

Note: If you're left-handed, follow these instructions as written, replacing "right" with "left" and "left" with "right", which you're probably used to by now. Don't even bother to look for left-handed chunkers.

Scissoring a Cockapoo, Step-by-Step
(these instructions will actually work for any Poodle cross)

choose length and start trimming here

Add length toward bottom

With the dog standing on the table with his head to your left, lift the hair along the spine just behind the shoulders with your Poodle comb, which you should be holding in your left hand. Decide how long you want the hair to be, and with the scissors in your right hand, start cutting from the shoulders toward the tail at that length, keeping the scissors parallel to the spine and remembering to use the whole blade. (Instead of the single cut you'll make with a plain shears, you will need to make two or three rapid cuts with the chunker, moving the scissors very slightly each time to create a natural feathered finish to the hair.) Lift each area with the comb before you start cutting. Trim until you've got a swath about four to six inches wide cut down the back all the way to the base of the tail that's the length you want. Now "fluff and comb" through the whole area in the direction the coat grows to remove any cut hair that didn't fall off and touch up where needed.

With the scissors pointing down, start moving down the side of the rump closest to you, remembering to fluff the hair with the comb before each cut. Trim this hair to approximately the same length as the back. Make sure the tips of your scissors are not dipping in to the coat, and that you are cutting with the entire length of the blade.

Still working with the scissors vertically, move down the leg, trimming all the way around and making a straight column to the foot, leaving this hair slightly longer than the "jacket". Blend the coat at the elbow to get a smooth transition between the jacket and the leg. (This is easier than it sounds.)

Brush the hair around the foot straight down and pick up the foot, wrapping your hand around it. With your straight scissors, trim off all the hair that sticks out below the foot, and trim any excess hair between the pads. (Use your little ball-tipped scissors to do the pads.) When you put the foot back down, you should have a nice round circle with maybe a tuft or two sticking out. Starting with the blade of your straight shears nearly flat on the table, tip it up about 45 degrees and trim neatly around the foot. The resulting angle will make the dog appear "well up on his toes".

Next move to the ribcage, and work your way down that area (again keeping your scissors pointed down), fluffing as you go. To maintain the proper outline, you want to leave it a little longer starting about halfway down the ribcage. Now working with your scissors parallel to the table, trim the underside, blending it into the sides and leaving enough length behind the ribcage to avoid a "poodley" or "greyhound" look. (In other words, you don't want to carve a lot of tuck-up under the loin.)

Move to the shoulder and trim the front leg pretty much as described in section 3. Lift the front foot and trim the same way as you did the back one.

Working from the head down, trim the neck, throat and chest, taking the throat and neck area down to the length of the back and leaving the hair slightly longer as you move to the chest. (Remember, you can always shorten an area afterwards, but you can't put hair back on!) Lift the ear and trim the entire area under it, blending into the neck.

Now stand back and check out what you've done so far. Make sure the line of the back is level, and neaten up the outline. Turn the dog around, and repeat the process on the other side.

Now check your work from the front and the rear, to make sure both sides match, trimming as needed down the shoulders, hips and sides of the legs to get there.

Trimming the tail

Natural (undocked) tail:

- **Stand the dog up and brush through the tail** from root to tip. Now scoop all the tail feathering near the base into your hand, slide your hand all the way out to the tip and hold the tail out straight behind him.

- **Trim off everything in your hand** that extends beyond the end of the tail about an inch from the tip. Now comb the feathering down and trim it into an elongated triangle from base to tip at whatever length you prefer.

- **Use your ball-tipped scissors to trim** the first inch or so on the underside of the tail. **Carefully trim around the anal and genital areas** for hygienic purposes. (This ideally needs to be done every couple of weeks even if you are having your dog professionally trimmed.)

Docked tail:

Because the Cockapoo is descended from two breeds whose tails have been traditionally docked, some breeders still dock the tails on their Cockapoo puppies, although it is becoming less and less common.

A docked tail is generally trimmed fairly short all the way around like a Cocker's, leaving no more than an inch at the end, neatly rounded. Pompoms are generally avoided.

The Classic Cockapoo Head Trim

First decide what length you want here, and keep a photo handy- tape one to the wall (a photo taken from the angle shown is most helpful) so you can look at it as you work. You'll get better results if trim the whole head at once rather than one side at a time, so you want the dog facing you dead-on for this part. He can be sitting down for this.

- *Lift the hair on the top skull with your comb and trim it to the desired length, starting at the center of the head between the eyes and working front to back, trimming in an arch that follows the line of the skull rather than straight across. Now lift the hair between the trimmed area and the ear to your left with your comb. Turning your scissors so the tip is pointing to the ear, blend this hair into the top of the ear, again working in a curve rather than straight across.*

- *Next, brush the hair on the muzzle and beard, brushing toward the nose. Using your chunkers so that you get a natural finish, trim it to the desired length, trimming in a half-circle on each side rather than chopping it straight across. Some owners prefer to shorten the hair more around the jaw behind the muzzle, while others prefer a fuller face—there's no rule here, so go with your personal preference...you can always start fuller and remove more later if you like.*

- **Now, using your ball-tipped scissors with the tip up rather than down, trim the hair between the eyes into an inverted V shape.** *(It helps to cover the dog's eye with your left hand as you're doing this on each side, as it will keep him from jerking back.)*

- **Trim the bangs to the desired length,** *always working in a half-circle shorter in the center and longer toward the ears to avoid the Mamie Eisenhower look.*

- **Trim the ears to the desired length** *with the chunkers, making a rounded curve rather than a straight-across cut.*

OK, you're done! Remember to give your newly gorgeous dog his special grooming treat, praise him lavishly for being such a great dog, compliment him on his good looks and take him out to play fetch for a couple of minutes.

It's also good to remember that, depending on your own temperament and the patience of your four-footed buddy, this trimming does not have to be done in one marathon session (although it really shouldn't take more than an hour tops once you've done it a couple times) but can be broken up into several sessions.

As with regular grooming, the important thing is to keep it from becoming a drag for the dog. And the best way to accomplish this is to *talk* to him while you're snipping way or combing...unlike everyone else in your life, *here's a friend who never tires of the sound of your voice.* He thinks you're brilliant, witty and the smartest person on the planet and your voice is music to his ears. Tell him about your job, or your love life, or practice chatting to him in a foreign language—at least he won't laugh at your accent! If you can carry a tune, you can sing the entire score of The Sound of Music while you're grooming. Come to think about it, you can do that even if you *can't* carry a tune...odds are good he's never heard Julie Andrews anyway, so he'll have nothing to compare it to.

"Grooming" Involves More Than Hair

In addition to an attractive tangle-free coat, a well-groomed dog also has clean ears, clean teeth and short nails. These are all things that you can and should tend to between regular haircuts, to avoid problems down the road.

Routine Dental Care

A mere decade or two ago, anyone who suggested actually *brushing a dog's teeth* would have been widely considered certifiable. Today it's an integral part of responsible 21st century dog ownership.

Vets now suggest periodic professional cleanings at least once or twice a year (at $250-$500 a pop, depending on where you live), and there are now a wealth of doggy toothbrushes, special doggy toothpastes and doggy mouthwashes on the market, all of which you are supposed to use daily to prevent *periodontal disease*, which vets claim are associated with a host of other life-threatening diseases in dogs.

Is this just a new way for vets to make more money, or is it truly necessary for a dog's health and well-being? After all, dogs went for thousands of years without dental care and survived just fine. Unlike people, dogs don't even get *cavities*. And as older dog owners know well, not too long ago most dogs died of old age with all their teeth intact; simply gnawing on bones kept those teeth shiny and white. *Not so much any more.*

Veterinary data reveals that periodontal disease is now the most common disease found in dogs, and affects an astonishing 80% of dogs over the age of three.

OK, it appears this dental thing is pretty clearly not hype. So what's going on?

A wealth of new evidence now suggests that periodontal disease in both man and beast is an *autoimmune disorder.* Really.

Basically, what happens is the same old bacteria that have always adhered to the teeth and formed plaque are now causing an inappropriate response by the immune system (sound eerily familiar?), which then overproduces cytokines like *TNF-alpha* and *interleukin 1 beta*, probably not coincidentally the same pair also involved in allergies.

Ordinarily important for healing, in excess these cytokines produce inflammation and ultimately destroy the *periodontium*, the tissues that support the teeth. It's that same inability of the immune system to distinguish between self and non-self that is the hallmark of all autoimmune diseases.

This also explains the association between periodontal disease and heart and other organ problems that have been noted. It's not so much that periodontal disease causes heart and liver problems, but that all of them are caused by the same *underlying inflammatory processes.*

Armed with this new knowledge, it should be pretty obvious that the BEST way to avoid periodontal disease is *to protect your dog's immune system in the first place* through careful choices in food, vaccination and anti-parasitic regimens, rather than trying to use band-aid solutions to treat the symptoms of an autoimmune disease after the immune system is overstressed by environmental factors

That said, brushing your dog's teeth is not a bad idea, and if you want to do it, by all means have a go—just make sure and use toothpaste made especially for dogs, because fluoride is toxic and dogs can't spit.

The main problem with doggy tooth brushing is that most dogs hate it and most owners don't really *do* it— they mostly just buy the toothpaste and toothbrush from the vet and then feel *guilty* about not actually brushing their dog's teeth.

A little casual research quickly reveals that the Canine Toothbrush is right up there with the AbBlaster in the "Least Likely to be Used After Purchase" department.

If that describes you, all is not lost…luckily there are several products out there that will pretty effectively remove plaque and tartar that you can just spray in your dog's mouth a couple times a week.

One that a fair number of vets (who probably know damn well that their clients are not really going to brush their dogs' teeth every day no matter what they say) carry in their office is made by *Petzlife*; it comes in both a gel you can rub on the dog's teeth and a spray, which is hands-down the easiest. If your vet doesn't carry it, Amazon does.

Actually buying this and using it a few times a week may well preclude the need for professional cleaning under general anesthesia, which both your dog and your pocketbook will appreciate, even if your vet does not!

Maintaining Healthy Ears

Your Cockapoo's ears should be ideally be cleaned whenever he gets a bath. This is easily done with a cotton ball or two dipped in coconut oil. Coconut oil (which you can buy almost anywhere) is great stuff, and should be part of any holistic dog owner's dog kit. It's non-irritating and yet has strong anti-fungal, anti-bacterial and anti-viral properties.

The inside of a dog's ear is a little like the gut— there needs to be a balance of flora in there for optimum ear health. When that balance is upset (most often by strong antibacterial products) yeast overgrowth occurs, and you can end up with a secondary yeast infection. If he's shaking his head and scratching at his ears a lot, or if you detect a "yeasty" odor in his ears, he'll probably have to be treated for an ear infection. (If the vet puts him on a course of oral antibiotics, be sure and give him probiotics or Greek yogurt for a week or two after treatment to rebalance intestinal flora.)

Because of their Poodle ancestry, some Cockapoos carry a lot of hair in the ear canal, which blocks airflow and consequently provides an ideal environment for infections. Groomers routinely pull this excess hair from the ears using a hemostat, which some vets agree with and others think is a really bad idea because it can cause inflammation.
However, like so much else, susceptibility to ear infections are a reflection of a dog's immune function at any particular point in time, and stressors like vaccination will often trigger them.

Trimming Nails

For some reason, this is one aspect of dog ownership that causes more anxiety on the owner's part than it needs to. Dog's being the intuitive creatures they are, this owner anxiety is transferred directly to the dog, and nail-trimming then becomes a Major Event, when it really should be no more traumatic for the dog to have his nails trimmed than it is for the owner, who rarely screams and carries on like she's being murdered during a manicure.

Because of this, most pet dogs are forced to endure nails that are too long, which is not good for them at all. Here's the rule of nail trimming: ***If you can hear the nails click when the dog walks across the floor, they are too long.*** When this happens, your dog is going to have to adjust his entire skeleton to compensate, because he needs to put his weight on the *pads* of his feet, not the nails, and it will eventually cause him to break down at the pasterns, and can actually cause spinal and joint problems.

Keeping your dog's nails off the floor is easy to do if you take a little bit off once a week, and if you cut them *at the correct angle*, which 99% of people do NOT do. Cutting *correctly* will actually cause the quick to recede.

The diagram below shows the *correct* angle to cut a dog's nails.

If you hold the nail trimmer in the correct position and cut the nails **vertically** as shown, you can get them back where they should be in a couple of weeks without cutting into the quick. On the other hand, if you cut at a 45 degree angle, as most people do, your chances of bleeding the nails go way up, and you still won't be able to get his nails off the floor. (If you do cut into the quick, a dab of Qwik Stop will stop any minimal bleeding that results in short order, and odds are your dogs won't even notice.)

So here's the technique:

- *With your dog's head in the grooming loop, lift each foot in turn (without much ado) and quickly snip off the end of each nail at the angle shown..*

- *Follow with a couple of quick swipes of the file to smooth out the rough edges and you're done.*

- *Reward him with one of his special "grooming treats".*

If you start trimming nails regularly when he's little and approach it with an air of cheerful confidence, it just won't be a big deal for the dog. Or you.

To Sum Up.....

As you've probably figured out, keeping your Cockapoo well-groomed is not rocket science, and is well within the average owner's capabilities. But it DOES require a commitment to investing a fair amount of time and effort on at least a weekly basis, even if you plan to use a professional groomer for the "haircut" part. If you are frankly unable or unwilling to make that commitment, this is probably not the right breed for you.

CHAPTER ELEVEN:

Beyond Basics Training
(cool stuff you can do with your Cockapoo)

Because Cockapoos are intelligent and extremely social dogs who actually *enjoy* training, there are lots of other really fun things you can do with yours once he has mastered basic obedience.

Dogs were developed over thousands of years to work and thrive on it – because of their hard-wiring, dogs without a job are more prone to anxiety and health and behavioral issues than dogs with one. In other words, chronic unemployment is no healthier for a dog than it is for a person. This is especially true for breeds descended from working dogs. So get your dog off the dole and put him to work!

The Entertainment Industry.... AKA Stupid Dog Tricks

Everybody loves dog tricks...including dogs! Dogs are natural performers, and learning tricks is a huge confidence-builder for them, especially if you start when they're puppies. Any dog who has mastered the sit/stay and a decent indoor recall can learn a plethora of tricks.

Although people have been teaching dogs tricks on their own for eons, a good place to start if you want help is with the book *Dog Tricks*, by Captain Haggerty and Carol Lea Benjamin.
Any dog who works his way through these eighty-eight tricks, some very useful and some just plain

Silly, can go on to do absolutely *anything* in the world of dogs, since all these tricks involve a lot of the basics used in "real" work. Plus every trick your dog successfully masters will make the next one easier, because of a phenomenon known to behavioralists as *chaining*.

It's probably worth noting that Chapter Two in this book (which was written back in 1978) involves teaching the "retrieve" command using a collar twist, which is controversial in today's "positive-only" world of pet dog training, although many serious professionals still use it for working dogs.

Since Cockapoos are generally pretty good natural retrievers, you can easily teach him the "take it" command, which is necessary, without using a collar at all by simply tossing the desired object a very short distance and working your way *back* to dropping and then placing it directly in front of him instead of the other way around. (Forced retrieving is really only necessary for working dogs who don't naturally put things in their mouths, and odds are pretty good you don't have one of those anyway.)

Teaching him "out" to release an item on command is also critical, and the instructions given for doing that are pretty time-honored. But for heaven's sake don't try to teach "take it" or "out" with food treats. A simple "good dog!" will suffice.
Tricks are fun for dogs and people….just remember to *keep* it fun!

Agility, Obedience and Rally

Once entirely the province of purebreds, the AKC opened competition in their three Companion events to mixed-breeds under their new Canine Partners Program in 2010, much to everyone's surprise.
This decision effectively allowed Cockapoos to enter and compete for titles as long as their breed is listed as "All-American" rather than as a Cockapoo or a Spoodle or whatever. (Hey, it's a start...and as we all know, once Lady Sybil married the Irish chauffeur, things were never quite the same at Downton Abbey.)
In addition to the Companion events, dogs listed with the Canine Partners program are eligible for AKC's new Therapy Dog title.

Undoubtedly one of the better financial decisions they've made in several lifetimes, over 20,000 entries by mixed breeds were recorded around the country in the first year alone, so you don't have to worry about feeling like the Lone Ranger if you decide to enter this Longtime Bastion of Purebrededness.

UKC is also accepting mixed breeds in Companion Events under their LP program, and also allows them to compete in dock-diving and weight-pulling events.

And not surprisingly, there are a TON of Cockapoos out there doing really well in Agility, Rally and Obedience, earning lots of titles, and between the two organizations there are trials in nearly every part of the country on any given weekend.

Virtually every city in the US has Agility and Obedience training clubs where you can learn the basics even if you don't want to compete for titles. (AKC-affiliated clubs are listed on their website. Go to their homepage at www.akc.org , click on Clubs and Delegates, then click on Club Search.) Most Obedience and Agility Clubs, even if AKC-affiliated, have long accepted non-AKC registered dogs in training classes as long as you pay the fees.

OK, so my dog is maybe cut out for this stuff... but what about ME?

Unlike AKC's Conformation shows, which operate on the competitive principle that "the last dog standing" is the winner (much like beauty pageants for any species), all of these sports are non-competitive. Each dog "qualifies" by achieving the required score rather than by beating the other dogs, and a predetermined number of qualifying scores need to be accrued at each title level. You can enter as many trials as you need to in order to get your green (qualifying) ribbons.

In general, **Rally** trials are the easiest and least formal, and it's a good place for beginners, kids... and people with bad backs and dickey knees. Your dog should know how to heel and sit while on a leash. Basically, you and your dog follow whatever directions you find on the signs set around in a seemingly random and ever-changing pattern in a fenced-in course. And you can chat merrily away with your dog on the course, which is sort of frowned on in Obedience trials.

Obedience trials are more formal and precision-oriented (with half-point infractions for things like crooked sits) in their set routines, and the sport appeals to some human and canine temperaments far more than others. Speed is not of the essence here, except maybe for the dog's recall, so you don't have to be particularly athletic to compete, although you'll occasionally need to bend over and/or trot a bit.

Agility trials are about speed as well as agility, as runs are timed. This sport does require both the handler and dog to be in pretty good shape, as the handler runs sort of beside the dog, although not through the tunnels and weave poles or over the jumps, thank Heavens. Basic obedience is required for this one, because the dogs are by necessity working off leash.

More information on all of these programs for mixed breeds can be found at both AKC's website at www.akc.org and UKC's at www.ukcdogs.com , including dates and locations for trials near you.. Be sure and tell 'em I sentcha!

Dock Jumping

If your dog likes water and retrieving out of it (which lots of Cockapoos do) this may be the PERFECT sport for him!
One of the newest and fastest-growing dog sports, dock jumping as a competitive sport "officially" began in 1997 when Purina added it to their Incredible Dog Challenge Program, and most people have seen dock diving on TV.

Several organizations quickly emerged in the last few years to sponsor events and competitions, the best-known of which are probably Ultimate Air Dogs, which is affiliated with Purina and the UKC, and Dock Dogs, which is independent. Both groups have maps on their websites showing event locations.
Both organizations welcome newcomers to the sport and allow practice time for novice dogs in the pool between competitions. The whole sport is fun and casual and all breeds of all sizes are welcome…the only requirement is that your dog be a strong swimmer, although life jackets are allowed.

Canine Freestyle

If Dock Diving is a sport that generally appeals to men (and a majority of its participants are males between the ages of 24 and 54) Canine Freestyle is a sport almost entirely dominated by women. More specifically, *women who like to dance.*
Canine Freestyle, often called "dancing with your dog", began in the 1990s and spread rapidly, with many local Obedience Clubs now offering classes. With choreographed routines performed in often flashy costumes to music, it probably resembles pairs figure skating more than anything else on the planet, except that it's done on the floor rather than ice and one of the pair is a dog.

Although any dog can learn freestyle, an agile dog with a love of performing will be easiest to work with, and the Cockapoo fits the bill here perfectly!

You can find a class near you by simply googling "canine freestyle" along with the name of your nearest midsize city or your state. The Canine Freestyle Federation also maintains a list of classes available around the country on its website, which can be accessed at www.canine-freestyle.org.

If, on the other hand, this is something you maybe want to fool around with first in the privacy of your own home, the absolute best place to start is Sandra Davis's website at www.caninefreestyle.com. Sandra Davis quite literally wrote the book on canine freestyle, which is available for purchase here, as are several instructional DVDs.

If you'd like to see how good Freestyle can get (and you've somehow missed them on TV) you can go to YouTube and search for one of Sandra and the amazing Pepper's many videotaped performances.

(As a side note, Ms Davis, who was one of the early pioneers of Agility in the 1980s before introducing a huge chunk of the dog world to Freestyle, is now pioneering a fascinating new sport she's calling **K-9 Dressage**. If you have a background in dressage and your interest is piqued, you can find out more about that also on her website.)

It's probably not surprising that in addition to their dancing skills, Canine Freestylers are often certified as Therapy Dog teams, and enjoy "taking their show on the road" to nursing homes and other health care facilities. And of course Therapy is another activity where Aussiedoodles shine, so let's move to that one n

Animal-Assisted Therapy

Therapy dogs do not perform specific tasks for people with disabilities, but rather visit facilities like hospitals, special needs centers, schools and nursing homes with their owners. The Cockapoo's low-shedding hypoallergenic coats and extremely social nature makes him especially welcome.

Although they certainly don't need to be able to dance, therapy dogs DO need to have exemplary temperaments and good social skills as well as basic obedience.

And after a few visits with their Therapy vests on, Therapy Dogs quickly grasp the importance of the job they've been asked to do, and clearly look forward to it. An amazing number even know when it's "Therapy day" as soon as they wake up that morning—is it because dogs have an internal calendar, or are they reading the handler's mind? No one knows, and it really doesn't matter, but it's certainly cool.

Therapy work is one of the most singularly rewarding things you can do with your dog, and there is a shortage of certified Therapy Dogs in many areas, as health care facilities have begun to realize their immense therapeutic value. Beyond merely brightening the days of those confined to a medical facility, the regularly scheduled presence of a Therapy Dog can initiate very real healing, for reasons we simply do not yet understand.

There are three large national organizations that partner with local groups to train, test and register dog/handler teams across the US. You can visit their respective websites to learn exactly what required to prepare for therapy work and to find a group near you.

- **Therapy Dogs Inc:** Founded in 1990, they boast 12,000 handler/dog teams in the US and Canada. They can be found on the web at www.therapydogs.com

- **Therapy Dogs International:** The oldest and largest, TDI was founded in 1976 and has 24,000 handler dog teams registered. Their web address is www.tdi-dog.org.

- **Pet Partners:** Founded back in 1977 and long known as Delta Society, their name was changed in 2012 to better reflect the work done by their 10,000 registered dog/handler teams across the country. They can still be found at their www.deltasociety.org web address, however-er.

Service Dogs

When most people think of Service Dogs, the first thing that comes to mind is the classic Labrador retriever in harness to guide his blind partner through a maze of city streets, or perhaps a Golden retriever in a bright orange jacket performing a variety of complex tasks like opening refrigerator doors and pushing elevator buttons for the wheelchair-bound.

These highly-specialized Service dogs are traditionally donated by breeders to training facilities as puppies. They are often raised by volunteers until old enough for formal training, and then placed with selected disabled owners as adults once their training is completed. This whole process takes the better part of two years, and is obviously not something we can (or even wish to) do with our family pet.

But the world of Service Dogs has expanded greatly in recent years, and dogs now perform a variety of tasks for people with a wide range of physical and mental disabilities that can greatly enhance their ability to lead normal lives.

What Defines a Service Dog?

There's a lot of confusion floating around about the "legal" difference between a Therapy Dog and a Service Dog. This matters in terms of where they are allowed access, because Service Dogs are protected under the Americans With Disabilities Act, *while Therapy Dogs are not.*

The main difference is that a Service Dog is trained to perform *specific physical tasks* for the benefit of an individual with a range of disabilities. In other words, although the owner's disability need not be physical, the task for which the dogs are trained must be— simply being there to provide "emotional support" does not count. (Emotional Support Dogs are not covered by the ADA.)

For example, dogs trained to assist veterans suffering from PTSD usually are trained to turn on light switches, because entering a dark room can be a trigger for PSTD. Those working with kids on the autism spectrum are trained to physically block self-injurious behaviors, while others are trained to "signal" when blood sugar levels start to drop. (With small children, they are trained to alert the adults in the household.) Some are trained to pick up dropped items when the owner cannot, while others alert the hearing-impaired owner to a range of noises such as smoke alarms, doorbells and phones.

And the Cockapoo is especially well-suited for a *lot* of these newer forms of service. (Their innate patience with kids makes them especially well-suited for Autism Service work, and lots are doing it.) These new jobs in the "Canine Service Industry" are called:

- Medical Alert Dogs (most often Diabetic Alert Dogs)
- Seizure Response/Alert Dogs
- Autism Assistance Dogs
- Hearing Dogs
- Mobility Assistance Dogs
- Allergen Alert Dogs (sometimes called "peanut dogs")

This last group often surprises people, but it's a skill whose time has definitely come. Literally thousands of Americans (many of them children) now have, for some weird reason, a life-threatening allergy to peanuts. A Cockapoo can be easily trained to detect them in anything, as well as detecting peanut residue on surfaces that may trigger an anaphylactic reaction.. And his size is an advantage here, because he's pretty portable. Peanut dogs can sweep a classroom or a playground for traces of peanuts, allowing some highly allergic kids who haven't been able to attend school to do so safely as long as the dog is with them.

And although many are unaware of it, once trained, all of these dogs are granted the same public access rights as the better-known Guide and Assistance Dogs under the Americans with Disabilities Act of 1990, ***whether trained professionally OR owner-trained. (***If you are interested in learning more about any of these newer kinds of Service Dogs just Google their name –there's lots of information on the internet.)

There is also a lot of *misinformation* floating around about Service Dogs and the law, so let's address that here first, just so you don't end up confused by conflicting information you may encounter from the usual internet "experts" The following information is from the US Dept of Justice and is current at the time of writing.

- *The definition of "disability" for purposes of public accommodation under the ADA is broader than that of agencies like SSA.* *It essentially covers anyone with "a physical or mental impairment that limits one or more major life activities". (Since "breathing" is actually on that list of activities, potentially life-threatening food allergies are covered, just in case you were wondering about Allergen Alert Dogs.)*

- *By Federal law, Service Dogs do NOT require any "certification" by any organization, nor do they need to pass any tests.* *In order to be protected under the ADA along with their owners, they just need to be "individually trained to do work or perform tasks for the benefit of an individual with a physical, sensory, psychiatric, intellectual or other mental disability", at least according to the US Dept of Justice, which has the last word, bearing in mind that "the work or tasks performed by the service animal must be directly related to the handler's disability."*

- *Service Dogs are not pets.* *Because Service Dogs are not considered pets by the DOJ, municipal, county and state "no pets allowed" laws do not apply to them.*

- *"Psychological Support dogs or Emotional Support Dogs are NOT considered Service Dogs and are not covered by the ADA.* *Providing comfort or emotional support, while certainly useful, is insufficient—the dog has to be trained to perform specific tasks.*

- *Contrary to popular belief, do you need "a letter from your doctor" in order to have a Service Dog.* *In fact, the ADA prohibits anyone from requesting one.*

- *Service dogs are not required to wear identifying vests or ID in order to be allowed public access.* *However, since most people are not mind readers, it's a very good idea and will usually make access automatic.*

- *Service Dogs in Training are not automatically guaranteed access under the ADA, although many state statutes grant them the same rights as trained Service Dogs. In states that do allow access (California and Florida are two states that do) the dog must be accompanied by his trainer.*

It is, however, illegal to *pretend* your dog is a Service Dog, or to identify him as one with a vest or a tag, just to get him on a bus or allow him to ride in the cabin of the plane for free, even if you have a letter from your doctor claiming the dog provides needed emotional support. *Doing so is against the law in most states, and will result in heavy fines and possible jail time, so don't even THINK about it.*

The most up-to-date and accurate information on federal laws concerning Service Dogs is available at: www.ada.gov/service_animals_2010.
If you use a Service dog, it's worth printing it out and carrying it with you for reference if needed.

Or you can now also buy a handy laminated card listing the rights granted Service dogs under the ADA right on the internet– in fact, along with Service dog tags, collars, vests and other identifying information, they are all available on Amazon.

So, all that said…if you or your child have diabetes, or if you have a child with a severe peanut allergy (or *any* life-threatening food allergy for that matter) or autism or any other disability and you enjoy training, there are lots of resources available to help you train your own dog to be a Service dog, which will probably please him no end, since dogs *like* to have a job.

And if the truth be told, with the exception of seizure alerting, which some dogs just seem to be born with, it's really not all that difficult to train dogs for a variety of service tasks…for example, the average dog can be trained to do reliable scent detection with passive or active signaling in *8-12 weeks*, maybe working with him an hour a day, by anyone with fair-to-middling training skills and a minimum of equipment.
There are at least as many ways of training an alert dog as there are trainers, and no real evidence that one works better than the other, so just find a method you and your dog are comfortable with..

The reason trained Service Dogs are worth anywhere from $10,000 to $25,000 is not because the dogs are somehow special—in fact, Hearing Dogs have traditionally come from shelters!— or because the training is extremely complex. The high price tag on trained Service Dogs actually reflects the total costs of *raising that dog from puppyhood* – including early socialization, food, grooming, routine vet costs, health screening, and the basic obedience required before he begins task-specific training— which are all factored into the cost.

But you already *have* the dog, and you've *already* invested all that time and money and done the basic obedience work yourself, so you can move right to the fun stuff…and finding things is truly one of the great joys in a dog's life. To him, it's just another Stupid Dog Trick. Think about it—dogs unerringly detect drugs, bombs, peanut or dairy products or low blood sugar levels not because they intrinsically understand that these are "bad" things, but because they think it's FUN and he wants to please you.

If training your dog for a service job for yourself or another family member sounds like something you would like to try, one place to start is actually with the Pet Tricks book mentioned earlier.

If you're a "visual learner", there are also wonderful YouTube videos put together by pros showing the basics of scent detection training and lots of other tasks…just go to You Tube and search for "detection dog training". There's a website at www.owner-trained-service-dogs.com that's a good place to start. Or you can work with a local search and rescue group or an experienced trainer of detection dogs, because the basics are the same.

Bear in mind while researching that there are at least as many *methods* of training a Service dog as there are trainers, and no real empirical evidence that one works better than the other (although law enforcement dogs are never food-trained for a wealth of reasons), so just find a method you and your dog are comfortable with. (Do beware of trainers who claim their particular method is the only one that will produce a reliable dog, though, because odds are they haven't been at it very long.)

And a lot of this work can actually be started when they're still puppies. Learning the basics of searching is well within the capabilities of puppies 3- 4 months old, and once they've grasped the concept, they can be trained to search and signal for anything. Cockapoos in particular love it. It's about the most fun a dog can have, so even if you don't need a "real" Service Dog, it's a fun thing to do with your dog. And you'll never have to wonder where you left your #$%& keys again….how cool is THAT?

So............ there you go.

That's almost everything you need to know about Cockapoos.

Truly a GREAT little breed.

~ Index ~

~RESOURCES~

Gene Testing:

Prcd/PRA:

The only lab to offer this test in the US is Optigen, in NY. (www.optigen.com). In the UK and Europe, Laboklin (www.laboklin.co.uk) or (www.laboklin.de) offers prcd/PRA testing as well as PFK and FN tests.

PFK (Exercise Intolerance) and FN (Familial Nephropathy) :

Most of the labs in the US that offer color testing also offer tests for these two recessive diseases. Prices vary by lab, so it's worth checking around.

DLA Diversity:

This test determines the level of heterozygosity at the MHC II locus and can be used to assess DLA diversity levels in multigenerational breedings. Currently only available from Genoscoper in Finland. Tests can be ordered online and they accept PayPal. (www.genoscoper.com).

Color and coat gene tests:

In some breeds, coat type and color gene testing is used to avoid producing colors and coats that are disallowed by their standards. In Cockapoos, where all colors are allowed, these inexpensive and non-invasive tests can be used to identify dogs carrying colors the breeder wishes to produce, as well as avoiding inadvertently breeding merle to merle, or producing "spaniel coats" in multigenerational dogs.

The following labs are two of many that now provide a wide array of color gene and coat type testing. Prices vary from lab to lab, and many offer discounts on multiple tests.

Vetgen, Ann Arbor, MI (www.vetgen.org) offers testing for both the curly and furnishings genes as well as most coat colors. Information on ordering test kits is available on their website.

VGL, Davis, CA (www.vgl.ucd.edu) offers testing for coat variations and color genes, including piebald. Information on ordering test kits is available on their website as well.

IDEXX is currently the only lab testing for the merle gene. Test must be ordered through a vet with an IDEXX account. Code # for merle test is 3341.

BAER testing:

A wealth of information on Congenital Hereditary Deafness, including various published research papers and a list of BAER testing sites can be found at the website of LSU's Dr George Strain, who is unquestionably the world's leading authority on the topic: (**http://www.lsu.edu/deafness/deaf**)

CERF testing:

Beginning November, 2012, OFA began a new Eye Certification Registry (ECR). The new ECR is a joint effort between the OFA and the American College of Veterinary Ophthalmologists (ACVO) and their member Diplomates. Since these are the same guys who've been doing CERF (Canine Eye Registry Foundation) exams for the past 30 years, it seems pretty likely that the traditional CERF number is being replaced by OFA's new ECR number. The criteria for *getting* a number hasn't changed, but the organization registering the results of the exams has. More information is available at OFA's website (**www.offa.org**).

Patellar Luxation:

Breeders who want to register the results of a patellar exam (this exam is manual and does NOT require an x-ray) with OFA can download the form for their vet to sign and instructions for submission at **www.offa.org.** (Note: The Cockapoo breed has its own database at OFA and does not need to be submitted as a generic "hybrid". A registration number is NOT required by OFA.)

Cockapoo Clubs with active breeder listings:

Although there are several Cockapoo clubs both in the UK and the US, the following ones maintain current and fairly extensive breeder lists, which are good places to start looking for a breeder near you.:

The American Cockapoo Club (ACC) has a lot of information for buyers and new owners as well as an interactive map of breeders. They can be found at **www.americancockapooclub.com**

The Cockapoo Club of Great Britain (CCGB) maintains an informative website with lots of great photos and a wealth of breed-specific health information as well as a list of member/breeders at **www.cockapooclubgb.co.uk.**

Made in the USA
San Bernardino, CA
27 March 2014